MW00635678

READY TO ROLL ...
READY TO DIE

By Paul F. Cook
District Chief, *Ret'd.*
Boston Fire Department

Unpublished work Copyright 1988 to 2002 by Paul F. Cook

All rights reserved. No part of this work may be reproduced or
transmitted in any form or by any means whatsoever, except for brief
passages which may be quoted by a reviewer.

Requests for permission, inquiries or correspondence should be
addressed to:

Paul F. Cook Enterprise
c/o Conrad Associates
P. O. Box 184
East Walpole, MA 02032

ISBN: 0-9728909-8-X

Explanation

This book was written to coincide with my retirement from the Boston Fire Department.

Pre-publication advertising listed it with the "Coming Books." While it was being prepared for distribution, the publisher filed for bankruptcy, and it took some time before my manuscript was returned to me. It was placed on a shelf at home and procrastination set in.

The contents of this book are as relative today as they were the day they were first written, therefore, the only change is the addition of "Rekindle" as a closing chapter.

With the events of September 11, 2001, there came a new respect for firefighters and their devotion to duty. It also inspired me to take my book off the shelf, in hopes it would provide some people with a clearer view of a firefighter's life as he serves his fellow man and makes extraordinary acts routine. There were a few close calls in my career, but God spared me from paying the Supreme Sacrifice.

"Greater Love Hath No Man"

FIREFIGHTER
PAUL F. COOK
APPOINTED:
JAN. 22. 1947

TO
DAD
CHRISTMAS
'91
LOVE,
Jonathan

INTRODUCTION

Paul Cook is a friend of mine, a fact that became a personal boast with the turning of each page of *"Ready to Roll ... Ready to Die."*

I am not only proud of what my friend has done, but I am in awe of it as well. It is powerfully, poignantly, beautifully written, a history not only of a man, but of his department and his city, too.

What started out to be an autobiography, envisioned as a legacy for generations of Cooks to come, gradually evolved into this magnificent finished product, a labor of love that became a love story, thanks to the author's keen eye for detail and wonderful willingness to place his heart upon his sleeve, making no bones about his love of God, love of country, love of family and love of the firefighting profession, as well as his unabashed affection for colleagues in it.

In ways he never intended, for self-promotion is foreign to his nature, Paul emerges as a personification of those values and beliefs that have defined his life, and in so doing allows the rest of us to vicariously experience the incredible journey he has taken, one that had its beginning in a time some say no longer exists, a time when patriotism and citizenship were as commonly understood as the concept of honor.

When Tom Brokaw coined "The Greatest Generation," it surely had to have been with men like Paul Cook in mind.

Red Auerbach, the legendary patriarch of the Boston Celtics and one of Paul's contemporaries, once expressed a great regret, not for himself but rather for succeeding generations, like the one now coming of age.

"I feel sorry for kids today," Red said. "When we were their age we had heroes; today kids have celebrities and there's such a difference. The biggest difference is, a hero doesn't practice being a hero."

This is a book about Red's kind of heroes, selfless and unassuming, many of who engaged and defeated America's enemies in World War II, then returned home to serve and protect their communities in a calling every bit as noble, firefighting.

It is written by a man who landed on Normandy's Utah Beach, a soldier who would later march victoriously with his Allied comrades into Hitler's conquered Berlin, then come to Boston where he would spend the next four decades knocking down fires; it was like living in another European Theatre that was every bit as perilous as he would discover again and again, such as the night five brethren answered their final call at Trumbull Street, or the day another nine responded to their last alarm at the Hotel Vendome.

Yet through it all, the recollections of searing heat and bitter cold and grief still wrenching to recall, there flows the surpassing sense of a life well-spent, bounding from the anecdotes and observations that richly grace his reminiscing, whether it's the courting of his wife, or the births of their children, or paeans to that camaraderie unique to fire houses everywhere, barns where brotherhood and caring are the orders of the day, all of which have enabled him to conclude, as he does with conviction, "by God's grace my cup has been filled."

How great a run did Paul Cook have?

The passion that was born in the days of his youth, back when he was just a spark hanging around the neighborhood station in Egleston Square, still resonated within him the day he retired as a District Chief, and it has clearly guided his pen in "Ready to Roll . . . Ready to Die."

This is a deeply moving, genuinely inspirational book, as warm and informative and disarmingly introspective as the unpretentious jake who authored it. You will come to know him in a way that will leave you feeling as if you, too, had the great privilege of calling him friend.

Characteristically, he made certain his story was complete, meaning there was no avoidance or soft-pedaling of the role his faith has played in his life because it's absolutely the essence of who and what he is.

In his closing pages, a chapter he calls "And Omega," Paul tells of his certainty that a day is coming when "I, too, will have to stand before God and give an account of the serious things of my life."

But since that's one chapter he obviously won't be able to add for posterity, here's guessing what he'll be told that day: "Well done, thou good and faithful servant!"

And that's exactly what readers of his book are going to tell him, too.

Well done, indeed.

- **Joe Fitzgerald**
Columnist, Boston Herald

ACKNOWLEDGEMENTS

Although written by one person, this book could not be finalized without help from others. I have been greatly assisted and encouraged by both my family and by fellow firefighters. In addition to their individual encouragement, I am particularly grateful and indebted to the following:

Rev. Bob Davidson, present Chaplain of the Westwood Fire Department, who taught me to use a Word Processor which speeded up my writing.

Commissioner Stapleton, of BFD, and Joe Fitzgerald, of the Boston Herald, who suggested proper text changes.

Bill Noonan, BFD Photographer, for the use of pictures from his private collection.

Joy Christensen, an English teacher, who proof-read it and corrected my Spell Checker.

Norman Conrad, for his enthusiasm and publication guidance.

Our sons Bruce, Frank and Jonathan, who pushed and shoved their Dad to do something about getting the book off the drawing board and into print. Bruce, for his research and statistics. Frank, for his formatting and layout suggestions. Jonathan, for his illustrations.

Likewise, my older brothers, Charles and Richard, both Baptist ministers, who provided guidance in my youth and pushed me to finalize this book even as Herb pushed me to study for promotions.

Rick Peterson, who zipped it all together fourteen years after it was written.

My wife Dorothy (now of 55 years) and daughter Janna Peterson, the two lady loves of my life, who nagged, as only women can, to bring this book to the "All Out."

READY TO ROLL ...
READY TO DIE

DEDICATION

This report is respectfully and sincerely dedicated to my brother Herbert. The oldest of the five Cook boys, his life work was devoted to banking, but his heart was devoted to the fire department.

For each rung I reached on the ladder of promotions, he was beneath, pushing me with all his might. In 1981 he ran out of strength and I never climbed that final rung to Deputy Fire Chief.

To put the record straight, it was my fault, and I apologize to you Herb.

Herbert E. Cook, 1908 – 1981.

SECOND ALARM ON DEDICATION

It has been suggested that nepotism is acceptable as long as it is kept within the family. My intent is for this book to go beyond personal family biography and so a second dedication may be in order. This being the case, this book is dedicated to firefighters everywhere --- and their families.

Whether full or part time, paid or volunteer, suburban or urban, big city, small town or Forest Service, firefighters are a special breed of men who have placed their "Calling" above their personal comforts and all else. Part of each week they have voluntarily forsaken their families and all things they hold dear in order to protect the public they serve. Notwithstanding the long-range consequences, they have willingly accepted startling statistics affecting themselves and their loved ones.

The three major diseases that kill and disable firefighters are cancer, heart disease and lung diseases. Cancer is becoming the greatest long-term killer of firefighters. Cancer deaths have increased 20% for the general public but have increased 38% for firefighters during the same thirty-year period of 1950-1980.

Since 1950, the average age of death for firefighters from cancer or heart diseases has dropped from 49 to 44 years of age. The average firefighter lives ten years less than the public he seeks to serve.

This is an antithesis when one considers that these men are some of the population's most physically fit when they come on the job. To make these facts more relevant, it is expected that of the 2,435 full time firefighters in Orange County, California, 937 will die from cancer. This is 440 more than would die if firefighters died at the same rate as the United States population in general.

As firefighters, we are accustomed to being smoked, baked and broiled, but we will never become accustomed to watching fellow firefighters slowly die of cancer.

This book wishes to humbly acknowledge the sacrifices made by all firefighters and their loved ones, and pay homage to these unselfish people who accept an early death sentence for the firefighter, in order that their fellow man might be served.

The Firemen's Creed

"I have no ambition in this world but one, and that is to be a fireman. The position may, in the eyes of some, appear to be a lowly one; but we who know the work which a fireman has to do believe that his is a noble calling. There is an adage which says that 'Nothing can be destroyed except by fire.' We strive to preserve from destruction the wealth of the world, which is the product of the industry of men, necessary for the comfort of both the rich and the poor. We are the defenders from fire, of the art which has beautified the world, the product of the genius of men and the means of refinement of mankind. But, above all, our proudest endeavor is to save lives of men - the work of God Himself. Under the impulse of such thoughts, the nobility of the occupation thrills us and stimulates us to deeds of daring, even at the supreme sacrifice. Such considerations may not strike the average mind, but they are sufficient to fill to the limit our ambition in life and to make us serve the general purpose of human society."

Firefighting

"Firefighting is a hazardous occupation. It is dangerous on the face of it, tackling a burning building. The risks are plain... Consequently, when a man becomes a fireman, his act of bravery has already been accomplished. Everything else is his daily duty."

Edward F. Croker
Chief
New York Fire Department
(1889 - 1911)

CONTENTS

FOREWORD

(or, I Wish I Had Said That)

In the Year Book of the Class of 1941 at Jamaica Plain High School, one of my fellow students listed his goal in life as being "to write a successful book." Not being much of a reader in those days, this did not strike me as a particularly imaginative or ambitious goal, even though he was a good friend. I don't know if Bob ever wrote his book but now having muddled through this sizable conglomeration of assorted pages, there is a new respect for my friend's early lofty goal in life. As for this book being a success, either as a literary or financial undertaking, the readers, or lack of them, will let me know soon enough. In reality, neither of these thoughts motivated me to write, but rather, just a desire to share with others what has been a most delightful lifetime experience.

There are several reasons for my writing this book. First, on occasion something funny, tragic or unusual would happen while my Group was working. Sometimes the event would have already been reported by the radio, newspapers or television so the event was no longer secret - although the reporting most likely was not an accurate account of the unfolded event. My experience as a chief in charge of fires, and thus an authorized spokesman for the fire department, has been that the media is not particularly interested or concerned about accuracy so long as the story is newsworthy, or more important - sells.

If there was a lull in the conversation at the dinner table at home, or if one of the kids asked about what they had read or heard, I might fill in some details. If my version was more exciting or picturesque, one of them was sure to comment, "Dad you should write a book." My stock reply was that the best stories about fire house happenings couldn't, or shouldn't, be written - and so these have been omitted from this book. On the other hand, it seemed that in forty plus years, enough writeable events had taken place to fill a few of these pages.

Second. As our children grew taller and older, and I trust wiser, they would wax nostalgic at times and reminisce about their comparatively recent youth in which television had a prominent place. In all innocence they would ask Mom and Dad what we had watched on TV, and what had been our favorite programs when we were growing up. It was almost impossible to convince them that when their parents were kids, the family sat around the kitchen table listening to the radio (if the family was fortunate enough to have one) and allowed our imagination to conjure up pictures of what we were hearing.

"Amos and Andy" was a very popular program on the air at seven o'clock each evening, Monday through Friday. It was so popular that one could walk down the street on a summer evening and not miss a word of the script because nearly every house had their radio tuned to that station and their windows open.

The absence of television when Mom and Dad were growing up gave birth to more questions about other conditions in those dark ages. The answers sometimes provoked disbelieving laughs among our kids. It also caused them to begin asking serious questions about life without electric blankets, refrigerators, hair blowers and boom boxes, let alone computers and microwave ovens, dishwashers and a host of other conveniences and luxuries that are all taken for granted by today's generation. So, some of these pages will be devoted to enlightening our children, and grandchildren, by providing them with written evidence of conditions and happenings that were part of their ancestors' aging process. It should incite some laughter in their grandchildren as they look back on the early part of the twentieth century.

Third. Since my transfer to Fire Headquarters in April of 1985, I have at times felt like an oracle as more and more associates drop into my office to talk and quite often ask if I remember such and such an event or person who has been associated with the department. The latter requests were most often precipitated by the Signal 10-15 (see Gloss---ary) and many times it has been easy to say "yes" and then fill in some information or an anecdote about the individual.

When I started this book there was a bulletin board in my office on which there was a list of the men appointed with me, and those appointed before us. It was captioned, "last of the MEN who worked the eighty-four hour week !!!" The list which had once numbered in the hundreds had by that time dwindled to just nineteen names. One of my visitors spotted it one day and remarked that he had been a participant in a conversation a few days earlier when the eighty-four hour work schedule had been discussed. They could find no one familiar with how it worked, and he wished I had been around that day to explain it.

All this questionable historical trivia can be found with a little research but this takes time, which isn't always worth spending, and sometimes it is difficult to know just where to begin to search. It would be so much easier and simpler if someone had just thought to communicate it, verbally or in writing. So some of these pages will be trivial information for such enlightenment.

Fourth. I have been hesitant to reduce some happenings to writing. With the passing of the years, many of my hypothetical characters have gone on to their rewards. It is my wish, and hope, that any reader detecting a similarity to events or persons, living or dead, will let it go at that - a coincidental similarity.

It is not my intention to belittle, berate, embarrass or malign anyone or, to tell tales out of school. Actual happenings, if any, have been related to hopefully bring remembrance and honor to persons who brightened my path as I trudged through life. I am appreciative of all whose paths have crossed with mine, and in most cases wish we could have traveled a longer road together. Most of what is written has been fun. For the serious part of life, each of us will have to give a personal account in the hereafter. So some of these pages are imaginary; some stretched truth. I leave it to the reader's discernment to separate them, but, as you read on, remember, "truth is stranger than fiction."

Fifth. A Forum. There is a term familiar to all firefighters which is "firehouse lawyers." There are other names for them as well but they all pertain to the same individuals. Their court room is usually the fire house kitchen, and it is there that all the local and world issues are settled by the assembled donut dunkers. It matters not what the subject is or which portion of the universe is involved as they can resolve any problem by the third if not the second cup of coffee. They really shine when the subject is they themselves and the fire department. All the decisions and policies promulgated by the "Brass" at headquarters, as well as officers in the divisions and districts, will be dissected and discredited. The combined analysis will prove beyond a shadow of doubt that the positive should be negative, the left should have been right and the white black. They can spend ages (unless saved by the bell) trying to figure out how anyone so stupid as to make such decisions could possibly have been smart enough at one time to have risen to the rank of authority. The simple answer is for them to study for promotion and find out just how easy it is.

When I became an officer I refrained from taking part in those discussions and decisions. That silence did not mean thoughts were lacking, just that my input was withheld. It is probable that some of those cooped up thoughts will sneak into this dissertation. We will see.

Sixth. The final motivation was procrastination. From time to time in recent years the thought of writing a book entered my head - probably prodded by my family's continual urging. Concerned about my ability to arrange and rearrange enough words, enough times, into enough sequential order to produce enough pages to constitute a book, it was easy to put off the decision and the labor until tomorrow, but more and more tomorrows somehow turned into yesterdays.

January 1987 arrived. As tradition dictates, the retiring year was depicted as a bearded old man leaving the scene as the diapered baby new year romped in. With it came the realization, that even if I stayed on the job as long as allowed, it was the start of my last full year in the fire department. The year would mark the completion of my fortieth year in the blue uniform, now adorned with the gold of Chief's rank.

That year Fire Commissioner Leo D. Stapleton reinstated the long neglected tradition of honoring those men who reached that mile stone by awarding them a Forty Year Service pin to be worn on the dress uniform. Feeling that a more public recognition was in order, he went a step further and arranged a luncheon for the forty-one men who would reach that high water mark during 1987. January 22nd was chosen for this event as it was the anniversary date of the first 1947 appointees, in preparation for the forty-eight hour workweek. Each member to be honored was invited to have his family join him and be part of the recognition ceremony.

I was looking forward to the day for it would likely be the last time that this group of fire veterans would respond and assemble as a unit. Two days before, my brother Richard called from Georgia to tell us his wife Helen had passed away. Needless to say, this took priority. My wife and I flew south for the services and missed the event of the year that took place at Florian Hall, during the heaviest snowstorm of that winter.

Still saddened and sombered by the passing of yet another contemporary, my work took me to the quarters of District Ten in West Roxbury one day later in January. The chief on duty that tour was Bob MacInnes. He too had been appointed in 1947. We had been promoted from the same lieutenant's list and assigned to Brighton where we worked the same Group but in different fire houses. In 1967 we were made captains the same day and were both transferred to engine companies in the down town section of Boston. When I made district chief in 1971 and stayed in District 3, Bob was still the boss of Engine 10 on my Group. There never was a finer gentleman or a finer fire officer, and so it became my goal to push and assist him in studying to make chief, which he did in 1977.

The thought, which kept running through my mind as we talked that January day, was that Bob was a year younger than me, and so would have a year longer to enjoy the job. In a sense I was envious, but shortly after our conversation, the fickle finger of fate struck and Bob had a serious fire which took its toll on his health, and he died in May. His short illness and untimely passing reinforced the reality of the uncertainty of life, and the futility of procrastinating. If my thoughts were ever to be put into writing, I had better get started. So if this book has any merit, my long time friend and fellow District Fire Chief, Bob MacInnes, deserves some credit.

So for better or worse, here is the potpourri of fiction and non-fiction, the current events and past history, the trivia and the tragedy, past practices and present procedures, the satirical and the sad, fantasy and forum, the ridiculous and the sublime. And for good measure, a little biography and a lot of bull---oney thrown in.

GLOSS---ARY

(or, Shining Explanations)

If you are a firefighter, and even more so if you are a spark, you will be familiar with all the vernacular used in this book. To assist the lay person, who may lack knowledge of the lingo, here is an education for nothing. If you skip over these definitions now, you may not understand some of what follows. So why not take the time and get glossed before you begin.

Further, as you read on you will discover that almost everything, by coincidence, is mentioned at least twice in this book. So if there is something that is not clear at first, be patient, a later reference should clarify the picture. This dual approach is probably a subconscious application of a lesson learned while taking promotional tests. Civil Service examinations for captain and chief included a fire problem in which you were given a series of circumstances relative to a structural fire. One of the secrets of getting a good mark was to comment and elaborate on every fact mentioned. Solving the problem, or fighting the fire, required you to put in writing your every action, and reason for it, from "Points to be considered while responding" to completion of reports. You were given three hours to put your thoughts in writing - which usually wasn't enough time.

AERIAL LADDER - the fixed ladder mounted on a ladder truck. The lower section, or base ladder, is attached to a turntable on the truck frame. The extension ladder is known as the fly, or tip. Special alloy ladders, which have replaced the wooden aerials, now come in lengths exceeding one hundred feet

ALARM (of fire) - may originate with a telephone call or someone pulling a fire box on the street

ALL OUT - coded signal denoting the end of a fire or incident. It is two blows followed by two blows, a pause, and two blows followed by two blows, followed by a box number. It is transmitted by FAO on orders of the officer in charge at an incident. It is sent over all tapper circuits and radios. For example, All Out on Box 1246 would be transmitted as follows:

APPARATUS - fire engines

APPARATUS FLOOR - first floor of a fire house, where the fire engines sit waiting for an incident to which they can respond. Also referred to as the Main Floor of a fire house

APPARATUS OPERATOR - see Pump Operator

APRON - the paved ramp in front of a fire house. It is recommended that the apron be of sufficient length to hold the longest piece of apparatus to be housed there. If this Standard were followed to the letter, some city ladder trucks would have to be shorter than the width of the sidewalk in order to comply

AUTOMATICS - refers to the single button at the patrol desk in olden days which put on all the lights in the fire house

BABY BANGOR LADDER - twenty foot short extension ladder without halyard for raising the fly section. This upper section must be raised by hand and is then held in position by engaging the pawls. Can be separated into two ten foot ladders for getting over fences or where short ladder is needed - chimney fires

BACK STEP - the platform at the rear of wagons and pumps on which the men rode in olden days

BAGGER - multiple alarm fire. Today in Boston it could be a two, three, four, five, six, seven, eight or nine bagger

BANJO DRILL - snow shoveling time

BATEAU - a flat bottom boat carried on the fire boats and used for getting under piers

BAZOOKA - or foam applicator. A device for applying high expansion foam in volume at an effective range of 10 to 12 feet

BELLS (or bell alarms) - there are many new Hi-Rise buildings in Boston and all have heat and/or smoke detectors and sprinkler systems. The detectors are quite sensitive and in residential areas are often set off by heat or smoke from cooking. Likewise in office buildings they can be triggered by various conditions, not only fire. In every case a series of bells begin ringing throughout the building when an alarm is transmitted. Throughout the city this occurs many times every day and each time the fire department responds. The ringing bells annoy tenants and they want them shut off quickly, but the Incident first must be investigated. There are so many of them the men refer to them as bells

BFD - Boston Fire Department

BIG LINE - a two and a half inch line of hose

BOOSTER - short for the water tank and line on the wagon. Early tanks held forty gallons of water and the line was two hundred and fifty feet of three quarter inch red rubber hose in fifty foot sections. Tanks always leaked. This gave a good indication as to where the wagon went and made it easier for the pump, truck and chief to follow. As distances to fires grew longer, they had to increase the capacity of tanks so there would be enough water to last. The newest pumps have tanks which hold seven hundred and fifty gallons and more. The spilled water also helps some firemen find their way back to the fire house

BOX ALARM - notification of a fire (or false alarm) received at the FAO when someone pulls a fire box on the street. Because of the increased use of telephones, some politicians would like to do away with street fire boxes to save money. The fire department is against this. The main reason is the increased number of languages spoken and the difficulty at times to get a correct location by phone in an emergency. When any person pulls the hook on a fire box, there is no language problem, and an exact location is known

BRASS - another name for superior officers. Also something that has to be polished in a fire house - and there is lots of it

BRESNAN NOZZLE - a brass globe which is revolved by water pressure. It has nine holes allowing it to spread water in all directions as it revolves

BUGLES (also referred to as toilet plungers) - used to designate rank in the fire department:

> One silver bugle   - Lieutenant
> Two silver bugles - Captain
> Two gold bugles   - District Chief
> Three gold bugles - Deputy Chief
> Four gold bugles   - Assistant Chief
> Five or more gold bugles - Chief of Department

BUNK ROOM - dormitory or resting quarters for firemen. No telling what it is since the fire service became coed

BUNKING IN - sleeping at the fire house

BURST HOSE JACKET - a hinged, two part, rubber-lined, metal jacket which, when clamped over the burst part of a hose being operated at a fire, forms a seal to prevent the loss of water and pressure. This is the theory: in practice, they don't work

CALL BELLS - forerunner of the P.A. system in fire houses. Consisted of door bell type buttons at the Patrol Desk and in the officer's rooms, plus small bells that could be heard throughout the fire house. Each company member was assigned a number and when wanted, his number was rung. His number followed by one short ring meant to report to the officer's room. Two short rings denoted he had a phone call

CELLAR PIPES - appliances used at fires to send water under piers, in cellars windows, through holes cut in floors, roofs, decks or other difficult locations. Besides the Bresnan nozzle, there are the Carey, Hart and Baker pipes

CHARGED LINE - a line of hose filled with water

CHEMICAL TANK - forerunner of booster water tanks on wagons. Consisted of a cylindrical tank under the driver's seat. It held thirty gallons of water mixed with sodium bicarbonate. A smaller cylinder containing sulfuric acid was locked in an upright position within the larger tank until a mixture was made at the fire location. It was in fact a big portable fire extinguisher with the chemical action providing the pressure to push the water mixture through the hose. It was strange how the wagons with boosters always got to the same fires before the wagons with chemical tanks

CIRCUITS - wires connecting all fire boxes and fire houses in the city with the FAO. In olden days when there was trouble with a circuit, the FAO notified the companies which circuit was "out." The officer would check to see if any boxes in his sub-district were on that circuit. If there were, he sent a man out to hang an "Out of Service" card on those fire boxes to let the public know that pulling the box would not bring help, and directing them to the nearest fire box in service or to a telephone. Because the FAO would usually restore the circuit in a short time, officers would try to delay sending a man out. What usually happened was that after a reasonable wait, the officer would send a man out with the cards and right after he left, FAO would call to report the circuit was restored. Since there was no way to contact the man, when he returned, he was sent back out to retrieve the cards. Somehow most circuit troubles were on stormy days, and after a while it was very difficult to find the "Out of Service" cards

CITIZEN ALARM - notice of fire received verbally from a citizen

CITY GONG - up until the 50s and 60s (depending on the particular fire house) there was an eight inch brass gong at the Patrol Desk. A box alarm was transmitted three rounds on the tapper circuits and two rounds on the gong circuits. The gong was much louder and slower than the tapper and had a "silence" switch on it. S.O.P. required that the first two box alarms transmitted each day, after 8 A.M., were to strike on the city gong. This was a test to make sure it was in working order. The gong was then silenced for the rest of the day. It was a mortal sin if the chief found the gong "off" before the first two boxes of the day had been transmitted

COMPANY - unit designation, such as Engine Company 3 or Ladder Company 2 or Rescue Company 1

CONDUCTION, CONVECTION, RADIATION - the three ways by which heat is transmitted at fires

DAY TOUR - the men working from 0800 hours to 1800 hours

DEQE - Department of Environmental Quality Engineering

DISTRICT - one of the eleven sub-sections the city is presently divided into for fire suppression. In 1947 there were fifteen districts

DIVISION - one of the two sub-divisions the city is presently divided into for fire suppression and administration. The area north of Massachusetts Avenue comprises Division One and south is Division Two. At various other times in this century there were three divisions and for a period there was only one

DOG MAN - member of a ladder company assigned to "dog ladders" which means securing it against sliding, moving or falling

DONUT ROLL - fifty-foot length of 2-1/2" hose rolled with both couplings on the outside. Taken to upper floors of high-rise buildings and into subways for connecting to standpipes

DOT - to some, the Department of Transportation. To me it is Dorothy, my wonderful patient wife of forty-one years as of 1988

EIGHTY-FOUR HOUR WORK SCHEDULE - this was the fireman's work schedule in Boston from 1924 to 1947. It replaced the so called "Day in Three" and was termed the "Two Platoon System" because each man had a partner and one or the other was on duty at all times. The way it worked, you were on duty:

Monday - 8 A.M. to 6 P.M.

Tuesday - 8 A.M. to 6 P.M.

Wednesday - 8 A.M. to 8 A.M. Thursday. This was the "Long Day" and men working it were granted one hour and fifteen minutes for supper (not all men at once)

Thursday - 6 P.M. to 8 A.M. Friday

Friday - 6 P.M. to 8 A.M. Saturday

Then off for twenty-four hours until Sunday 8 A.M. when it started all over again

EL or BOSTON ELEVATED RAILWAY - forerunner of Massachusetts Bay Transportation Authority (MBTA)

E.M.T. - Emergency Medical Technician. With much additional training some become Paramedics

EPA - Environmental Protection Agency

FALSE ALARM - the pulling of a fire box when there is no fire or emergency. Could also be by telephone

FAO - short for the Fire Alarm Office - located in The Fenway. This is the nerve center of the fire department where alarms are received and retransmitted to fire stations

FEEDER LINE - hose stretched from hydrant to pump

FIRE BARN, FIRE HOUSE, FIRE STATION - all synonymous. Early designation was fire barn because it housed horses and men. The animals were usually given the most consideration. It was the start of a tradition

FIRE BOX - a red box usually at street corners and used by the public to summon the fire department. In early days the door was locked and before the "hook" could be pulled, the key had to be obtained from a local citizen who was entrusted with its care

FIREFIGHTER ON PROBATION - today, the first twelve months on the job

FIREMAN, FIREFIGHTER - one and the same. First called fireman. Somewhere along the line someone reasoned that men who shovel coal into a furnace were called firemen. Their work made fires bigger - even though contained. Our work is to make fires smaller - hence firefighter. This change made some people very happy, but now there are some other very unhappy people who want the name changed to "fire person." My feeling is, fireman is shorter, simpler to say, and it is what every good little boy wants to grow up to be

GENERAL ALARM - a single switch at the patrol desk in many fire houses which replaces the older AUTOMATIC and HOUSE GONG switches. It puts on all lights, sounds the electronic alerting device, opens doors, controls traffic lights in front of house, and sounds an outside warning device. After a few minutes the doors are closed automatically and lights shut off

GENERAL ORDER - official communication originating with the Fire Commissioner. They deal mostly with the administration of the department, including appointments, promotions, transfers, retirements, discipline and fire box changes

GOOD FIRE - a relative term used by firemen to rate the magnitude of a fire. It could relate to a one room fire or one involving a city block. Also, the more worked involved, the "gooder" the fire. In reality there is no such thing as a good fire -- unless it is one barbecuing steaks

GROUND LADDERS - assorted ladders carried on "trucks" to be raised by manpower. They range in length from Baby Bangors to fifty-five foot. Those carried on ladder trucks add up to two hundred and forty feet

GROUPS - way of dividing men on a company to balance manpower:

> 84 hour schedule had 2 groups
> 48 hour schedule had 7 groups
> 46 hour schedule had 11 groups
> 42 hour schedule has 4 groups

HALLIGAN BAR - a multi-purpose tool, approximately 32 inches long and 8 1/2 pounds in weight, consisting of a bar which terminates at one end in a claw and at the other end in a head which has an adz and a hook at right angles to each other. It is suitable for use under conditions calling for the use of a claw which can be driven in to penetrate heavy materials, under conditions calling for the use of an adz to open doors or to remove baseboards, trim, roofing, etc., and under conditions calling for the use of a hook to remove locks, hasps, staples, etc., or to lift manhole covers

HIT GAMEWELL HIT – fireman's plea for action from the tapper

HOSE CLAMP - a device for squeezing hose so tightly that the flow of water is stopped. It is used to replace sections of burst hose, add pieces of hose to extend a line, or to drain a line of hose so that it will not be necessary to carry a charged line to upper floors, without having to shut down the pump or hydrant supplying water

HOSE HOIST - a roller device which serves to facilitate the hoisting of hose, ladders and other heavy objects to the roof or upper floors of a building. It eliminates the chafing of the hauling rope on rough edges of roof or window sills. Although used regularly in olden days, you will have a hard time locating one today

HOSE LINE - a device for securing hose to ladders or other objects to prevent the hose from being moved by sudden pressure changes and to relieve the strain on its couplings. The device consists of a piece of one and three-fourths inch rope about thirty inches long which is equipped with a metal ring spliced to one end and a metal hook spliced to the end. Note: the size "one and three-fourths inch" refers to the circumference of the rope and not the diameter

HOSEMAN - in olden days, the men assigned to an Engine Company. Men assigned to Rescue Companies were also designated as hosemen

HOTEL VENDOME FIRE - on June 17, 1972, after this four alarm fire was "knocked down," a corner of the building collapsed killing nine members of the Boston Fire Department

HOUSE GONG - now referred to as house alarm. In olden days it was a large brass gong about two feet in diameter. It made a lot of noise as it summoned the men from rest to action. Present house alarms are dainty electronic noise makers, that have no clamor or glamour

HOUSE PATROL - in Boston there is a member on watch in each fire house twenty-four hours a day (except when they respond). The "watch" is broken up into approximately three hour units. Man on watch records all activities of the house in the Journal, and is available to meet the public and direct them according to their needs. He is the one responsible for dispatching men and equipment in that fire house to Incidents - correctly

INCIDENT - a fire department response. It may be one piece of apparatus to a wash down or a nine alarm fire. Boston averages close to fifty thousand Incidents a year

IN-SERVICE INSPECTIONS - a program in fire departments by which companies systematically visit each building within their sub-districts to become more knowledgeable about them and their hazards. Radio contact is maintained with the FAO as companies are in service and ready to roll

JAKE - another name for a fireman/firefighter. Also rhymes with "break," as in "Officer, will you give a jake a break?" There seems to be no positive identification as to the origin of the term "Jake"

JOURNAL - a red bound book containing two hundred and eighty lined and numbered pages. It is in this book that the man on patrol records everything pertaining to fire house activities. It includes status of every member assigned to the company as of 8 A.M. and 6 P.M. Roll Calls, "alarms" and "all outs" received together with the times, visits of chief officers to quarters, Incident responses with duty performed and who responded, injuries received, and a lot of other happenings that would fill a book

KINK MAN - usually the rookie of an engine company whose first job at a fire is to straighten out bends in the hose so it won't bind, or kink, when the line is charged with water

LADDERMAN - in olden days, the men assigned to a Ladder Company

LIFE NET - a metal ring to which is attached, by approximately two dozen springs, a landing mat of canvas, usually padded and with a red bulls-eye to aim for. The circular ring is divided and hinged so that it may be folded when carried on the apparatus. To use the net, it is unfolded and the ring is locked into shape by sliding ferrules that cover over the hinged points. Opened, it has a diameter of about ten feet. When used, it is held neck high by ten or more men - if they are available. Earlier versions of about the same size were woven of rope and carried on each engine and ladder company. Inflatable air bags have replaced them both

LINE OF HOSE - one or more fifty foot lengths of hose with a nozzle attached

LNG – Liquified Natural Gas

LONG RING - given on Call Bells and indicated all members are to report to the main floor for a non-emergency reason

LOWRY HYDRANT - a male threaded large pipe, with a controlling valve, extending from a water main to a box just below street level. It is covered by a round metal plate to keep out dirt and debris. When the fire department needs to use it, the plate is removed and a Lowry chuck is screwed onto the pipe, allowing it to be used as a regular hydrant. Following a snow fall, these plates are covered with rock salt by the fire department so they can be easily found and used in the winter. On a nearby wall or pole, an "H" is painted with a number under it. The number indicates distance in feet to the plate. By coincident, if there is only one car parked on the street, you go to it first when salting because the law of average says the car will be parked on the plate. Most Lowry hydrants have now been replaced with a regular post hydrant

LOWRY HYDRANT CHUCK - a portable hydrant carried on Boston engine companies. The device, made of heavy brass, is screwed onto a special water main connection and then functions as a regular hydrant. It has one or two 4-1/2" outlet for the pump connections and two or three 2-1/2" outlets (total 4 outlets). There is a smaller version known as a "Coffee Pot Chuck" which has only a single 2-1/2" outlet. It was used for a detail line so the larger chuck did not have to be left at the fire

LYCEUM HALL FIRE - Maverick Square, East Boston fire at which six firemen lost their lives on November 15, 1942

MAN ON PROBATION - in olden days, the first six months on the job

MEN - although the fire service has become coed in recent years, this book will continue to refer to the personnel as "men." First, it is difficult to teach an old fire dog new tricks, and second, because no matter how much the fair sex may beautify the surroundings, it is still, and always will be, a "man's job." Politically Correct - be damned. (May have lost a few readers before the book even starts)

MORNING CALL - wake up time at 0700 hours in fire houses

MULTIPLE - a fire requiring two or more alarms. Or, the means by which parking lots are created

NFPA or NATIONAL FIRE PROTECTION ASSOCIATION - an organization devoted to fire prevention and safety. They produce volumes of publications dealing with fire subjects, including the National Fire Protection Handbook (currently the sixteenth edition). This textbook contains nearly two thousand large pages and fire officers are expected to know it cover to cover. To make this task easier, there is a several hundred page guide to it - which fire officers are also expected to know

NIGHT HITCH - a combination of rubber boots with pants over them. When bunking in, the pants are rolled down over the boots and the combination is placed beside the bed. When responding, the man steps into the boots, pulls up the pants and he is dressed for fire duty. For better or worse, these have been replaced with new "Turn-out Gear"

NIGHT TOUR - the men working from 1800 hours to 0800 hours the next morning

NOZZLE or PLAY PIPE - device screwed onto the end of a line of hose to straighten the stream and control the flow of water

OFFICERS - Lieutenant / Fire Lieutenant
Captain / Fire Captain
District Chief / District Fire Chief
Deputy Chief / Deputy Fire Chief

Based on previous reasoning (FIREMAN), it was only logical that officers should be more positively identified so the word "Fire" was inserted before designated ranks. In reality they are usually shortened to "Luf" for Lieutenant, "Cap" or "Cap'n" for Captain and Chief is still "Chief." I never cared what they called me as long as the paymaster had it right and showed up on Fridays

OLDEN DAYS - in this book, about 1950 and before

OSHA – Occupational Safety and Health Administration

PARKING LOT - building location before fire was discovered

P & L - Planning & Logistics Division

POLE, FIRE POLE, SLIDING POLE - vertical brass pipes (now sometimes aluminum) about three inches in diameter which connect floors in firehouses. Used by firemen as the quickest way to apparatus floor when house gong sounds. (When Ladder 17

was housed alone on Harrison Avenue it had one pole from the third to first floor)

POMPIER LADDER, SCALING LADDER - ladder for scaling walls by engaging hook portion over window sills. Consists of a single wood beam 16 feet long banded with metal and having a 30 inch steel gooseneck hook, with teeth to prevent slipping, at the top. The rungs are wooden crossbars, 12 inches long and set through the beam. Two curved metal plates on the hook side, one at the top and one at the bottom, keep the ladder two inches from the wall to permit the hand to grasp the beam. When using this ladder, the beam should be grasped and not the rungs. This ladder is used now for training new recruits to give them confidence and to help overcome fear of height. In the fire service it is referred to as "the pomps"

PUMP, PUMPER, PUMPING ENGINE - second unit of a two piece engine company (now mostly extinct) or the only unit of a single piece engine company. This unit is intended to be connected to a hydrant, either by a soft or hard suction hose or a longer feeder line, and supply water at sufficient volume and pressure to extinguish a fire. Sometimes it takes quite a while to accomplish this feat

PUMP OPERATOR or APPARATUS OPERATOR - man who drives the pump, and once at the fire gets the water from hydrant into the pump. In olden days he was also responsible for tending the coal furnace in his fire house. He was paid an extra hundred dollars a year

RAKE or PLASTER HOOK - a tool which is used for removing plaster ceilings and partitions and for other cutting operations calling for the use of a long-handled tool. Consists of pole which has, on one end, a long hook having a tempered cutting blade. Ladder companies carry an assorted length of these to reach various height ceilings

REGISTER - used in conjunction with the tapper at the patrol desk. Coded signals of the tapper are duplicated on a one-inch wide paper tape passing through the register. Signals are indicated by triangular shaped punched holes

ROLL CALL - once held each day at 0800 and 1800 hours in every fire house in the city. Members lined up in uniform on the apparatus floor, according to rank and height, where the senior officer present called the names of all members assigned to the house - and hopefully heard "here" at least a few times. He also read any new General or Special Orders and relayed any other information he wanted to impart to the men. In a lot of fire houses today, "Roll Call" has been replaced with "Donut Call"

ROSS THAWING DEVICE - a unit used to melt ice in the barrel of a hydrant. It consists of a container holding a mixture of water and alcohol, a tank of acetylene gas and a short length of reinforced hose. By controlled burning of the acetylene, the mixture in the container is heated to produce steam, which then passes through the hose and is directed into the barrel of the frozen hydrant. Steam is produced in a matter of seconds using this device

RUN - another term for a fire department response to an Incident

RUNNING CARDS - at every Patrol Desk there is a box containing these cards. There is a card for every fire alarm box location in the city. The response or covering assignment of every company is indicated on the cards. Present cards provide for a nine alarm fire response. Instructions from FAO do supersede card assignments

SAVED BY THE BELL - term indicating that whatever was being done in a fire house, it was stopped because members had to respond

SCUBA - Self Contained Underwater Breathing Apparatus

S.O.P. or STANDARD OPERATING PROCEDURE - printed guide lines for how things ought to be done

SPAGHETTI - term used to describe the many lines of hose that are run at a big fire. Looking down at the street from an elevated position the massed hose lines resemble a plate of spaghetti

SPARK - one who is interested in or chases after fires. In some cities they are referred to as "buffs," or other names. Little sparks have been known to cause big fires

SPECIAL ORDER - communication originating in the office of Chief of Operations. Deals with day to day operational instructions and orders that govern company and members duties and responsibilities

SPITOON or GARBOON - brass receptacles that decorated every room in olden fire barns. They sat on little round black rubber mats and were used by the tobacco chewers - who were plentiful in the olden days

STICK or AERIAL LADDER - were once seventy-five and then eighty-five foot wooden mounted ladders, usually spring raised. Today they have been replaced by hydraulic raised metal ladders extending up to a hundred and twenty-five feet or more

STILL ALARM - notice of fire received by telephone

SUB-DISTRICT - districts are divided into a number of smaller areas, determined by the number of companies in the district. Each company is responsible for building and hydrant inspections within their sub-district

SWAP - exchange tours of duty with another man. Not to be confused with WASP

TAPPER - the device which receives coded signals on a bell for identifying a box alarm or Special Signal. For example, Box 1246 is one blow followed by two blows followed by four blows followed by six blows:

For example, Special Signal 10-15 is ten blows followed by one blow followed by five blows:

TEN FIFTEEN (10-15) - Special Signal denoting death of a department member, (either active or retired). It is struck two rounds on the tapper and is followed by an announcement on department radios identifying the member. Upon receiving the signal, all department flags are lowered to half staff out of respect for the departed member

TILLERMAN - the fireman who steers the back end of the ladder truck. Actually all he has to do is follow the front end. Very glamorous job, but becoming an extinct species

TRUCK or LADDER TRUCK - in children's books it is called the "hook and ladder"

TRUCKIE - another name for Ladderman

TRUMBULL STREET FIRE - five alarm fire on October 1, 1964 during which the front wall collapsed in the first few minutes of the fire killing five Boston firemen and a spark

TWENTY-FOUR HOUR CLOCK - takes twenty-four hours for hands of the clock to make one revolution instead of two twelve hour trips around the face. The Armed Forces Network once explained it this way. "It is now two thirty P.M. For you Navy men, that it is five bells. For you Army men, it is fourteen hundred thirty hours. For you Officers, the little hand is on two and the big hand is on six"

WAGON - short for hose wagon, which was the first unit of a two piece engine company (now mostly extinct). It carries hose, booster tank and line, and assorted other equipment. It is also something some firemen fall off

WASP - White Anglo Saxon Protestant

WHO: ALWAYS PRECEDED BY A FIRST NAME - a retired firefighter, like Paul "who"

WORKING FIRE - a fire needing additional help beyond the first alarm but not requiring a second alarm - yet! It is designated by the coded signal 4-5 followed by the box number. For example:

Note: Some equipment definitions are from the old Massachusetts Red Book for fire department applicants.

So now you know!

ALPHA

(or, Let's Get Started)

"Once upon a time" is not the way for this book to begin, and the ending will not be the fairy tale conclusion that "they all lived happily ever after." The setting for this book is more the "Camelot" style. The endings of the individuals referred to vary, but all have the consolation that they lived happily during most of these happenings, even if not "ever after."

To most people, October 23, 1988 was just another day on the calendar but it marked another anniversary of my birthday and with it came the realization that there were only eight more days of my career as a Boston fireman. Only eight more days to savor and enjoy the work that had pleasingly dominated two thirds of my life.

With the mindless mechanical movement of the hands of time from one minute to the next, from the end of one hour to the start of another, from one day to the day following, from Monday, October 31, 1988 to Tuesday, November 1, 1988, I would move from District Fire Chief Paul F. Cook, Chief in charge of the Planning and Logistics Section at Boston Fire Headquarters to Paul "Who?" That which had taken over forty-one and a half years to attain in rank and respect, would pass in the ticking of the second hand of time from 2400 hours to 0001 of a new day. To put it more dramatically, the ladder of rank, which took me that many years to ascend, I would descend "in the twinkling of an eye."

My appointment date to the Boston Fire Department was January 22, 1947. It had to be the happiest day of my life to that time, and probably of all times, for it was the fulfillment of not only a boyhood dream but also of the deep desire which had burned within me for twenty-three years.

Along with a few hundred other returned veterans of World War II, my appointment to the department was in preparation for a reduction in the work week of the city's fire suppression force from eighty-four to forty-eight hours, as voted by the citizens of Boston. The vote was in response to a most vigorous all out effort by the firemen of that time who campaigned with the slogans, "Vote Yes on 4" and "Give a Vet a Job."

It came as no surprise that The Occupant of City Hall, who was the "Purple Shamrock" (otherwise known as James Michael Curley), was not particularly pleased over this expensive change that was voted, but it was the will of the people and thus became law. As a way of showing displeasure, the city administration delayed appointing and training any new men for as long as possible, but time eventually caught up with them and our first weeks in the department coincided with the ending days of the eighty-four hour schedule which was so inconveniently arranged that the men were in the fire house at eight o'clock every morning unless on vacation or injured leave.

Starting salary for us was two thousand dollars a year, or thirty-eight dollars and some change each week. It figured out to about forty-six cents an hour - and this was with a Union! Fringe benefits included all the smoke you could eat and the promise of a reasonable pension at the end, if you were among the fortunate who survived. Most of us wanted so much to be firemen that we gladly accepted a cut in pay and more than doubled weekly work hours just to be part of the action.

Our Civil Service list had not yet been "established" so our appointments had to be "Provisional." Because of this technicality that we were not "Permanent" firemen (Hosemen and Laddermen in those days), we were not covered by the new law. So when the work week for the old timers was finally reduced in February, the city made us work a sixty-eight hour schedule so as to provide us with additional time to learn the ropes. Eventually our list was "certified," we were made "Men on Probation," and we too enjoyed working forty-eight hours a week. Mathematically this amounted to a pay raise from forty-six to eighty cents an hour. It constituted a 73% increase, but somehow we still received the same amount of cash on Fridays. Because of this quirk, we have the dubious distinction of being the relatively few firemen who have worked 84, 68, 48, 46 and 42 hour schedules during our careers.

But here it is forty-one years, nine months and eight days from that starting point. Where did the years go? They say time flies when you are having fun. It must be true because the years have flown and we did have fun. What was accomplished in those years? What can be shown for them? Hopefully, this report will provide an accounting of my stewardship as a firefighter for the citizens of Boston.

For my family it will also be an explanation, and apology, for the time we spent separated - the nights, the weekends, the holidays. The important events, which are part of every family as it grows up, and which in this case, mother had to cope with alone. It also includes a special apology for other special family events that dad missed because he was working. My thanks and appreciation to each of you for your understanding and acceptance, albeit reluctant at times, of the fireman's work calendar which does not recognize weekends, holidays, birthdays, anniversaries or other special occasions.

In my forty-one plus years in the department there have been a couple thousand fellow firefighters come and go. Of course all those that were there when I was appointed have since become "Whos." Many hundreds more who came during my years in the department remain to carry on the traditions. With most of them, our paths at least crossed or ran parallel for a spell. Some of these "jakes" had spectacular moments in their careers, some with lots of publicity and some with none. Too many had their careers shortened by having to pay the "supreme sacrifice." Some came, did their job and left, leaving no particular monument to their service other than the personal satisfaction that they had served their paymaster well. Sadly, all too soon they became Phil "Who" or Joe "Who" and a myriad of other names that always end with "Who."

Some of the "Whos" remained firefighters their entire careers - because that is the way they wanted it - - or because fate dealt it that way. Some rose in rank to become Chief of Department - and that is the way they wanted it. Others, like the writer, ended up somewhere in between - and that is the way we wanted it. So, my career can be stereotyped as being ordinary, typical or a happy medium, but like every other fireman's, mine had its own uniqueness, and for sure it was never boring.

As for the accounting, first and foremost, thanks to the citizens of Boston who made it all possible - first in voting and then in paying. Thanks for my wife Dorothy, our home, our three sons and one daughter, plus now their spouses and our grandchildren.

Thanks to the people of Boston for the food we have eaten, the clothes we have worn, and the rugs and furniture we have worn out in forty plus years of marriage. Thanks from our children for the toys, once new, that were played with, broken and discarded, or replaced and preserved. Thanks also for their education. Thanks for the vacations we were privileged to enjoy, the places we visited at home and abroad, the sights we have seen and the history learned. Thanks for the doctors and dentists we were able to afford when their services were needed and thanks for the autos, used and new, that have been part of our life.

Thanks most to God, who spared me serious injury, or worse, during the thousands of fires and other Incidents to which I responded. It is said that God has a plan and a purpose for every life. I am grateful for the life He planned for me, and I hope the purpose has come close to what was intended.

Finally, there must be a special thanks for the men I worked with through the years. Those men who were there before me and those who remain at my departure. Firefighters, whom I grew to respect and admire as we shared both pleasant and harrowing moments together. Each one contributed his part to the tradition and heritage that is part of the fire service in Boston. I am glad I was a part of their lives, and consider myself specially blessed because they were part of mine.

Chances are the tax payers never knew, or realized, they were providing us with all the necessities and niceties we have enjoyed, but they did and with our grateful thanks, in the weekly paychecks they provided --- even when it was only forty-six cents an hour when it all began. Fortunately the weekly rewards progressively increased with the passing years, but this had no bearing on my choosing to remain a fireman.

And just what did the tax payers receive in return? It is my hope this record of my Stewardship will show that the citizens of Boston received their money's worth - at least from the writer. Probably the best way to check off the credit side of the journal is a chronological review, as best can be remembered, of the years that flew by so quickly, while I was having fun.

So it is with great anticipation, and hopefully a satisfied curiosity, that I begin this journey to recall the past. It will be interesting to see how many happenings can be retrieved, and with what degree of clarity. It may bring some laughs and provoke a tear or two, but hopefully it will serve as a pleasant reminder of what was involved in a life spent in service to the citizens of Boston.

Everyone has to be born somewhere
SOMEWHERE
(or, Why Not In Back of A Fire Barn)

There comes a time in most families when someone brings up the question of the Family Tree. This usually happens after the children have grown up, left the nest, made you grandparents and their children get curious about whence they came. Alex Haley wrote a book that became a TV mini-series about this very subject and called it *Roots*.

Now the trouble with most families is that when someone starts asking questions about the Family Tree, the two people that first planted the dumb bush can't be found to supply the desired answers. In fact, even the more recent bearers of the family name who might be expected to fill in some of the blanks are no longer around either, or they have forgotten. About the only solution is to have a family conference, or even a series of them, and try to recreate the tree with the bits and pieces of information that can be gathered from those still able to communicate. Aunts and uncles can usually be a big help in this sort of project but even with all available assistance, the end result is often a lot of twigs and very few branches. Any four-year-old with a pad of paper and a box of crayons could produce a better-looking tree. The tree put together by the joint family efforts usually bears no resemblance to the ones about which Joyce Kilmer wrote.

Along the same line, whenever the fruit of the subject tree produces something great - or produces bad apples as sometimes happens, someone is sure to raise the question as to whether inheritance or environment can be credited or blamed. If the harvest was unfavorable to the family, the blame is quickly placed on the spouse's side; but when there is a really noteworthy achievement, then naturally full credit should be given to your noble side of the ancestral lineage.

It would appear Dr. Sigmund Freud leaned toward environment as being the dominating element in life and perhaps he can pick up a brownie point in this case. When we shook our family tree, a few nuts fell from the branches (what family doesn't have them) but no firemen, so my vocation cannot be attributed to inheritance. On the other hand there is environment.

At the time of my arrival, the family house was on Beethoven Street in the Egleston Square section of Boston, right on the Jamaica Plain / Roxbury line. Our back yard abutted that of the city's fire barn, which fronted at 3089 Washington Street and housed Engine 42 and Ladder 30, together with the horses that pulled them. The barn was built around 1893. At least that is when it was first occupied by BFD. Not too long before my arrival, the fire apparatus had been motorized.

The lot line between the two properties was marked by a fence, and some prize-winning dahlias that were my dad's pride and joy - until yours truly came along. After five boys (although the second oldest, Emerson, died on Christmas Day when he was seven, before I was born), my parents, Frank and Florence Cook, were really hoping for a daughter to grace and complete the family. When the fifth son put in his appearance in 1923, Dad bowed his head and prayed, "Thank you Lord for another healthy son, and I don't mean to complain, but this is getting monotonous" - or so I was told. In all fairness it must be added that Mom later said, after we had all grown up and married, she was most pleased that she had all boys. Perhaps it was just said to make the runt of the litter feel good - and if so, it worked.

The environmental effect (if there was one) really started the following summer. The family album contains pictures of the future chief in his carriage, absorbing sun and fresh air, with the fire barn in the background. Surely my carriage was within hearing distance of the house gong, but I didn't respond then.

Now brother Herb was a different story. When Herb heard the house gong, he did respond - right through Dad's dahlias and over the fence. He also responded, before going to school in the morning, to clean out beneath and behind the horses. Strange how "sparks" will willingly perform otherwise undesirable tasks just because it allows them to play the role of fireman for a little while. Also strange is the fact the firemen didn't care if he did it!

More Environment. Next door to the fire house was the old Egleston Theatre. It was a large wooden structure that disappeared one night in a beautiful multiple alarm fire (Box 2445). Rather than turn the vacant space into a permanent parking lot, the Littlefield family, who owned the property, decided to replace the burned out movie house with a new larger brick edifice. To do this they needed more space so they bought our house and moved it to what is now Mendell Way, off lower School Street, and there it still stands.

They provided the Cook family with an apartment on upper School Street, at reasonable rent, and included a ten-year pass to the new theatre for the family. More about the theatre will follow but the fire environment persisted in the School Street house. Prior to our moving there in the second year of my life, there was a serious fire in the house one Christmas night that was started by lighted wax candles on a Christmas tree. When our family moved in, there was a white marble mantel in the "parlor" which still bore heat scars on the underside from that fire. No amount of cleaning would remove them and often in my youth I relaxed on a couch under that mantel and looking up at that blackened reminder of the earlier fire, dreamed of being a fireman.

Anecdote:
Years after we moved, the house was destroyed beyond repair in a two alarm fire (Box 2448) and the remains were torn down. Today the land is being used for parking.

Brother Herb also dreamed of being a fireman but circumstances were different in those days of the Great Depression, as this continuing saga will reveal.

The real supporting limb of the Cook family, our Dad, died of pneumonia at 9:00 P.M. on February 23, 1932. Herb was the only one of the boys out of school and he had plans to marry in

November, so responsibility lay heavy on his shoulders. Brother Charles would be graduating from high school that June, Richard was in the sixth grade at the George Putnam School on Columbus Avenue and the runt of the litter was in the third grade at the Ellis Mendell School on School Street (where else).

The Depression was taking its toll following the Wall Street crash in 1929. The economic catastrophe had spread throughout the entire world. In the United States, businesses were closing and jobs were becoming scarce. In 1932 Franklin Delano Roosevelt had been elected President and he was taking steps that would change America forever. If a person had a job, he did nothing to jeopardize it. Some companies would promptly dismiss an employee if they found out he or she was seeking, or even considering employment elsewhere. There were just too many people looking for permanent work to keep an employee on the job who might leave on their own volition.

Following his graduation from West Roxbury High School (later changed to Jamaica Plain High School), Herbert started work as a "Bench Boy" (inside messenger) with the National Shawmut Bank. In his forty-six years with the bank, he moved up on his ladder of promotions to become a Vice President before reaching mandatory retirement, but at the time of Dad's passing he was a teller in the Boylston Street Branch. Although he too wanted more than anything to be a Boston fireman, he felt he could not afford to risk detection by taking the Fire Entrance Exam.

Besides, the fire department was also suffering from the same conditions that were plaguing the rest of the country, so there was a drought as far as adding new firemen. No firemen or policemen were laid off during the Great Depression and this gave rise to the belief that these jobs assured security. This balloon was shot down in 1981-82 when firefighters were discharged, officers were demoted and about a third of the fire companies were deactivated in Boston, under the guise of Proposition 2-1/2 and Affirmative Action. It was all very political and almost made firemen yearn for the good old Depression days when the city fathers and the courts respected public safety and dedicated men.

Going back to the Depression days, the first men added to the fire department in nearly four years were the Famous "96" who were appointed in July 1937. Soon after, many of them volunteered or were drafted into the Armed Forces as the war in Europe spread following Germany's attack on Poland on the first of September 1939 and the first Peace Time Draft was begun in our country. After the Japanese sneak attack on Pearl Harbor in December 1941, many more firemen joined the military ranks and this resulted in a further reduction in the manpower of fire companies. The men serving their country were carried "On Military Leave" as the Journal was written up each morning at eight o'clock and evenings at six following Roll Call.

Most of these men returned to the fire department when they were separated from the service and soon became the strong nucleus of officers who would guide the department in the coming years. Having had their apprenticeship with the real old timers, some of whom had worked the "day off in seven" schedule, they had a strong influence for good in our early years in the department.

It is quite likely that Herb might have been among those appointed then if he had felt at liberty to take the Fire Entrance Exams during the Depression. How he would have loved to have been one of those Famous "96." He would have gladly given up all the plaudits and accolades that later came his way, in banking and associated fields, to wear the blue uniform of a Boston fireman.

It is getting way ahead of the chronological order, but to digress a moment, these men were highly commended in General Order 13, series 1979. It read:

GENERAL ORDER   HEADQUARTERS FIRE DEPARTMENT
NO. 13   MARCH 13, 1979

THE "96"

The retirement on March 1, 1979 of Fire Captain Robert W. Collins, Ladder Company 8, will bring to an end the presence within our ranks of a group of men who were referred to and were justly proud to be called the "96."

To the members of the department who are not aware of the "96," they were a group of 96 firefighters appointed July 16, 1937, a time when appointments were few and far between.

Over the years these men, by example of courage and experience, kept the spirit and camaraderie of this department alive and well. Furthermore, they had the foresight that brought positive changes within the department that are enjoyed by all members today, changes such as creation of Local 718, Celeste Blood Bank, establishment of the Credit Union, and changes in Relief Fund elections.

On behalf of all members, I am pleased to highly commend these men and wish them good health in their retirements.

BY ORDER OF FIRE COMMISSIONER/CHIEF GEORGE H. PAUL

The environmental impact struck the Cook brothers long before DEQE and EPA became household words. Herb was born in Boston in 1908 (Boy that seems a long time ago!) the same year the City of Chelsea experienced one of its several major fires. At the time, a Boston newspaper assembled a collection of photos depicting Chelsea and the devastation caused by the conflagration. There were about a dozen pictures printed on a three-foot by four-foot piece of heavy paper, suitable for framing, and it came in a cardboard cylinder ready for mailing.

Someone of our ancestors thought it appropriate that the baby boy born in 1908 should have a set of the Chelsea commemorative prints as a souvenir of the other historic event that took place the year he was born. It was preserved in a safe place until Herb came of age (about seven) to decorate his own room, and there the pictures had a prominent place both as a decoration and an inspiration. Herb became a "spark."

Sparks, or buffs, come in a variety of ages, sizes, shapes and sexes. Just about everybody will stop to watch a fire if it occurs in the neighborhood they happen to be in. Some even get caught up enough in the excitement of watching the firefighters' battle that they become full-fledged sparks.

Sparks come in various degrees of commitment. Some are content to listen to scanners and just be aware of what is happening before they see it on the eleven o'clock news or read it in the morning paper. Some listen to their scanners with the intention of going to the fire. There the classification of sparks is further delineated.

First there are the "observers" who just watch as long as there is action to hold their attention. Lots of flames are the attraction but once these are beaten back the novelty is over and home they go. Next might be the "student" sparks who are impressed by the systematic procedures that are followed and that eventually make man master over the flames. They have learned to appreciate that firemen don't break windows to satisfy an adolescent frustration, but rather to facilitate the technological approach of ventilation which is providing avenues for heat, toxic fumes and smoke to be removed from a structure so firefighters can enter and attack the fire. As these sparks observe and better understand the science of firefighting, and then discuss their observations with their acquaintances, they perform a worthwhile public relations service for fire departments. After the "students" might come the "critic" sparks who may have started out as "students" but soon became self-appointed experts who stand among the spectators at a fire and outspokenly vocalize on how the fire should be fought - in their opinion. They may sound quite knowledgeable to the uninformed within hearing distance, but they do a real disservice to dedicated firemen.

Some sparks spend their time at a fire house doing nothing more than enjoying the atmosphere of those sacred halls. This is probably a carry over from smaller towns where the fire departments are often made up partially or entirely of volunteers and the fire station is the social center of the community.

And then there are the elite - the "working" sparks who enjoyed special privileges in their "off-the-record" role. They have become a dying breed because of the changing firefighting profession which now requires all men entering a fire building to be more or less encapsulated. "Working" spark was a plateau that many sparks aspired to, but few attained. It was a special acceptance, unofficially granted, on an individual basis within a particular fire house and was usually limited to that domain. The privilege came with strict responsibilities and could be terminated quicker than it was granted. Herb was a "working" spark - one of the "elite!"

Scanners are a short wave radio innovation that came on the market a few years ago and promptly became a must for sparks to own. Instead of having a radio that could receive only one fire department station at a time, the scanner, as its name implies, is capable of monitoring several frequencies. When a particular department is transmitting, the scanner stops and picks up the signal and when the message is finished it resumes scanning.

The early models did this by means of individual crystals set to the frequency of a particular fire department. This limited the number of communities or public safety departments that could be monitored, but it was better than a separate radio for each one. Changing crystals took a little time and a little money as each crystal cost about five dollars then. Less expensive and more convenient are the programmable scanners that are on the market today. Top of the line models cover several bands and up to a hundred channels. Frequencies are added or changed simply by punching the desired numbers into the program. They are reasonably priced in the two hundred dollar range.

Some eager-beaver sparks keep two or more scanners going all the time and will drive almost any distance if indications are the fire will still be burning when they get to it with their marshmallows. Taking along a camera, and now camcorders, provide a means of reliving their hobby experiences and also sharing them with audiences unable to view them first hand.

The availability of scanners to know about fires and the abundance of autos to get there are the tools of the modern spark, but they cannot compare with the thrill of being a "working" spark. Scanners and autos in abundance were not available fifty years ago so sparks had to be more ingenious about means to alert sparky friends that a multiple was in progress.

Herb had a friend, whom we will refer to as Bill. Bill was also a spark, and a rarity in those days, he had a car - about a 1925 Ford rumble seat roadster. One Saturday they spent all day installing what might be called a house gong in the School Street home of the Cooks. It consisted of three, one and a half volt dry cell batteries connected in series with a large door bell in Herb's room. From there one wire from the bell side and one from the batteries ran in parallel out the window and down the back of the house where they terminated about ten feet from the ground.

Bill also had a radio that picked up Boston Fire, which at that time broadcasted on a single channel at 1630 kilocycles on the regular home broadcast band. There was no two way communication, or even voice at that time, so all that could be heard was the beep beeps that were simultaneously sent over the tapper circuits. It permitted listeners to know when there was a multiple struck and when the "all out" was sent. Bill kept his radio on at all times, like a good spark, and when there was a multiple he would drive to School Street to pick up Herb.

Bill was rather short in stature so when he got to our house he had to climb up on the fence and then with a key reach up and touch the two parallel wires they had installed on the back of the house. The key connection completed the circuit, the bell rang in Herb's room and he got up and went to the fire. This arrangement was supposed to allow Herb to learn of a fire and leave the house without disturbing the rest of the family. In reality, Mom slept with one eye open and it was impossible to sneak in or out of the house without her knowing it. Herb and Bill should have saved their time and money that Saturday and just let Bill ring the front door bell when there was a fire.

Anecdote:
Although Bill was not accorded the privilege of being a "working spark," he too dreamed of becoming a Boston fireman. He often spent evenings in a fire house shooting the breeze or playing cards. One rainy night he was doing just that and the tapper had died. Around midnight, Bill left to go home. It was so quiet in the department that evening that as he was leaving, one of the firemen, out of character, jokingly remarked, "On your way home will you pull a box so we can see if the tapper is still working?"

Bill was walking that night and passed a half dozen fire boxes on his way home in the rain. Just before turning into his street, there was the lighted red globe over a fire box. The fireman's remark sneaked into his head. He looked around and saw no one. Without suspecting the possible consequences, he pulled the hook and ran for his house. Naturally the tapper worked and the apparatus was on the way, but as Bill crossed the street a policeman, who had been ducking in a doorway to keep dry, stepped out and grabbed him. Bill was arrested for his first, and only, brush with the law. At his trial he pleaded guilty and was sentenced to six months in jail, even though he had no previous record.

Even more tragic to Bill was the fact that he now had a police record and so was for ever barred from realizing his dream of becoming a fireman. For quote, "Justice sake," compare this sequence of events, and the consequences of a relatively minor infraction, with what the State Department of Personnel Administration, and our courts, overlook today with regards to some individuals with repeated felony convictions. They then force cities and towns to give these individuals a public safety job - all under the guise, or more accurately disguise, of Civil Rights and Politically Correct.

Upon his release from jail, Bill was persona non grata in the fire house. This was adding insult to injury, and although he avoided fire houses, Bill remained sparky and best friends with Herb.

One year for Christmas, in the early thirties, there was a Buddy L truck under the tree for me. People who grew up in those years will know of what I write, but for the rest, it was the trade name for a rugged little steel toy truck about two feet long. They had rubber tires and a steering wheel which actually controlled the front wheels. My truck took the form of the American Express delivery trucks of that era, complete with a genuine wire mesh cargo area with a small padlock to secure the rear doors. When the novelty of the delivery truck wore off, I used it as a fire engine - with a lot of imagination.

Seeing this, Herb and Bill offered to turn it into a real fire engine for me. They had it at Bill's house for six months before returning it to me as a replica of Engine 42's wagon, complete with gold lettering on the hood, BOSTON FIRE DEPARTMENT ENGINE 42, a black canvas windshield and headlights. There were wooden ladders on the side, a rake and axe in mounted holders on the sides of the hose bed. The back step included a reel with booster hose plus a brass lowry hydrant and fire extinguisher. On the right running board was a covered metal tool box filled with miscellaneous equipment including a copper "hose hoist." On the left running board were the traditional wooden battery box and a "Kelly door opener" in brackets.

The hose bed was covered with three removable floor boards and a canvas cover to protect the hose. The cover draped over the end of the hose box and was authentically marked E.42. On the deck was a rope life net, wood wheel chocks with straps, a deck gun and of course the standard cylindrical gas tank and the brass bell over the driver's head.

The fifty-foot lengths of two and half inch hose were fifteen inch pieces of cotton clothes line. Couplings were spent twenty-two caliber long shells forced onto the ends of the rope. Small dressmaker snaps were soldered onto the ends of the shells to make them male and female. This allowed my hose to be shortened or lengthened as necessary to reach the "fire." My "fire house" was the space under the kitchen stove. Mom sure was a patient lady!

Meanwhile, when Herb went to the fire house for a night of sparking the tapper usually died, but over the years he caught his share of workers and multiples and relished them all. As Herb moved up the ladder of success in the bank and became more valuable to them, he had to cut back on his active firefighting. His direct superiors knew his blood-shot eyes and hung-over appearance was the result of having caught a good fire the night before, but they feared customers would suspect other causes.

They were also concerned he might get hurt and the bank would lose his services for a spell. He never fully obeyed their dictum but as a compromise he became active in the Red Cross Disaster Service so he could continue going to fires, even if he couldn't work at them. Typical of him, Herb ascended in the Red Cross ranks as well.

He headed the Disaster Service Unit in Boston for a number of years and brought it to such high standards that it is still exemplified as the goal of excellence to try to duplicate. He went on to National office in the Red Cross where he was recognized as an authority on Disaster Service. All this as a forty-five year Red Cross volunteer.

His picture hangs in a prominent place at the Brookline Avenue Red Cross Headquarters and I am told that hardly a meeting is held without some reference being made to Herb and his unselfish devotion and contribution to the Red Cross. The bank was delighted with his community involvement and gave him time off to attend to his multiple volunteer activities, and took credit for their donation to worthy a cause.

Anecdote:
The Red Cross Disaster Service of Mass Bay has established the "Herbert E. Cook Award for Outstanding Leadership." It is given in recognition to those volunteers whose Leadership has: enhanced, (1) service delivery to disaster victims, and (2), the professional image of Red Cross in the community. In 1987 it was my privilege, on behalf of Mass Bay, to present the Award to the first recipient, Don Walker.

The *Sunday Herald Magazine* ran an article on Herb entitled, "The Banker Who Goes To Fires." In it they pointed out that Herb spent about a hundred and fifty nights a year in his volunteer work helping people. In later years, some of his spare time was spent as an active Emergency Medical Technician and he was honored by being given the first "Massachusetts E.M.T. of the Year Award."

For years he spent Thursday nights as a volunteer in the Emergency Ward, first at Boston City Hospital and later at Peter Bent Brigham Hospital. His normal job on the emergency floor was to take vital signs and do basic first aid until a doctor could see a patient but during the war, with many doctors in the service, his role expanded to include using his advanced first aid knowledge. He was fond of telling about one night at Boston City during the war when an inebriated man was brought in with some cuts and Herb patched him up. The man became appreciative of the fine care Herb had given him and when a doctor finally got to see him, the patient became resentful of the change in his "doctors." He belted the real MD in the face and told him he would stick with his first "doctor."

Long before it became a menacing problem, Herb was a pioneer in bank security and established much of the basic principles that are the accepted guide governing bank security today. When approached by a local university to teach Bank Security, he declined because they would not restrict the class to bank security officers only. His reasoning was that by opening the course to everyone, the bad guys could also learn all the secrets for the cost of the course. Herb is named as a contributor to the Bank Protection Manual of the American Bankers Association and a copy can be found in every national bank in the country.

Meanwhile Paul was growing up and becoming fascinated with Herb's hobby of sparking. *The Boston Post* newspaper included in the morning edition, the "Daily Fire Record," which was a report of all fire alarms in Boston for the previous day. It included the box, time, fire location, casualties, loss and cause - but being the "media" it was never fully accurate or complete. Each day I went to that page of the paper with scissors and pasted the dated clippings into a scrap book for future reference.

Anecdote:
Years later when I returned from the European Theatre of Operations following World War II, my wife to be had faithfully, and unknown to me, saved all the "Daily Fire Records" that appeared in the Boston Post during my two plus years overseas.

Eventually my sparking became more active, but I couldn't just walk into a fire house, hang around and tell them I wanted to spark - particularly at the ripe old age of about ten years. They would have thrown me out bodily. My approach had to be more subtle. Of course the chosen target fire house was the one closest to home, Engine 42 / Ladder 30 in Egleston Square.

There were no "general alarm" switches in fire houses in those days. Just two buttons in brass switch plates at the patrol desk, one put on all the lights in the house and the other one was for the house gong. The apparatus house doors were manually opened by the officers or senior men, who then preceded the apparatus onto the apron where they mounted the moving engines. This procedure was in compliance with the Department Rule Book and provided me my "in."

Outside the fire house there was a siren that could be heard for quite a distance. The man on patrol pulled a lever when they were responding and the siren outside gave five seven second blasts. The purpose was to clear the traffic in front of the fire house and alert any men who might be out of quarters. No matter where I was or what I was doing, when that siren went off, I ran for the fire house. My chosen task was to close the doors, put out the lights and wait for the apparatus to return; then put on the lights and open the doors. Actually it was the police officer on the beat who was supposed to do this. The men appreciated the doors being closed in the winter to conserve heat and before long they were sending me on errands. My acceptance had begun.

The Cook brothers were not the only sparks in the Egleston Square area. In fact, there were four others who lived on Weld Avenue and probably a dozen more in the general neighborhood. During the Depression, with limited work opportunities, a lot of men became more or less interested in the fire department. First it gave them something to help fill the void of long empty days, and second, some maintained their interest and eventually became firemen.

One of the neighborhood sparks was Fran Quigley whose father was deputy chief in Division Two, which was located on Warren Avenue along with the then District 7, Engine 22 and Ladder 13. Fran was older than me, having already graduated from Boston College and had spent some time during the Depression in the C.M.T.C. (Citizen's Military Training Corps). Age difference has little to do with sparks as their common interest overlooks the years. Fran and I had one other common interest - going to the movies, and this was the way we spent most Fridays (after I got out of school) and Saturdays (after I finished my chores at home) for several years - if we had money.

The first stop on Friday was the theatre in the South Station because that was the day they changed their program. Admission was twenty-five cents, for which you saw about a dozen short features on a variety of subjects. The reason for this arrangement was that people waiting to catch a train could kill a few minutes or a couple hours in an enjoyable fashion for a reasonable cost. If we had the money we might go to another movie in the evening, or if his father was working we might visit him, and hop in the back of his red car if he had a run. On Saturdays we would try to get in town to a theatre before one o'clock because that was the bewitching hour for admission to jump from a quarter to forty cents. If money was short, we would walk to some section of the city to become more familiar with the different neighborhoods.

On some warm summer evenings we would go to East Boston by the ferry. Cost of the ride from the ferry slip at the end of Battery Street was one cent. When it docked, we would hide somewhere on the boat and then reappear when it pulled away from the slip for the return trip. In this way we could cruise back and forth across the harbor all evening for a penny.

Anecdote:
Quig joined the Army when the war clouds gathered and when the war ended, he was among those veterans who were appointed to the fire department on January 22, 1947. He became a lieutenant before he developed a heart condition and was retired. Like an old fire horse, he continued going to fires and in the seventies he had a

heart attack and died, while watching a three bagger on Heath Street in Jamaica Plain.

We had an agreement to alert each other of multiple alarm fires and the duties of the man on patrol in fire houses gave us an assist in this direction. In every Boston fire house there was a blackboard on the wall outside the patrol desk. At Engine 42 there were engraved brass plates over sections of the blackboard indicating what current information was to be posted, such as "Water Off," "Streets Closed" and "Last Alarm." This latter section was the one most important to sparks. It was the duty of the man on patrol to post with chalk the last alarm received on the tapper. When a chief officer came into quarters, he was given a salute and the last alarm. He usually glanced to see if it was posted - and it better be!

In the days before radios, even in chief's cars, this information was vital. When a second and then additional alarms were struck, the man on patrol added this info to the Last Alarm board along with the time received. Since I was by far the youngest of our group, it was easy, and expected of me, to frequently check the last alarm and alert the sparks when necessary.

Once in a while one of the others might have access to a car, in which case it was a much faster means to the fire. Often we had to rely on the old Boston El street cars and buses. If the fire was downtown, there were plenty of open trucks going through the square and hooking a ride on the back of one was a toll free way of getting to the fire while there was still something to see.

No matter how hot the weather, or how appealing an ice cream cone, or cold drink might become, we always made certain there was a dime in our pocket. This way we always got to the fire and it didn't matter if we had to walk home from Charlestown, South Boston, Hyde Park or any other section of the city.

We approached this problem philosophically and concluded that it provided us with an opportunity to better learn the city. In reality, we would have much preferred a second dime in our pocket, and to heck with philosophy. In coming years I would get a ride home with Engine 42 or Ladder 30, if they were at the fire, but that was still an eon down the road.

Avon calling
(or, It Only Costs Five Dollars)

In the middle nineteen thirties my interest in fires followed two separate paths, like the parallel railroad tracks that appear to merge at some distant point on the horizon. Fortunately mine did merge.

On one hand, my goal was to be accepted as a "working" spark, but since I was only about eleven years old at the time, it was necessary to wait for biological processes to add age, height and weight to my body. In the meantime, the other path I would follow was that of a student spark. At the Secretary's Office at the State House, anyone wanting to be a fireman could purchase a Red Book, which was the manual used to study for the Fire Entrance Examination. In later years it would be declared irrelevant, and the vast amount of knowledge it contained for exam questions would be replaced with tough minded bogglers like, "Do you love your mother?" But in those days it was still the bible for fire department aspirants and so I made a visit to the State House and purchased my first Red Book. The fact that ten years would have to elapse before I would be eligible to take the exam was immaterial. When it comes to education, you can never start too early. Mom wished her youngest would apply that same logic to his three R's in grade school, and forget the distant future for a while.

During this time Mom was having her own problems trying to make ends meet and coping, through no fault of hers, with what is today termed "single parenthood." She was an excellent self-taught dressmaker and earned some money making and altering women's apparel at home. About this time the Boston Public

Schools began an Adult Evening Education Program which men and women could attend at no cost to learn a trade or improve their skills in one. Mom became a Sewing instructor at the Mary E. Curley School for three dollars a night. At first it was just on Wednesday nights, but as the Program grew in popularity, Friday nights were added to the schedule. She continued teaching two nights a week for over thirty-five years, during which time the nightly stipend increased to about twenty-five dollars a night.

In those Depression days every little bit helped but it was never enough to meet the needs of a family of growing boys. One day a woman stopped by the house and said she had been given Mom's name to contact relative to her becoming an Avon sales lady. Then it was a relatively new company specializing in cosmetics and some cooking products, and developing a new twist in marketing - ladies selling lady's products door to door. It cost five dollars to become a "Representative." There was no salary but commission on sales was forty percent, which was quite generous. The five dollars to start in the business didn't come easy but with Divine leading, Mom signed on the dotted line and became Avon's second Representative in New England.

The five dollar cost provided her with a black leather bag containing about three dollars worth of sample Avon products, catalogs, sales book, order forms and other items necessary to become a successful seller. Mom became just that and within the year Avon came calling again and wanted her to become the first "Supervisor" in New England. Her new job would be to persuade other ladies to come up with the magical five dollars so they too could start "Avon Calling" on their own. For a start Mom's territory would be the Boston area, but also Eastern Massachusetts and as much of the rest of the state and New England as she was able to cover. She accepted the challenge, and the job, which was quite an undertaking considering her background and work experience.

Her new career caused her to start out each day with two Avon black leather bags under her arm and using public transportation, head for some section of the city or suburbs in her attempt to entice other ladies to become Avon Representatives. Supposedly her salary was a hundred dollars a month at the start, but the five dollars she was expected to collect from each new recruit was deducted from the hundred. Naturally

Avon hoped she would place at least twenty new representatives each month, which meant their outlay would be zero.

Unfortunately this was not easy to accomplish. To encourage interested individuals who just couldn't afford the five dollars all at once, Mom would often take an I.O.U. in the form of a dollar a week, or wait for the lady's first sales before collecting the five dollars. In those poverty days, most people were still honest and eventually she collected most of the fives. Sometimes the barter system came into play and that is the way I took violin lessons. Mom should have waited for that five dollars in cash, no matter how long it took!

To keep track of her growing number of sales ladies, and so as not to saturate any one area, Mom purchased a large map of the city, had it mounted on fiberboard and hung it up in the kitchen over a chest of drawers. Colored pins were used to mark the location of her growing number of representatives. It soon became an impressive indication of Avon's growth and progress in the Boston area - until our cat, sitting on the chest of drawers, discovered it was good exercise for his jaws to sit and pull out the pins. Naturally the pin holes remained and it was easy to recreate the picture. The feline's pin pulling practice was resolved by hanging little tags on the pins, which the cat didn't like and he left the pins in place. The map also came in handy for me to learn my way around the city.

With much hard work and determination, Mom started quite a few ladies on their profitable way as Avon Representatives, and several of them did quite well for themselves. The company started Supervisor's meetings in different cities of the Northeast and brought Mom and her counter-parts, which then numbered about a dozen, to these gatherings. On each successive meeting some Supervisors were replaced with new ones, but in Massachusetts, Avon was expanding nicely and they decided there should be a Boston office.

Following one of the out of town meetings they instructed Mom, on her return, to select and furnish an office and move in. She chose the Little Building at 80 Boylston Street and set up operations in a tenth floor office. The office price range she was pointed in did not provide much of a window view but it was a start. Her additional instruction was to begin training and transforming Representatives into Supervisors whose job would be to go out and get more ladies to sell Avon at five dollars a start. Avon's Boston business boomed, as did the eastern part of the state, so the adjacent office was rented and Mom settled in.

The out of town sessions now became Managers' Meetings and Mom was commended time and again for her leadership accomplishments. As Avon grew in Boston, it also prospered in other parts of the country and its management became more sophisticated and very progressive in its marketing. They had a Managers' Meeting in Washington (as I remember) and only Mom and one other of the original Supervisors were still hanging in. Following this meeting, she was directed to enlarge the Boston office and include an Executive office for herself and furnish it as is fitting a lady executive. For a girl who never graduated from high school, Mom was becoming quite an entrepreneur. She moved Avon into a suite of offices on the Boylston Street side of the Little Building with a commanding view of Boston Common. Avon's Executives were delighted with her choice of location and decor when they came for the opening.

We all figured Mom had now made it in the business world, but shortly after the grand opening of the new enlarged Boston office, she received a very formal letter expressing management's thanks for her years of efforts in their behalf, but her services were no longer needed. They would be sending a lady from New York to be the new office manager, and please turn everything over to her.

This again put the axe to the financial branch of the Cook family tree in no uncertain terms, but Mom accepted this traumatic ending in the same way she had accepted the unexpected beginning, as Divine leading. There was a reason for it all and she would trust God for the future as she had in the past. "And we know that all things work together for good to them that love God..." (Romans 8:28).

At least there was still a good map of Boston on our kitchen wall in which I could push new colored pins to keep track of fires - and I had to remember to hang little tags on the pins lest the cat relocate the fire target areas. Mom harbored no ill feelings towards Avon, and did not resent their map continuing to hang in her kitchen.

Years later, when there was a little money in my pocket with which to dabble in the stock market, Avon had grown into a blue chip company which was recommended by brokers for long and short term investments. I couldn't bring myself to become even a minuscule stock holder in a company without a heart, that greedily prospered and profited without concern or appreciation for the little guys (or gals) who made them big. Of course Avon was not alone, as it has become the norm for big business in America.

It may have been cutting off the nose to spite the face, but one has to have principles. In the eighth grade at the Theodore Roosevelt School, also on School Street, I had a teacher, Miss Bacon, who each week wrote a different saying on the blackboard. One of the many that impressed my young mind was, "I have to live with myself, and so I want to be fit for myself to know." These were words of wisdom to guide a life. So even though there was a chance of making money by getting in on Avon's ground floor, I declined because I have "to live with myself." It was putting character principle before monetary opportunity and I have never regretted not opening that door when Avon called.

Abraham Lincoln said, "No man is poor who has a godly mother." To that I will add my Amen.

CHARIOTS OF FIRE IN A TAJ MAHAL

(or, This Is For Me)

Story wise, the preceding Avon commercial gave my body time to grow a little and my relationship with the fire barn to grow a lot. My visits to the fire barn were more frequent and lasted longer as the men became accustomed to seeing more of "Young Cookie" around the main floor and that became my nickname, or perhaps designation is a better term. Herb, who now became "Old Cookie," never resented my elevating him to senior status so quickly.

He gave me some advice when I first showed serious interest in hanging around the fire house. If it was my desire to be accepted, there was one responsibility that went with the privilege. At the fire house, you see nothing, you hear nothing and most important you say nothing. The rule is, "Don't carry tales!" If stories or events on one platoon reached the other platoon, any spark would be suspected and if there was reasonable, or even unreasonable suspicion, that spark would be finished! I was determined that I would be the perfect model for the three monkeys, with two hands over my ears, two hands over my eyes and two hands over my mouth. That should keep all of my hands busy.

There was no reason to doubt Herb, but his message was driven home again and again in my early days as a "visiting fireman." During the ensuing months and years more errands were entrusted to me and my observations taught me much about the fire house and how it operated. It totally fascinated me. My presence was being accepted and my willingness to help where I could was appreciated. This became evident, as one by one perhaps a dozen or more firemen took me aside, and though maybe using different words, all came across with the same message that Herb had given to me. It was "You are welcome, so long as what you see and hear in the fire house, doesn't go out the door with you." You can be sure I always left empty handed, and empty headed. Years before, Herb must have been taken aside a number of times by the old timers of that day and given the same lecture and advice. My new role was so enjoyable, and so unique for a boy just entering his teens, that I was determined to do nothing that would jeopardize it.

My determination was so set and cemented in those early days that it lasted long after the transition from being a spark to being a paid fireman. In fact it pretty much still exists today. At home, my family long ago learned to accept silence about my work. If I did choose to talk about something that happened, they listened and learned not to press for additional details beyond which I spoke. At work it was my practice not to repeat a story until I had heard it three or four times, by which time it was either a well established rumor that could not be traced, or it was fact. It is said that anything ceases to be a secret once a second person learns of it, and this is definitely true in the fire service.

The fire department that I was introduced to in the thirties was far different than the one existing as I leave the relationship more than fifty years later. Back then it was still a department of wooden ladders and iron men and in my young eyes, all those men stood at least ten feet tall. The fire service has always been considered a "semi-military" organization, and in those days it was more "military" and less "semi." Spit and polish was the accepted way of life in the department. The Rule Book was still in vogue - actively adhered to and seldom tested. Officers merited a salute and were accorded the respect of rank, regardless of the individual. Officers were not expected to be good fellows, just good officers!

It is said that one never really gets over their first love. This may or may not be true in all cases, but I fell in love with the fire department that existed then. Some of the changes that have taken place during the last fifty plus years kind of eases the pain of having to leave that glamorous first love. This may sound a little reminiscent of the general in the movie "Patton," but the corollary gives me an understanding of how the general felt about his years of service and those changing times. Incidentally, during World War II one of my assignments was with General Patton's

Third Army, starting with the breakout at Avranches in Normandy, and then the dash across France and the liberation of Paris. Ah, What a day -- and night!

By today's standard, the fire department that existed in the nineteen thirties would be considered primitive but it should be remembered that all over America, and in fact the world, there was a slow but steady progression into the mechanical age. The transition from horse drawn to motorized apparatus in Boston began in 1910 and was completed in 1923, when they bid adieu to the last faithful horses and put them out to pasture.

Some of the new apparatus looked just like the name implied - the horses were unhitched, the motor installed and they became "motorized." Perhaps it is symbolic, at least to me, that the year I was born the last Boston fire horses departed the scene. Those that remember them, including brother Herb, say it was truly a magnificent sight to behold as two or three steeds raced down the street dragging a highly polished boiler that was spewing out glowing sparks all over the route, as it built up sufficient steam pressure to operate the pumps once it reached the fire.

Old pictures show the ladder trucks generally drawn by a team of three horses. Between the clatter of the horses' hoofs on the cobble stones and the rattle of the wooden ladders and other loosely secured equipment, it produced a distinctive and unforgettable sound, as it dashed towards its fiery destination. Ladder trucks were often referred to as "hay racks."

Even now it is difficult to determine just what the magical attraction was that first drew me to the fire house. Undoubtedly it was a mixture of reasons and circumstances that defies easy explanation. Environment has already been alluded to as one of the probable causes and the excitement that is generated in every boy at the sight of racing fire engines must have also played a significant part. From the very first time my father took me to the fire house to see the engines, I was hypnotized by the whole scene and intoxicated by the aromas that were, and still are, part of that scene.

The distinct aroma that intrigued me in those days must have been a blend, which included the smells left over from the horses, the pipe tobacco of the men, the new rubber tires, the sulphanapthol disinfectant, the brass polish and the waxed engines, the rubber lined cotton hose that may have recently been scrubbed to remove mildew, the canvas covers and windshields, the distinct odors of various smokes that had permeated the fire gear of the men, the pleasant smell of gasoline and the nauseating exhausts of those early gasoline motors, plus the acid chemicals used to charge the extinguishers and chemical tank on the wagon. Intermingled with these were the inevitable fire house cooking odors and the ever perking coffee pot. There must have been a lot of other fire house accessories as well that blended into the atmosphere and added to that sweet perfume which caused me to inhale deeply and savor the air whenever I entered the fire house.

The many routines of the fire house life fascinated me as well. It intrigued me to see the fire gear of the off duty platoon placed on the clothes racks. All were neatly arranged, with the black rubber coats on hooks, boots lined up under, and their leather helmets placed on the shelf over the coats. All of the shields faced front, so that there was a row of white 42s on the Engine's rack and red 30s on the Ladder's rack. Often as I looked at that impressive array, it made me feel like a general reviewing his troops -- and I dreamed that one day my gear would hang among that assembled army.

The patrol desk was the nerve center of the fire house, even as it is today. One man was on watch all the time, even as today, but there the similarity ceases to a degree. In those days the man on watch wore his dress uniform until nine o'clock at night and only the man on watch was allowed on the main floor once house work and other apparatus floor duties were finished. The exception to this rule was "Men on Probation," who were not allowed to leave the patrol desk area until they had learned to count boxes and do watches by themselves. The running cards with the "reversed pyramid system" took a little time to understand, but they had to be mastered before the captain would trust a new man with the watch.

Smoking was not allowed on the apparatus floor so if the man on watch wanted a smoke, he had to get another man to come down and "hold the floor" while he went upstairs and lit up. That was one way I got to practice "holding the floor" and thus began to earn my keep. The man upstairs grabbing a smoke would stay close to a pole so he could return to the apparatus floor quickly, like when the chief was due. When a chief officer visited quarters he was always given the "Last Alarm" and a salute - but by then "Young Cookie" was hiding out of sight at the back of the fire house.

The width of the apparatus floor at the Egleston Square fire house probably measured less than thirty feet. The patrol desk on the right side was no more than thirty inches wide and about seven feet long. It was barely wide enough to hold a regular fire house chair, which were "Captain" style wooden chairs made at the Charlestown State Prison. Small as the Patrol Desk was, it was still efficient and impressive. On the side wall were the tapper and register by which alarms were received. Under the register was a round metal waste basket to catch the used paper tape and other refuse. Also on this wall were the brass City Gong, call bell buttons and circuit switches. The small desk area was just large enough to hold a goose neck lamp, a two hand telephone which rested on a small triangular shelf above the desk, a writing area just large enough to hold the journal, a small horizontal blackboard plus chalk and eraser, and the traditional red and black ink wells with dip pens. (There was always an ample supply of small advertising blotters - from the National Shawmut Bank, thanks to Herb).

Crammed into the right upper corner of the desk area were two buttons, one marked "House Gong" and the other "House Lights." When responding to an alarm of fire in the day time the man on watch would push both buttons at the same time, but for night responses the lights would be put on first as most firemen would react to them and be awake before the house gong clanged. This unheralded procedure was an early attempt to reduce stress - long before it was known to exist.

With all these essentials, there was hardly enough room left on the desk for the feet of the man on watch. Everything possible in the patrol desk area seemed to be made of brass and was polished several times a week. To my eager young eyes it was all very impressive and I was anxious to learn all about it - and use it.

The apparatus doors were of heavy pine wood, hinged with solid panels on the bottom and glass sections on top. These were supposed to be kept closed at all times except when apparatus was passing through but sometimes in the summer, the upper portions would be swung back to allow air to circulate. The district chiefs knew this and out of an unspoken courtesy, they scheduled their required daily visits on a regular time pattern so the man on patrol could have the upper halves closed when he arrived, and thus not get caught violating rules.

At the bottom, on the outside of each door was a metal flange, which hung down and scraped the floor. There were grooves cut into the cement floors so arranged that when the doors were open the flange settled in the groove. The reason for this arrangement was that when responding, the doors were unlocked and swung back and the flange would settle into the groove and hold the door open. Without this arrangement, the doors would have hit the wall, bounced back and been knocked off their hinges when hit by the apparatus -- which still happened from time to time. Rules required that the officer or senior man open the doors and precede the apparatus out of the fire house to be certain there were no persons crossing on the apron. He would mount the apparatus outside of quarters as it was responding. Too many times there were injuries because men slipped and fell as they reached for the apparatus. In my early days of sparking a senior man on Ladder 30 was jammed between the ladder truck fender and the fire house door. He received internal injuries that resulted in a disability retirement. Later, his wife presented him with a set of twins, so it would appear his injuries were not totally incapacitating.

At the back of the main floor was a small room where rolled hose was stored on racks and the gasoline pump was located. Before using it one had to first get the key from the officer on duty. A five gallon open can and a funnel were hung on the pump spigot. Gasoline was brought to the surface by cranking a large handle and then the five gallon can was filled. It was carried to the piece of apparatus and passed up to the driver who stood on the hose bed deck and filled the round tank using the funnel. Sound like a rather antiquated system? It was the accepted practice until we moved to the new fire house at 1870 Columbus Avenue in December 1952.

In the cellar of that old fire house was the hose drying racks, a coal fired furnace and the necessary coal bin, rock salt storage (which came in a hundred and twenty pound bags in those days) and the "Orange Crate Office" about which there will be more later.

On the second floor were the four officer's rooms. Each officer had his own room on the two platoon system but they shared the shower and toilet. The rest of the second floor was taken up by the men's locker room with its black soapstone sink with four sets of brass hot and cold water faucets, shower room and toilets. Hanging on the toilet partition wall was the traditional cloth roller towel for drying hands. It was changed every two or three days, whether it needed or not! There was also a wall mounted device to hold shoes for shining.

On the third floor was the then called "smoking room" which contained a pool table (provided by the city to all fire houses - in olden days), a table suitable for card playing, several of the "prison" chairs and a library box. Each month the Boston Public Library delivered a box of books, on assorted subjects, to each fire house and left them there until they brought replacements. Thanks to this contribution by the library, most firemen were well informed on a variety of subjects.

Also on the third floor were the kitchen and the bunk room. I was mesmerized by the bunk room. It was "L" shaped and contained a dozen beds all neatly made up the same with white linen and pillow cases, a gray blanket, white bed spread and a rolled red blanket at the foot. In the center of the bunk room was the brass sliding pole that was held in place by four rounded brass supports, which gave it the appearance of a brass cage over the pole hole. This large amount of brass literally sparkled and in my later sparking years, when I progressed to "bunking in," I often laid in one of those neat bunks and willed myself to stay awake just to be able to delight in that special privilege which was mine. In later years, I willed myself to sleep in that same bunk room - and learned who kept that brass sparkling.

Between the "smoking room" and the bunk room there was a small closet referred to as the "boot locker." It contained cubicles, one for each man, to hold his night hitch. Opposite this was a second good sized closet which was kept locked, except for one day a year. The contents of this locked closet I learned years later after my appointment.

Each year there comes a time in the fire house that is known as "spring cleaning time." The entire fire house is scoured from the roof to the cellar, and then at Egleston Square came the day when that third floor closet was unlocked and opened. In it had been placed the harnesses when the apparatus was motorized. Our captain had been in the department when much of the equipment was still horse drawn and although he wasn't responsible for putting the harnesses there, he took it as his responsibility as captain of the house to be certain they were always ready and in usable condition.

On the last day of spring cleaning each year, the closet was unlocked, the harnesses were taken out and moved to the "smoking room," where we took cotton waste (a fire house product of the past) and laboriously rubbed generous amounts of neatsfoot oil into the leather to preserve it. The brass fittings were polished till they glistened. Then the harnesses were returned to their storage place for another year, and the closet locked.

Anecdote:
There was a heavy snow storm during one of the war years and motor apparatus was having difficulty getting around the city. Engine 42, along with a few other engines, was given a horse and wagon to respond with. When the horse arrived at Egleston Square, the closet on the third floor was unlocked and opened and a harness, in "mint" condition, was brought down and put into service. While waiting for an alarm, the horse was kept in the small room at the back of the main floor tied to the hose rack, where the ungrateful beast bit the fireman who was assigned to take care of and feed him. I was in the service and overseas at the time so missed even this opportunity to see "horse drawn apparatus" if one could call it that. The horse and wagon was loaned by the Park Department so the response certainly wasn't the breathtaking sight that was so awe inspiring in years now long gone.

Anecdote, Second Alarm:
Around 1950 one of the Assistant Chiefs from Headquarters headed a program to rid fire houses and the department of unnecessary and outmoded equipment. Throughout the city's many fire houses, many truck loads of once valuable items were discarded. When the chief came to 42's old house he asked what

was in that locked third floor closet. The key was produced and the door opened. He took one look at the specially preserved relics of the horse drawn days, and without hesitating said, "Add those to the trash pile!"

To complete the description of the fire house, on the roof was a wood deck where firemen and clothes hung out in the summer time. On the left side of the firehouse at ground level was a driveway long enough to hold four or five cars. To the rear was a small area just large enough to have an abbreviated horse shoe court. It should be pointed out that the previously mentioned driveway member parking separated the fire house from the new Egleston Square Theatre. Although the theatre was not part of the fire house, it played an important part in fire house life as well as in the life of the rest of Egleston Square.

You may or may not be impressed by my word description of those hallowed halls, but to me, and this is no reflection on the home Mom provided us, it was a mansion! A real palace! The Taj Mahal! The fire engines in that Taj Mahal would probably not impress too many people today either, except as antiques or as Americana artifacts. Let us look at them. On the left side was Ladder 30. In 1927 the so-called City Service type ladder truck was replaced with an American LaFrance seventy-five foot wooden aerial ladder truck. It had solid rubber tires and was a right-hand drive, as were all the fire engines of that time.

All the apparatus was chain driven and had two wheel brakes. On occasion these chains would come off the sprockets while the apparatus was responding, which of course put the piece "out of service." Replacing the big bicycle type chains was the sole responsibility of the driver, but usually with the help of other members. It was not considered a job for the Motor Squad but it had to be done quickly so the apparatus could continue to the alarm or return to quarters "in service." In the case of a two piece engine company, the driver would be left alone to replace the chain and the rest of the men would respond with the other piece.

There was a black canvas windshield, which was just that, something to shield the driver and officer from the wind, but the driver at least had to look over it to see where they was going. At that time the tillerman had no protection at all in front of him.

The headlights were big round lenses about ten inches in diameter, and of course did not have high and low beams. You were lucky if they lit.

There was a single small red light, which may or may not have flashed, to let the public know the on-coming vehicle was a fire engine. There was a hand operated siren for the officer to use. The harder he cranked the handle, the louder the sound and the higher the pitch. The desired warning sounds could not be attained by an officer passively sitting and twirling the crank so many times he would be standing up all the way to the location and work up considerable sweat before even reaching the fire. There was also a hand siren on the running board of the trailer portion which was operated by the man riding on that side. The conventional large brass bell was also on the trailer and a rope ran down the length of each side so men riding on the sides could make use of this important warning device. Going to the fire there was usually a strong continuous pulling on the bell rope which was accelerated if traffic conditions required it. Returning to quarters, the bell was sounded in intermittent strokes of twos indicative of the "All Out."

The tillerman had a leather cushioned seat which he had to swing out of the way when they reached a fire scene and the spring raised ladder had to be thrown. The wooden steering wheel for the tiller was a good two foot in diameter and the spindle for it passed through the bed of ladders and into a small hole in the trailer steering mechanism. As well as swinging his seat out of the way at the fire location, the tillerman had to remove the steering wheel, hang it on the side hook and then remove the spindle and place it in the keepers provided so the ground ladders could be removed from the bed if they were needed.

Before returning from the fire, the spindle had to be reinserted into the steering box. Sometimes when going over rough roads the spindle would bounce out of the steering box. The tillerman would have to be alert and quickly return it to the small hole so he would not lose control. Finding in a hurry that small hole, which you could not see, with the end of the spindle, which you could not see, was like looking for a needle in a haystack, but this was just accepted as part of the tillerman's job. No one complained, and no one thanked him.

Another hazard of that early apparatus was the crank. Self starters were just beginning to be added and sometimes they didn't work or the battery was low and it just wouldn't turn over the engine. Then one of the men had to crank the motor while the driver adjusted the spark and throttle to the right combination for a start. At this point the crank would sometimes kick back and if the man was holding it tightly, he might end up with a broken wrist or arm.

Equipment on ladder trucks in those days was simple and required a lot of strength to use. The wooden ground ladders were heavy and many were raised at fires in Boston - and still are today. Soda and acid extinguishers rode in metal containers on the running boards and later carbon-dioxide extinguishers were added, as were the H & H inhalators. Life nets were of rope mesh and were carried in a wooden box at the back of Ladder 30. Each truck carried two All-Service Gas Masks which were kept in boxes in the wire baskets which constituted the storage space under the ladder bed. About the only time masks were used then were at ship fires or very, very smokey cellar fires. Other equipment included door busters, cellar pipes, hand saws, axes, rakes (or pike poles) of various lengths, wire cutters and rubber gloves to use with them, brooms, water buckets, a box of elevator tools and a First Aid box.

Anecdote:
During World War II, Air Raid Wardens provided five gallon galvanized water pump cans to those requesting them. They were intended to be used by people to extinguish small blazes in their homes caused by incendiary bombs. Pressure to expel the water was created by means of a hand pump similar to a tire pump. Connected to the pump was about four feet of small diameter hose with a short piece of pipe for the nozzle. A short strip of flexible L shaped metal was welded to the pipe. The short part of the L could be depressed in front of the nozzle end so the straight stream could be deflected into a spray. Fortunately they were never used for the intended purpose, but following the war people found other uses for them around the house and yard. When they could get them, firemen used them to replace the water buckets mentioned in the previous paragraph. They held more water, were easily carried into the woods and provided a much more accurate application of water than throwing a pail of water at a brush fire. Many times it saved

running long lines of hose and then moving it from one hot spot to another.

One additional piece of equipment carried on all apparatus in a canvas bag was the hood cover. This was a large piece of canvas that was custom fitted to go over the hood of that particular piece of apparatus. It was well padded and on long winter stands it was the duty of the driver to be sure the engine was covered. Although the horses under the hood were then iron, the padded covers were a carry over from the days when the moving power was equestrian and padded blankets were draped over them for protection on their long winter stands.

Engine 42, on the right side of the fire house, was a two piece company, as were most of the engine companies at that time. In back was a 1924 American LaFrance 750 gallon rotary gear pump. This was modern, as evidenced by the pneumatic tires. It was a right hand drive, complete with drive chain, two wheel brakes and black canvas windshield. The brass bell was in the traditional place, over the round gas tank and both of these were above the driver's head. Today this arrangement would be certain to cause at least ringing in the ears of those riding the front seat and probably would result in head trauma with some time off on "injured leave," but in those days everything was silently, or in this case, noisily accepted.

In a trough on each side was a "hard suction" hose. These were four and a half inches in diameter and ten feet long and made of hard black reinforced rubber. Standard procedure was for all engine companies responding to multiple alarm fires to connect to separate hydrants using the hard suctions to the steamer outlet. Woe to the pump operator who didn't connect the hard suction at a multiple! Even when responding on a first alarm, if the fire appeared to be of large magnitude, the hard suctions were to be used. This was a judgement call and there were few reprimands for making a quick connection with the "soft suction" to get water fast on a first alarm.

In the hose bed were two, three hundred foot lines of two and a half inch hose, one reversed. This means the male thread faced out, with a nozzle attached. On the back step was the lowry hydrant and in the winter, the Ross Thawing Device was added.

There was a hinged wooden box that held an assortment of hose connections which could be adapted for various fire needs. Also on the back step was the sixteen foot soft suction hose for connecting to hydrants. Standing on that box, as an early teenager, I was just about tall enough to be mistaken for a regular fireman.

In front of the pump was the wagon. In 1929 the department had purchased nine booster wagons and Engine 42 was one of the lucky recipients. These were the first to have a forty gallon water tank and a small pump to propel the water through the two hundred and fifty feet of three quarter inch red rubber hose, and on to the fire with sufficient pressure to be effective. This hose was coiled into a recessed box on the back step with the first fifty feet hung in loops over the end of the ladders on the right side. On arrival at a fire the "booster man" grabbed the fifty foot loops over his shoulder and proceeded to the fire location. These booster tanks were a big improvement over the chemical tanks that earlier wagons had as their first line to attack a fire. They only required plain water to replace what was used, or later leaked out, and no mixing of chemicals or disposing of the remaining contents which was not used at the fire.

This wagon was also an American LaFrance piece of equipment. It was complete with right-hand drive, chain driven, two wheel brakes, black canvas windshield and with the round gas tank and brass bell both above the heads of those riding the front seat. It did have some modern improvements, such as one piece front fenders and a beacon of four rotating red lights mounted on a pole by the driver's seat. A flood light, which had little penetration, was mounted to the left of the canvas windshield. It had a portable deck gun over the hose bed and carried two five hundred foot lines of two and a half inch hose in the bed. The first fifty feet was three inch.

A metal box on the right hand running board contained various tools and other equipment. On the left running board was the wooden battery box. Under the front seat was a storage space about two foot square and accessible from both sides by metal hinged doors. In this was carried the "burst hose jacket"- which never worked. Nevertheless it was soaked in a bucket of water for several hours each week to keep the rubber pliable.

Also under the seat were the two All Service masks, in boxes, and the High Pressure Response Box assigned to Engine 42. The latter was a wooden box containing a high pressure gauge, main stem wrench, two or three independent gate wrenches and brass tags, marked E.42, on leather straps. Operating the high pressure hydrants in the down town area required the large wrench to unlock the bonnet and open the by-pass allowing water to enter the hydrant. The small wrenches were used to control the independent gates permitting water to enter the line of hose. Standard procedure was to place one of the brass tags on your line at the hydrant so it could be identified in case a change in pressure was needed. On the right side of the wagon was carried a short extension ladder and a short roof ladder. From time to time the thinking changed as to whether the wagon or pump should precede the other piece but for the most part the wagon went first.

These are some of the tools of the trade that intrigued me and during those early years I was an observer of the gradual changes that took place in the fire service, as improvements were invented and added.

It was always interesting to see a spare piece in quarters and then see what changes or additions had been made when the regular apparatus was returned. It took three visits to the shop for all the rubber tires on Ladder 30 to become airborne. First the front tractor wheels were done and months, or years, later the tiller wheels were replaced with innertube tires. Long afterwards, the rear tractor tires got inflated. Each such addition improved the ride over the rough roads.

A real safety innovation was the addition of sand boxes on the tractor portion of Ladder 30. They consisted of metal boxes filled with sand and mounted on each running board just before the rear tractor wheels. There was a pipe coming out of the bottom of the boxes and by pressing a button, the driver could release sand on the roadway in front of the rear tractor wheels, which included the two wheel brakes. It was primarily for winter use. Following other visits to the shop, the truck came back with a plate glass windshield, which was a great improvement for visibility, and eventually one was added for the tillerman, but this was not so successful as it was repeatedly broken or cracked by being hit with tree branches at night. Raising the aerial ladder before this piece of glass was swung out of the way also took its toll.

Glass windshields were added to the wagon and pump of Engine 42. These modern windshields were furnished with large rubber wipers which moved from left to right and back. They were operated by air pressure through a small rubber hose from the engine and from time to time this hose would disconnect from one end or the other and the wipers wouldn't work pneumatically. It was not an uncommon sight to see the officer standing up, leaning over the windshield in the rain or snow and manually moving the blades back and forth so the driver could see where they were going.

The pump operator, who usually had no one riding in the front seat with him, was at a distinct disadvantage. Often times if I was riding the back step, he would motion for me to join him in the front seat and become the power to move the wipers. If the driver was alone and his visibility became too obscured he merely drove standing up so he could look over the windshield and see to follow the wagon. Other added improvements over the years were electric sirens and much later, those lovable noise makers, the "buckeyes." Sealed-beam headlights were added when they became available. Overhead protection for the front seat or the back step were never even considered, but those were the days of iron men, rust-proofed and anti-freezed.

These were the Chariots of Fire that were housed in a Taj Mahal at Egleston Square.

Engine 42, organized in 1892. Pictured with 1893 Silsby Steam Engine capable of pumping 550 GPM. Note the church that later became the Egleston Theatre on the left side of photo.

Quarters of Engine 42 and Ladder 30 at 3089 Washington Street, Roxbury from 1892 to 1952. Note JA Café on the right side of photo.

Engine 42, American LaFrance 750 GPM pump, as it was when I was assigned there in 1947.

Ladder 30, 1927 American LaFrance with 75' wooden aerial ladder. Note canvas windshield, right-hand drive, crank to start it, and solid rubber tires.

APPRENTICESHIP
(or, This Is The Way To Do It)

In the early years I kept a diary of my sparking experiences. In my mind I was probably keeping my own journal but somewhere along the line those pages got lost in the shuffle. However, at the same time I also kept a record of the multiple alarm fires which occurred in Boston from 1934 to 1946 and these didn't get lost in the shuffle. While I was serving Uncle Sam in the Army and overseas, Herb faithfully maintained this bit of trivia for me. It came to light recently as some of my files were being cleaned out. Many of the major and interesting multiples recorded on those pages were vividly recalled and were a help in putting some of my experiences into the proper time frame for this book. At some of the fires I was a mere spectator, at some I worked, and some I missed entirely through no fault of my own.

My rushing to the fire house to close the doors when the men responded to an alarm began when I was ten years old and started my sparking career. This can be pinpointed because at that time you had to be twelve years old to be a Boy Scout and I was closing the fire house doors for a couple years before my twelfth birthday when I became a Boy Scout of America. Jamaica Plain Troop 3 met at the Boylston Congregational Church on Monday nights and I recall checking the "Last Alarm" slate before and after going to scout meetings. The pastor of the church at that time was the Rev. Howard Pomeroy, and he later became the first Protestant Chaplain of the Boston Fire Department.

Anecdote:
In the Boy Scouts, there was a "Firemanship" Merit Badge that could be earned for advancement in scouting ranks and long before I was even old enough to be a scout, I had the requirements for that badge down pat. The test for that badge had to be taken at the fire house on Centre Street and as soon as I was eligible there was a visit by me to Engine 28 and "Firemanship" became the first of my Merit Badges.

Another indication of the time factor is that, as previously mentioned, I never just walked into the fire house. Being a bit timid and uncertain of my grounds, I would wait until they had responded to an alarm before going in to close the doors and once they returned I promptly left. Gradually I started remaining in the fire house for longer periods after they returned, and finally progressed to the point to just walk in. Of course a lot depended on who was on house patrol, as some firemen were a little bit friendlier than others, and I quickly determined how far my liberties extended with each one.

So before age thirteen I could walk into the fire house, hang up my hat and coat and play fireman for a few hours, but of course not respond - yet! Work uniform for firemen at that time was blue chambray shirts and dungarees. So, coincidentally, my mother was persuaded that the ideal after school clothes for me was dungarees and blue chambray shirts. Convincing Mom of the wisdom of this selection was not easy. In those days kids wearing denim dungarees, particularly if they were faded, was synonymous with lack of family funds, and people did not want to advertise their financial status, even though most everyone was in the same financial boat. A sign that a family was becoming more affluent was when the boys began to wear regular pants instead of dungarees, or jeans as they are called today.

To help pass time on my visits to the fire house, I started making my own set of running cards by copying the then nearly two thousand box cards onto my own individual three by five inch lined index cards. These were kept in a metal file box on the chest of drawers under the Avon map in our kitchen. My Mom was a patient lady.

With much practice I also became a reasonable forger. The journal was handwritten, as it is today, by the man on watch. Alarms received and responses are entered in red ink and all other data is written in black ink. The penmanship of many of those men were a real work of art and it took a lot of practice to imitate many of them. With much determination, and a lot of "holding the floor," eventually I could quite accurately duplicate handwritings of most of the men and it became easy to add to my repertoire of signatures and writing as new men were added to the companies.

I tried to observe everything and file it away in my mind if it could be helpful in the future. It was impressive to see the quick thinking and fast response of the men as different situations arose.

One afternoon a man came in to the fire house and asked if he could borrow a fire extinguisher. When asked the reason, he said he had a small fire in a closet and could put it out himself if he could have the use of an extinguisher - it wasn't necessary to bother the firemen. As they pressed him for a location, he became adamant that he didn't want firemen messing up his home. One of the men took a fire extinguisher off the engine, and diplomatically handed it to the would-be firefighter, along with a piece of paper and pencil. He asked him to please write his name and address so they could pick up the extinguisher in case he didn't return it. The man quickly scribbled the information and left with the fire extinguisher. Once the address was known, the men responded to the closet fire, which turned out to be a three bagger - due to delay in alarm.

Contrast this with a man who often visited the Egleston Square fire house but lived in a house off Warren Street in Roxbury. One afternoon he breathlessly burst into Engine 42 to report a fire in his house. He had run all the way, passing one other fire house and at least a dozen fire boxes. After the fire was out, they asked him why he had passed Engine 24 and all the fire boxes which would have brought help sooner and reduced the loss in his home. His reply was that he knew the firemen in Egleston Square and wanted to give them the business. He did!

Running errands for the men increased my value to them but also presented a problem at times. Getting a sandwich at the

Egleston Square Diner or Kohler's Delicatessen was no problem, but if they wanted a pack of cigarettes I sometimes came back empty handed. The law prohibited selling cigarettes to minors and despite the fact I was wearing dungarees and a blue chambray shirt, many clerks would not sell butts to me even though I insisted they weren't for me but for a fireman. It was irritating and frustrating to me then but in retrospect it was nice growing up at a time when everyday people made a conscientious effort to live up to the letter of the law, even if it deprived them of a little business profit.

However it was a big day for me when I finally convinced Louie at the corner spa that I was just doing an errand for the fire house, and after that there was no problem. It probably helped that Louie was also a little sparky, and he could see that I did not smoke at the many fires we both went to watch. Incidentally, a pack of "Twenty Grand" cigarettes cost a nickel then. One big plus of running errands was that it gave me the opportunity to go upstairs in the fire house to deliver the sandwich or whatever and before long complete freedom of the house was mine.

Rolling hose at fires was one task I could perform without any problem and the help was appreciated particularly if the fire had been a long stand. Likewise, when they returned to the fire house with wet hose and I was there, my eager willingness to assist in racking the wet hose and re-packing with dry hose made further brownie points for me.

Anecdote:

Usually no one wore gloves when racking or re-packing hose but during the aftermath of the 1940 Valentine's Day Blizzard all men were held on duty. We returned from a good fire with a lot of wet hose and for some unexplained reason several of the men kept their gloves on while changing the hose this time. By now I was sixteen years old and still wanting to look the part of a regular fireman, I too put on gloves. Among the firemen present was a rough and ready burly hoseman who was highly respected at fires for his aggressiveness with the play pipe and well thought of as a fireman in general. Now there had been a little celebrating of the blizzard and the confinement of a couple days, and as we packed hose he caught sight of my gloves. With a smirk and a brogue he asked, "What are the gloves faar boy? You'll nevva make a fireman!" For me there was dejection and silence - and also a bit of loneliness, as all the gloved firemen ducked out of sight to remove their hand covers before they too were spotted. Jim later made Lieutenant and was a highly respected and decorated officer on Engine 23, but whenever the Valentine's Day Blizzard of 1940 was recalled, the glove incident was always included in the stories.

Through the years many of those gloved firemen who were present that night have greeted me with "What are the gloves faar boy?" Lieutenant Frank Bonner, Retired, who sang the National Anthem at the Annual Firemen's Ball, and other department functions, for many years, is one of the few men still around (besides yours truly) who was there that night in 1940. At the 1987 Ball he reminded me that I will "nevva make a fireman!"

The first time I rode on a fire engine was certainly a red-letter day in my young life and although the date is vague on the calendar of life, the circumstances that brought it about are crystal clear. In the fall of each year was the Annual Hose Test. Most men considered themselves fortunate if they were off duty on the selected day but I looked forward to it as another day I could play fireman. It was the one time each year when all the two and a half and three inch hose, belonging to a particular engine company, was taken to a specific location. There it would be connected into one or two long lines and water pumped through it at two hundred and fifty pounds pressure. The pressure was sustained for a specified period of time during which any weak lengths were supposed to burst. In practice some did burst at the test but in most cases they were just weakened by the high pressure and then burst the next time they were used at a fire.

The tests were held under the watchful eyes of the deputy and district chiefs and members of the "hose shop." Engine 42's test location was Franklin Park where there was lots of open space. When the test was completed the wagon and pump were packed with wet hose and the remaining hose was rolled and taken back to quarters to be dried. Since the total hose assigned to an engine company consisted of enough pieces to provide almost three complete changes for both the wagon and pump, there was plenty of hose to be rolled and lugged to the back step.

A couple times I went to the test and helped with the hose rolling and then walked back to the fire house to assist in racking. Then came the test I rolled hose at and as the apparatus was about to return to quarters, the pump operator told me to hop on the back and help hold the hose on. It would be difficult to determine just how much help my hundred or so pounds would be in holding down the hose, but I climbed up on top of the pile on the back step. As the motor started and we began to move back to the fire house, my heart began to pound and I must have been at least ten feet high on that first ride back to quarters. I couldn't wait for Herb to come home from work and tell him I had my first ride!

There is no recalling how long it was before my second ride and then the third and fourth and so on, but I remember that all my early rides were back to the station. It saved me a little carfare, which I didn't have anyway, and always was my reward for helping with the hose. As I rode, my feet were on the back step but my head and heart were way above.

As stated previously, in my young mind I made a study of the temperament of each of the men and officers, at least as they related to me, and determined that overall, one platoon was more friendly than the other. This was most likely a direct reflection on the district chief working. The two chiefs then assigned to District 12 (now District 9) were as different as night and day. One was a stern disciplinarian who seldom smiled and the men he worked with always appeared quite tense. The other chief, Timothy Donovan, had a more friendly nature and once he got used to seeing me around, he greeted me in a cordial manner - and looked the other way when I was doing something he would rather not see - like my riding. Naturally most of my sparking was done with this platoon but slowly I worked my way into the other as well and before long most of the men were taking advantage of my errand running and rewarding me with riding back privileges.

Anecdote:
Dot's daily letter of December 30, 1944, to me in Europe, included a newspaper picture and clipping of a three alarm fire the night before at 775-783 Centre Street in Jamaica Plain (Box 2475). It included the report of the death of District Chief Timothy Donovan, who succumbed at the fire from smoke inhalation and over exertion

partly due to the war time shortage of firemen. Because of the Battle of the Bulge, Dot's letter did not reach me until late in January, but the tardiness of the news did not lessen the shock or sadness caused by the Line of Duty Death of my "friendly chief."

If I was in the fire house when they had a run, it just meant the doors were closed sooner and I would wait for their return. The men on a long day were entitled to a meal period which meant that from three in the afternoon until about nine o'clock at night they rode one man short, which usually meant there was no one on the back step of the pump. It so happened that Al, who had first told me to hop on the back at the hose test, was alone on the pump for three of those hours on his long day. One afternoon they had a run and as I watched them prepare to respond, Al motioned for me to hop on the back and make sure nothing fell off - including me. If I was ten feet tall on my first return ride, I was surely twenty feet high on my first response to an alarm and so I remembered to duck my head going out the door. Again I couldn't wait to tell Herb of my latest accomplishment. He was delighted for me and it gave him opportunity to lecture me about safety and a lot of other things that were for my own good.

Naturally I did not take this first response ride as license to allow me to hop on anytime. My appearance was still that of a young boy and although Al continued to motion me to ride, I knew the officers were a bit less enthusiastic - so as much as possible I tried to avoid their seeing me.

Anecdote:
With my mother's permission I went to the fire house one Sunday afternoon. Normally this was a no-no, as Sundays belonged to God and it was expected of me to be at morning and evening church services. Just before five o'clock, a third alarm was struck on a downtown box. Engine 42's assignment was to cover Engine 26 on Broadway. I knew my mother would be looking for me at church but Al motioned for me to hop on. Decisions, decisions, decisions! I couldn't resist this opportunity and away we went. On the way down Columbus Avenue and then moving to Tremont Street at Roxbury Crossing, it dawned on me that the officer riding on the wagon wasn't really friendly. When we pulled up on the apron of

Engine 26 it was a little after five and no telling how long we would be covering. Another decision had to be made. My reasoning was that I had had another "ride" and if I wanted to protect my sparking privileges with Mom, I better get home and to church. But with no money - how? Solution, I ran all the way from Broadway to Egleston Square (about four miles) in the dark and got home in time to walk to church with Mom.

Most of my early riding was on the back step of the pump and then assisting the pump operator hooking up to a hydrant. Going into the fire building was out of the question, first because I actually still looked like a thirteen year old kid and second, the men's rubber coats all reached to my ankles if I tried to wear them, and the shoulders reached half way to my elbows. I would stand around watching the fire and learning how they went about ventilating and extinguishing. If the police were clearing the area I took refuge with the pump operator until the company was making up and I could help roll hose and then ride home.

Anecdote:
The only way you could get inside the Police lines at a fire was if you had a Fire Department badge. Of course all firemen had badges and there was a smattering of others around. It didn't seem logical, but the police assumed everyone with a badge was entitled to cross the fire lines with no questions asked. It didn't matter your age or appearance, if you had a badge, you got by. Somewhere along the line Herb had become the owner of a Boston badge which had an "O" where the number was usually stamped. One Saturday afternoon a man stopped at our house and since Herb wasn't home, asked me to give him the package he had for him. In the package was a brand new Boston badge that had "H.E.C." engraved where the number usually appeared. Herb was surprised and delighted, and for a long time it was a mystery to him where the badge came from. Come to think of it, to this day the origin of that donation is still a mystery to me, but for my fourteenth birthday, Herb gave me the "O" badge. I used it to get into fire lines until I was appointed and given a shiny silver badge numbered 1926. When our oldest son Bruce became a teenager and displayed an interest in chasing fires, the "O" badge was passed on to him, and he still has it.

Anecdote, Second Alarm:
A few years ago while still in Command of District 3, I found an envelope on my desk one day. In it was an unsigned note reading, "Thought you would like to have the enclosed" and with it was my original badge, number 1926. It was mostly plain copper by then because the silver had worn off with successive users, but the 1926 was clearly visible and it is still a mystery from whom that badge came.

No new men were added to the Boston Fire Department during the years 1934, 1935 and 1936 because of the Great Depression and so the strength of the companies slowly became depleted due to normal attrition. This suited me fine because my availability made me all the more useful around the station and at fires. It should be pointed out that by this time Herb was married and raising a daughter so his spare time for sparking had become limited. Also, it was around the late thirties that Herb moved to Forest Hills, not far from Engine 53, and he mostly moved his allegiance to that fire house where he was accepted as a working spark.

By 1937, one-way radio receivers were placed in the chief's cars. Two-way communications was completed in 1942. Fire Alarm was still broadcasting on 1630 kilocycles. Our Brunswick radio at home picked up this station and when home alone that was the station tuned in. It saved a lot of time in keeping track of the last alarm, and was a much quicker way to learn a multiple alarm had been struck and for me to start alerting our group of sparks.

1937 was also the year the Famous "96" were appointed "Men on Probation" on July 16th. One of them was Ralph Reis who was a member of the church we attended and as a boy I remember how proud he looked wearing his uniform to church that first Sunday. Little did I expect then, that in future years we would be responding to the same fires and other Incidents in Roxbury and elsewhere. He ended his career as a district fire chief and his son is now a lieutenant on Engine 39.

Two each of the 96 were assigned to Engine 42 and Ladder 30 and these four brought the house up to full strength. With no one missing because of vacation or injured leave the companies were riding 1 and 6, or one officer and six firemen, except during meal periods when they were short a man on each company. During vacation periods, plus injuries, the men available for work was usually closer to 1 and 4 or 1 and 5. This number still allowed me to ride without making the company look over-manned.

When these men joined the ranks, I was already pretty much of a fixture at Engine 42 and some of them found it easier to ask me questions, on the side, so they could appear quite learned when quizzed by the old timers. Naturally I was delighted to be of service to any fireman, and since I was there before 1937, all those who came after were not certain just what my status was, and so accepted my presence and freedom of the house and apparatus without question. If a member had an important errand that had to be done and I was in the fire house, he would mention my presence to the officer, and quite often I would be asked to ride on the truck or the engine depending on where my appearance was most needed. This didn't bother me a bit, and I worked on my versatility by perfecting Hoseman and Ladderman skills.

Anecdote:

In those days there were several department functions that were considered essential and men involved were allowed to attend them if there was sufficient manpower. I was aware of the scheduling of these events, and who usually attended them, and planned some of my fire house visits according to when I might be most helpful. The band practiced every Monday night - and the captain of Ladder 30 was a member. The Boston Firemen's American Legion Post 94 met on the first Monday night of the month - and the lieutenant of Engine 42 was progressing through the offices to Post Commander. On some first Monday nights, both officers would be working and looking to go to their respective meetings - I would be sparking. More than once the captain came down first and before leaving for band would say, "Cookie, ride the truck." He would be just about out of sight when the lieutenant would come down and before leaving for Legion would say, "Cookie, ride the engine." I would ride which ever one went out first, which I am sure both officers knew, but everyone felt better thinking all the bases were covered, and I was enjoying every minute and not caring which apparatus I rode.

The next red-letter day in my sparking career was Christmas 1937. By then I had grown big enough to wear the rubber coat and helmet of some of the shorter firemen but boots were a problem because some men kept them in their locker. For my "big" present that year, brother Charles gave me a pair of fireman's hip boots - which cost him four dollars and fifty cents. As soon as all the Christmas guests had left our house, I asked Mom if I could take my new boots and go to the fire house to break them in. With her usual admonition "to be careful and be home early" she granted her permission.

To my delight, they were riding light and shortly after I arrived, one of the men went to bed sick. Around nine o'clock we had a run to Boylston and Egleston Streets (Box 2443) for a chimney fire and I road the back of the pump. On returning, I hopped off and went in to open the doors. Ed Steidinger, who had been appointed that July and was to become one of the Famous "96" was driving the wagon. As I went to open the doors, the officer asked Ed where Joe was (he was supposed to be riding the back of the pump but had gone to bed sick). Ed said Joe had just gone in to open the doors. The officer remarked, "that isn't Joe, that's young Cookie."

It so happened that on the same run, when the other responding ladder truck turned right from Brookside Avenue into Boylston Street, the tillerman kept going straight - right out of the seat and over a fence into a yard, and then to the hospital. The chief called the officer at Egleston Square and instructed him to detail a tillerman to the other truck for the rest of the night. The officer held a roll call and sent one of the best men on detail - and sent the rest to bed.

Ed had the floor and just before midnight asked if I was staying all night. Being quick of thought, I said I forgot to ask my mother - but I would go home and check with her and be right back. (In the "dark ages" of my growing up, it was necessary to get parental consent to do anything out of the ordinary.) It took a little begging, and maybe some weeping, to convince her but with Mom's permission my "bunking in" began. We didn't have any more runs that night, but my new boots were made into a night hitch for the first time and stood beside a bunk room bed while I tried to go to sleep - but afraid I might not hear the house gong and miss a run. New boots of my own and bunking in. What wonderful Christmas presents for a fourteen year old!

When most little boys dream of being a fireman, it is certain that one of the attractions is steering the tiller. Many Hollywood pictures have used the scenario of a ladder truck careening down the street, swerving from side to side to avoid other vehicles, and then making dramatic turns - all as seen from the tillerman's view. It is impressive on the screen, but the first time in the tiller's seat is a little less dramatic and a lot more frightening. One reason being that you don't feel you are in complete control of your end. My first tillering was dramatic and a bit nerve racking.

Ladder 30 had some first alarm boxes over around Devon and Normandy Streets in Roxbury to which Engine 42 did not respond. As pointed out earlier, whichever company went out first, I went with it. This particular night there was a heavy snowstorm in progress and we had a good fire in a three decker. Walt Doyle and I had been sent to get a thirty foot ladder to the rear of the building, but the deputy called us and said to move Ladder 23 around the block, to the next street and the rear of the building. Riding on Ladder 30, I was wearing a red topped helmet and as I happened to be closest to the deputy, he told me to drive. Had the time for true confession come?

I was just about to tell him that I didn't know how to drive, even though my helmet for the evening was red, when Walt, sensing what was happening told me to hop up and tiller and he would drive. There was no fast careening and swerving. Just a slow plodding through deep snow, around a couple corners to get Ladder 23 to the next street and the rear of the fire building - but I tillered for my first time - - and before I was old enough to have a driver's license!

As a youngster it seemed to me that when a man was promoted to chief, he must have not only been given gold bugles to adorn his uniform but also a stern look to adorn his face. The above deputy was typical of this impression of mine and yet he did have a sense of humor. Probably eighty percent of the runs from the Egleston Square fire house at that time involved a left turn and then a right turn up Columbus Avenue.

One night they had a run and the pump wouldn't start. The wagon and truck responded to a 2400 series box, that meant a right turn from the house. After a while the pump did start but in the delay and confusion, the driver had missed the location. Following the law of averages, he turned left and then turned right, and went up Columbus Avenue, intending to cruise the areas most frequently responded to. In the meantime the wagon and truck returned from the False Alarm and wondered where the pump had gone. About fifteen minutes later the phone rang for the officer. It was the stern faced deputy chief and he said, "If a pump happens to go by your fire house will you please lasso it. One has gone by my quarters three times now and the driver looks lost." It was his way of letting the officer know, he knew!

The next main event in my apprenticeship took place in the summer of 1940, but let us lead into it gradually. Lest the reader get the impression that I spent all my time at the fire house, let me set the record straight. Sparking was a privilege that was granted to me not only by the firemen, but also by my Mom. There were certain tasks that were mine to do and it was only after these were completed that I could spark. Of course fires didn't always wait until I was available and Mom did give me certain leeway, but for the most part chores came first.

Brother Charles had graduated from Jamaica Plain High in 1932 and although we were in the depth of the Depression he was fortunate to get a job with the First National Bank of Malden. Mom was expanding her work with Avon so the household duties of cleaning, shopping, washing and cooking fell to my brother Richard and myself. Dick was taking pipe organ lessons and practiced a couple afternoons a week at the New England Conservatory of Music, and after graduating from Jamaica Plain High in 1938 he went to work at Paine Furniture. So though in theory Dick and I shared the house duties in our younger days, most of them fell to me as my brothers grew older and assumed other responsibilities.

Summers were different. During the thirties and into the forties, polio epidemics were the big worry of parents and kids alike. Going to places, even beaches and theatres, where large crowds gathered was avoided and pretty much you played with the same kids all the time to avoid new exposures. A lot of families in those days still had country cousins. Partial migration from the farm to the city was taking place in a lot of families, but enough of the family farms remained for many city kids to go visit in the summer. Some were in the northern New England states but in our family the farm was near the Pennsylvania Dutch country.

City parents would send their kids to the farm for the summer in hopes of avoiding polio and my Mom was no exception. At first Dick and I went together but in the late thirties I went alone. For me farm life was a complete change of pace with no electric lights, running water or toilets. Milking cows and working with a team of horses became my new chores, along with haying, threshing and the other laborious work that is part of farming. Recreation consisted of fishing and walking seven miles each way to the nearest city if you wanted to go to the movies on a Saturday night. Visiting the farmer's daughter was also recreation. Naturally I missed sparking, but I did see a lot of barn fires caused by lightning strikes or spontaneous combustion of hay. I learned to appreciate the efforts of volunteer firemen, and then the response of neighbors as they all turned out to build a new barn for the unfortunate farmer and his family.

Anecdote:

Above I mentioned visiting the farmer's daughter, but in my case it was the farmer's granddaughter. As I spent several summers at the Cook farm, there was a nearby farm where the farmer's granddaughter spent the same summers. When she was ten or eleven, I knew but didn't notice her, but when we were both sixteen we shared a one summer teen-age romance. Her name was Marjorie Rude and many many years later, Dot and I were at the Honesdale, Pennsylvania Historical Society trying to find some branches to put on our Family Tree. They had a registry book in which you added your name and address to the particular family name you were researching. The idea being that you might find a long lost relative who was also searching that Tree and contacts could be made. When adding our address to the "Cook" pages, imagine my surprise to find "Marjorie Rude Cook" with a Florida address. It turns out she married my second cousin and a year or so later, the four of us visited the Genealogy Library in Orlando and together learned that our grandfathers had sailed from Bremerhaven, Germany on the two masted barque "Albert" and six weeks later landed in New York City.

My mother would send me money for the Greyhound bus fare home at the end of the summer (about $3.50 Scranton, PA to Boston). Sometimes I would hitchhike home by way of New York City and catch a movie because they were shown there long before they reached Boston. It was there that I saw Judy Garland, Bert Lahr, Ray Bolger and Jack Haley on the stage as the "Wizard of Oz" had its debut at the Capital Theatre. On other stops I saw Glenn Miller and other "big bands" on the stage. In 1939 my stop was to visit the World's Fair, with it's spectacular Trylon and Perisphere, and used my Scranton to New York part of my bus fare for admission. That year I did take the bus from New York to Boston. Germany had invaded Poland on September first and World War II had begun. I bought the *New York Daily Mirror* to read all about it on the bus ride home.

Anecdote:
The next time I saw Glenn Miller was in Plymouth, England where his Army orchestra gave a concert at Raglan Barracks. Not long afterwards he was listed as "missing" when the plane he was on went down.

It wasn't long before the war in Europe began to effect life in America. More work was available as war industries began to start up and supplies to our future allies started to trickle overseas. Bombings of cities in Europe became more frequent and sinking of cargo vessels and tankers off the East Coast occurred regularly. Thoughts in America began to turn to defense and what needed be done. With more and more firemen entering the military and with the possibility of an attack on the East coast becoming more prevalent, the Boston Fire Department decided that the time had come for an Auxiliary Fire Department to be organized.

A public meeting was held at the Gardner Auditorium, at the State House, to explain what was being planned. There was a large turnout, including sparks from the Egleston Square area, which included me. Volunteers would be trained and assigned to fire houses to augment the regular force. Training would consist of taking the regular thirty day Drill School course that all new firemen attended. What an opportunity for a sixteen year old spark! Applications were distributed and those interested in joining the new Auxiliary could sign up. Now I was brought up to be honest and not to lie, as were most kids in those days. This presented a problem on filling out the application. I was most anxious to join and everything went fine until that part of the application that dealt with age. Based on my upbringing I could not bring myself to lie about my age. The solution - leave it blank.

This was in May 1940 and a few weeks later my friend Fran received notice he had been accepted for the Auxiliary Fire Department and to report for the thirty day drill school at Fire Headquarters on Bristol Street. No Pennsylvania farm for me this year. School was out for the summer and I would be reporting to Drill School with my friend, Fran.

Captain Nicholson, known as "Big Nick," was the Drill Master at that time and after calling out his list of names, asked if he had omitted anyone? Up went my hand. "What is your name?" boomed "Big Nick."
"Cook, Sir" was the reply.
"I don't have a Cook. What is your first name?"
"Paul, Sir."
"I don't have a Paul either. Did you get notice to report?"
"Why else would I be here? Sir."

He added my name to his list and so without telling a lie I became number "seven" in the first drill class of the Boston Auxiliary Fire Department.

Every morning I reported to the drill yard and progressed through the training. The smoke house with the All-Service mask, jumping into the net, advancing a two and a half inch line straight up five stories on a perpendicular fire escape, carrying a roof ladder up a straight ladder and placing it in position, learning to tie knots, how to operate and drive a pump, sliding down the rope from the eighth floor and then going back to do it again, only this time stopping at the seventh floor to pick up a man on the way down, and carrying your partner over your back down a thirty foot ladder.

Although only sixteen, there was no problem keeping up with the others. All the ladder evolutions were leading up to the big test - the "single pomp." The "chain pomp" is the warm-up for this. In this evolution, eight men wearing life belts, extend the pompier ladders up eight floors and when the top ladder is in position, all members hook in with their safety belts and lean back with hands behind them to prove they aren't holding on or afraid. Then comes the "single pomp" in which one man progresses from the ground to the eighth floor window alone using one pompier ladder. Floor by floor he sits on the window sill and pushes his ladder to the next window above, then climbs up and sitting on that window sill he pulls the ladder up and pushes it up to the next floor. On reaching the eighth floor, he again locks in with his life belt and leans back to show everyone how easy it is.

It was about the twenty-fifth day and I had just completed my "single pomp." I had it made! All that was left was a visit to the Fire Alarm Office, the High Pressure Station and some other minor ground evolutions, and then graduation on Friday. I never made it!

After completing my pomp, I was standing with a group of the other men beside "Big Nick." Most of the men in the drill class were on the list for appointment to the fire department and the day before several had gotten their notices to report for physicals and appointment. The following conversation ensued.

"Big Nick" asked me if I was one of the lucky ones being appointed.
"No" was my short honest reply.
"Why not?" he asked.
"Because I am not on the list."
"How come? I thought everyone in this class was on the list."
"Not me."
"Why not?"
"Because I didn't take the exam."
"Didn't take the Exam? Why?"
"Because I wasn't old enough."
"Not old enough! How old are you?"
"Sixteen" was my automatic, honest and mumbled response.

My honest upbringing had not allowed me to lie and there was no way to ignore his question.

As soon as the man that was then doing the "single pomp" reached the ground safely, "Big Nick" blew his whistle and called for a ten minute break. He disappeared into headquarters and returned a few minutes later, followed by Chief of Department Samuel J. Pope. They both headed in my direction. Confronting me, Chief Pope asked, "What is this Captain Nicholson has been telling me?"

"I don't know what he has been telling you, Sir."

"He tells me you are only sixteen. Is that correct?"

"Yes, Sir."

"Well I am sorry, but you are finished at drill school as of right now! If you got hurt, my neck and the City's would be in a noose!"

"But I signed a release, Sir," I protested.

"I know it and I have it right here, but you are a minor and your signature means nothing."

"I can get my mother to sign it, if that will help, Sir."

"Nothing will help at this point! You are all done!"

Then he mellowed a bit and said he was sorry but he had to stop me to protect the city and the fire department, and himself. If I wanted to stay around and watch I could, but no participation. He appreciated my interest and respected my enthusiasm, but he had no alternative and that was final. He never did ask how I got into the class and I never told - until now.

As the war clouds gathered over England, there was a lady there who raised Dalmation dogs and, seeking safety for some of them, she offered six of the pedigreed pups to the Boston Fire Department with hope, and instructions on how to breed them. The original six were placed in fire houses, and as the breeding instructions were followed, the results were distributed to other fire stations. Before long any fire house that wanted one had a thoroughbred spotted mascot.

"Neddo" was the offshoot given to Rescue 2 and he became a familiar sight, as he rode on the front seat beside the officer on every run. He developed a strong company spirit and when Rescue 2 arrived at a fire, "Neddo" took his place on the apparatus and wouldn't let any fireman take equipment off the piece, unless they were from Rescue 2.

"Tapper" was the black spotted white pup given to Egleston Square. He never really took to riding the apparatus but he did chase the men to the sliding pole when they had a run, nipping at the last man's heels. Many times his brakes didn't work in time, and he followed his target right down the pole hole, yelping all the way. Someone realized that "Tapper" didn't respond to the house gong when he was tired, so one of my tasks was to take the dog up to Franklin Park a few times each week and let him run till he was exhausted. A couple of the dogs got run over by the apparatus, or got hit by cars. Most of them eventually ended up going home with one of the men and became family pets.

So this was my apprenticeship. Not too bad for a teenager, and even a pre-teenager. Everything I saw and did in that apprenticeship only whetted my appetite for more and I still hunger for additional knowledge and experiences in the fire service. Even in retirement, I expect to follow it as closely as I have for well over fifty years.

After my appointment, and following a harrowing incident at a fire that will come later, I continued displaying my love for the job with an aggressive approach at fires. This caused one of my associates to remark, "Cookie, you won't be happy until you get killed on the job." This was the farthest from the truth, as I did not join the fire department to become a hero - either dead or alive. Further, I love life and the God who created it, and would do all within my power to protect and preserve it - whether it be my life or that of someone else - so long as He gives me breath.

THE CITY OWES ME FOR THESE

(or, Forget The Money, You Don't Charge When
You Are Having Fun)

It is said that time heals all wounds, but it does a lot more than that. It also erases the memories of people, or it might be more accurate to say that time erases the people with memories. When I first began listening to the repeated recalling of incidents in the fire house, the two most dramatic stories told were of the Molasses Tank and Pickwick Club Disasters. In the mid thirties there were many firemen still on the job who responded to one or both of these tragedies and even though fire played no part in either of these accidents, the fire department did.

On Commercial Street near North End Park there was a very large tank filled with molasses. If you have cooked, or otherwise been in contact with this liquid, you know how sticky a product it is and how slowly it pours. Shortly after noon on January 15, 1919 this large tank ruptured and two million gallons of the gooey stuff poured onto Commercial Street and into the North End neighborhood. The saying "Slow as molasses in January" proved paradoxical as a copious amount of the sticky substance surged forward fast enough to overcome fleeing people and drown them. Dozens of buildings were wrecked. Many more buildings were inundated by the sweet smelling syrup, which has lingered in some of those structures to this day. The Boston Fire Boat, Engine 31, was berthed next to the tank and the fire house was one of the buildings that was demolished by the cascading condiment. One fireman from the boat, George Layhe, was among the nineteen people who lost their lives that January day in a flood of molasses.

The Fourth of July has always, and rightfully so, been a festive and patriotic time during which fire departments experience an increase in activity. Contributing causes used to be fireworks, which were then legal in Massachusetts, and bonfires, some of which were legal community celebrations and others were neighborhood nuisances. The latter are the ones that gave workouts to the firemen as kids would spend days gathering materials to burn and then light them off just as it got dark on the Night Before the Fourth. The parents would watch and the firemen would come to extinguish the back yard bonfires to prevent burning embers from scattering and setting homes on fire. As water threaded through the hoses and onto the fire, the men would be greeted with hissing and booing from the spectators. In later years the verbal attacks would turn personal and physical and many firemen were injured. One lieutenant lost the sight of an eye when struck by a thrown missile.

While waiting to respond to bonfires someone usually recalled that the Fourth of July was the anniversary of the Pickwick Club Disaster. The Pickwick Club was a dine and dance hall located on Beach Street in the Chinatown section of the city. Early on that morning in 1925, the building collapsed killing forty-four people. Shortly before the collapse, there was a brawl out on Beach Street and many customers left the Club to watch the fight and perhaps had their lives spared. The fire department responded to locate and remove victims from the debris.

Anecdote:
Later, in attempting to determine the cause of the building collapse, partial blame was given to overcrowding and to the dancing of the "Charleston." Within a week of the accident the Legislature voted 99 to 1 to ban strenuous dances in nightclubs. It was also reported that the last dance music the orchestra played was, "All Aboard For Heaven."

Some of the more spectacular fires, that occurred during my early sparking days, include: a five alarm fire at Fenway Park in January 1934, the Central Congregational Church in Jamaica Plain in December 1934 (what a cold night that was), St. John's Seminary in Brighton in April 1936 (only four alarms), and the Grist Mill in Charlestown in November of 1936.

In December 1936 there was also a two alarm cellar fire in the Publix Market in Roslindale. Sulfur dioxide, used as a refrigerant then, was released by a broken pipe and twenty-five firemen were overcome as the gas combined with moisture in their lungs and caused severe respiratory problems. Many of them never returned to work from that fire, including one from Ladder 30. Both Engine 42 and Ladder 30 ran short of men for several months following this fire and it was about this time that my "riding" became more regular.

On Wednesday morning, March 10, 1937 there was a fire that could have spelled disaster for the city and its fire department. The "S.S. Laila," loaded with nitrates, was tied up at Pier 45, Mystic Docks in Charlestown, and it became involved in fire. Five alarms (Box 4191) were ordered in quick succession (the third alarm was skipped) as fears grew that the nitrates might explode. By early afternoon the fire had been sufficiently controlled by the Boston firemen on board to allow a tugboat to get close enough to get a line on it. Still fearing an explosion, the ship was towed down the harbor to a place where property damage would be less if the cargo exploded.

The fireboats followed along beside it pouring thousands of gallons of sea water into the holds, and finally extinguished the fire without further incident. This happened on a school day so I missed the fire, but I was waiting at the fire house when Engine 42 returned and after helping with the hose, sat spellbound as the men told of their battle with the nitrate fire aboard the "S. S. Laila."

Anecdote:

In April 1947 there occurred the Texas City Disaster. The "S.S. Grandcamp," containing 2200 tons of nitrates became involved in fire and after burning for just fifty-five minutes, the cargo exploded spreading fire and destruction to the industrial waterfront area. The ensuing fire consumed several nearby ships, a chemical plant and other industries, as well as oil tank farms. Damage was estimated at sixty-seven million dollars and it took the lives of 468 people including over fifty firemen.

Fires in buildings under construction are quite common and I had a good many of them later while serving in District 3, but on January 11, 1938 there was one that almost terminated my sparking. The fire was discovered about five thirty in the evening at the Suffolk County Court House, then under construction. Most of the steel framing work was completed and much canvas had been used to enclose the floors to protect workers and the stored building materials. Four alarms were sounded in eleven minutes as strong winds fed the flames and caused them to race from the sixth to thirteenth floor in a brilliant display of the speed and power of fire. Fran and I took the "El" into town and arrived in time to still see much of the action.

After the fire, Fran suggested that we go to a movie as the evening was young. Having been brought up to eat three meals a day, and I had only had two so far that day, I reasoned that it best I go home to supper - besides Mom would be looking for me. Fran was working part time so had some money and said supper was no problem. We went to the Hayes Bickford Cafeteria in Scollay Square and had something to eat, and then we went to the Scollay Square Theatre to see a Bob Hope movie.

I arrived home about midnight and Mom was not sleeping with one eye open this night. She was up, with both eyes open, and once she knew I was home safe, her mouth opened too. The deserved tirade that ushered forth, was all aimed at me and my thoughtless actions of the evening. In today's terms, my sparking was "grounded" and my school homework received its rightful attention for a while. Fortunately my grounding wasn't permanent, because on May 17, 1938 there was a four alarm fire in West Roxbury at the Gardner Street Ice House (Box 2797) and I was there rolling hose and riding home on the back step of the pump.

Anecdote:
In 1965 I was a lieutenant on Engine 28 in Jamaica Plain and on September 1st we responded to a four alarm fire at 1980 Centre Street in West Roxbury (Box 284). The fire involved offices of the Metropolitan Life Insurance Company and the New England Mobile Book Fair. This was the first four alarm fire in West Roxbury since the Gardner Street fire in 1938 and I worked at both of them. The residents of that community did not have to wait so long for the

next four bagger. It occurred on May 28, 1973 when the Congregational Church at Centre and Mt. Vernon Streets was destroyed in an early morning fire (Box 285). I was on vacation at the time but went to watch my brothers work.

In Boston, the periods of 2100 hours June 16 to 2400 hours June 17 (Bunker Hill Day) and 2100 hours July 3 to 2400 hours July 4 were periods of "Reduced Assignments," except in down town Boston. Because of the large number of bonfires and other minor fires that occurred during these periods, the first alarm response was reduced from three engines and two ladders to two engines and one ladder, plus the district chief. These four nights were always big nights for sparks, whether they were riding apparatus or not, as there was always the possibility that a fire would get a good start because companies would be tied up at nuisance fires. There was also the possibility that one of the bonfires might extend beyond what was intended.

On the night of June 17, 1938 there had been a few earlier runs and more were anticipated as darkness settled in. At 9:30 Box 2122 (Washington and Nawn Streets) was struck and the second alarm at 9:34. Off went Engine 42 with me on the back step of the pump. The fire was in a large old wood barn, at 27 Hunneman Street. It was then being used as a barrel factory. We ran a long two and half inch line to the rear and upstairs in the adjacent building. For the next hour or so we directed the stream of water through a small opening that was made in the common partition wall. As we sent water in, the fire sent smoke back and we spent an uncomfortable evening, but I thought it was just fine. That was the good part; the bad part was we missed a lot of other running.

Anecdote:
A third alarm was struck on Box 2122 at 9:40 for this fire, but at 9:39, Box 1294 (down town) was struck for a fire at 34 India Street. A second alarm was struck for this fire at 9:43 and the third alarm at 9:48. It was the first time in Boston that three alarms were struck on each of two successive boxes and it hasn't happened since.

September 21, 1938 was another memorable day. As I walked home from school, the wind was increasing dramatically and right away I determined that the fire house was the place for me. About four o'clock Ed Steidinger, who was due to work the night tour, came running into the fire house completely out of breath. He had seen a house on fire off Harold Street and had pulled several fire boxes but got no response. He tried calling Fire Alarm on the phone but couldn't get through. The officer tried to notify Fire Alarm on the department phone, but without success, so Engine 42 and Ladder 30 left for the fire location with Ed showing the way.

On arrival, there was a large two and a half story frame house, well involved in fire. The officer told me to help the pump operator hook up and then try to get help. Just as we hooked up, a large tree fell across the suction hose cutting off the water supply from the hydrant. For the next several minutes we went at that tree trunk, which measured about fifteen inches across, with axes and finally got water flowing again into the pump. Then I went on my assignment to get help.

It was then that I pulled a fire box for the first time - in fact the first dozen times, and always with the same results - none. I could hear the code wheel transmitting the signal but no apparatus arrived. Trying to call on telephones also produced nothing. Most overhead wires in the neighborhood were downed by falling trees so there was no lights or communication and a fire that probably should have had a second alarm was put out by the two companies, along with the help of the building occupants and a few other citizens. There are lots of stories that could be told about that first New England hurricane in many years.

As related above, I missed the ship fire on the "S.S. Laila," but all things come to those who wait. On Friday night, December 2, 1938 I was at the fire house and shortly after eight o'clock Box 4116 at Water and Gray Street, Charlestown, was struck. Second and third alarms soon followed and we left to cover Engine 10. At five past nine the fourth alarm was struck and we responded to Pier 43 at the Hoosac Docks. The fire was aboard the "S.S. Southlure" which was loaded with hemp, sisal and other cargoes. The hemp and sisal made a very heavy irritating smoke and the officer working was hesitant to let me go down into the hold, especially since the two All-Service masks carried by the company were already in use - but in all that smoke who could recognize anyone anyhow. Once down, the smoke wasn't as bad as above on deck, which is often the case. We got back to Egleston Square around midnight and after helping with the hose, headed for home - a weary but well satisfied fifteen year old spark.

On looking over the list of 1939 multiples, nothing triggers my mind as being particularly noteworthy but my sparking continued and I went to a number of fires throughout the city, either with or without aid of the apparatus.

Valentine's Day 1940 was the date of one of Boston's biggest blizzards. It was a Wednesday night and Mom went to teach her sewing class at the Mary Curley School and I went to the fire house hoping for winter action. Mom advised me to be home early, in fact, be there when she got home. I missed by five minutes.

Outside of shoveling the apron every hour there was little activity outside the fire house, but as the storm intensity grew and transportation bogged down, activity inside the fire house increased. More and more people became stranded and found their way into the fire house where they took refuge from the storm. Every flat space was used as a bed or for resting and the coffee pot did yeoman duty. When morning came and the local bakeries opened, a continental breakfast of sorts was served to everyone, and I went home.

Mom beat me to the house by five minutes. She had spent the night on the Dudley Street bus, and at daybreak had trudged home through the deep snow, walking along with other passengers of her night's ordeal. It would have been nicer for her if the bus had bogged down near a fire house.

The off platoons were held for a couple days until streets became passable and then regular tours were resumed, but Young Cookie reported for duty every night for about a week - hoping. I had gotten to the point where sound sleep came easy in the bunk room, but just after 3:30 in the morning of February 20th, the lights came on, the house gong sounded and we rode into the winter night to a two alarm fire at 70 Munroe Street. The fire was in a three and a half story wooden dwelling and we worked on the second and third floors.

When the fire was knocked down they sent me to get fifty feet of inch and a half hose and a play pipe, for overhauling. As I was going out the front door, Engine 14 was taking a line over a ground ladder to the attic. The pipe man was about half way up the ladder when a large section of the coping came off the front of the building and knocked him to the ground. Fortunately there was still plenty of deep snow and this broke his fall, but he was injured and covered with burning wood. Along with the men of Engine 14, I helped dig him out, put him on a stretcher and carry him a good distance through the snow to an ambulance. There was a photographer from the *Daily Record* who took photos of the coping burning, breaking away, hitting the member, and then his being carried on the stretcher. The series of pictures ran the next day in the afternoon edition, and I had my newspaper fire debut.

There is a saying that "rats desert a sinking ship." Well they will also desert a sinking building. As mentioned earlier, the patrol desk at Engine 42 was against the right wall as one faced the house. On the other side of that wall was the JA Cafe - which gained some notoriety following the Brink's Garage robbery as one of the owners was alleged to have been a participant. On the cafe's left side there was a flight of wooden stairs leading up to the second floor. About two A.M. on November 28, 1940, the man on watch was distracted by a strange sound coming through the wall. The cafe was closed, but there was a thumping of feet racing down those stairs, and then silence returned. Shortly afterwards the tapper came alive and punched out Box 2445 - the box outside on the fire house wall. At the same time the policeman who pulled the box began pounding on the door and pointing next door. When the apparatus pulled out onto Washington Street, flames were already leaping from the second and third floors of the JA Cafe and lapping up the side of the "El" structure. A second alarm was ordered and as the men forced the door to gain entry to the fire, a lot of good sized four legged critters rushed out the door, grateful to be rescued.

In June of 1941 I graduated from high school and went to work for Powers and Hall, a law firm at 30 Federal Street. The woman Office Manager who hired me said I was the first non-college graduate she had ever hired for the position, which was Office Boy. My duties included frequent visits to banks to make transactions for the many trust accounts they handled, and filing various legal papers in an assortment of courts in the greater Boston area.

My starting salary was fourteen dollars a week. Half went to Mom for room and board and the other half was mine for carfare, lunches, dates, church offerings (a tithe) and savings. By skimping on lunches, and probably dates, I was able to save enough money to visit the Albe Rubber Company and buy a fire coat of my own. In those days they had no pockets and no reflective tape but it did have large metal snap hooks which distinguished it from an ordinary black raincoat. They "gave" it to me at reduced price because there was a small area inside the coat on which the rubber vulcanizing had not taken. So for fourteen dollars, one week's pay, I made the first major purchase of my working life and went home very happy with my own black fire coat. It wasn't long before it was christened.

Shortly after six in the evening on September 18th, 1941 fire broke out in a warehouse shed on Rutherford Avenue. Within four minutes the chief ordered the second alarm to be skipped and a third alarm struck (Box 4156). The fourth and fifth alarms were ordered within the next six minutes, and shortly thereafter all off duty men in the department were recalled. The fire rapidly spread to several similar warehouse sheds. Each was several hundred feet long. Some of the sheds were loaded with canned food products of First National Stores, and these became rocketing missiles when they heated and exploded. There was a mixture of various flammable commodities stored in the other buildings.

Again I was with Engine 42 and we were operating the deck gun atop 42's wagon. We were positioned about halfway down between two of the warehouses. The deck gun was being supplied with three two-and-a-half inch lines of hose that we had stretched. There were a couple other wagons positioned in the same roadway. The deck guns on those wagons were all being supplied by either two or three lines of hose. There was little smoke but plenty of flames and heat and it was this radiated heat that was quickly contributing to the spread of the fire. For me it was a beautiful picture of firefighting strategy and team work as those powerful heavy stream appliances each poured close to a thousand gallons of water a minute into the inferno and I was delighted to be part of this action.

Suddenly the wind shifted and those flames that had been spiraling upward became a ceiling of fire directly over our heads. Looking up we could see nothing but brilliant red-orange flames and it seemed to be slowly dropping. The heat became intense and our fire coats began to smoke as the smell of burning rubber began to surround us. For the first time at a fire, I was scared, and if things hadn't happened so quickly I might have prayed, "Dear God, get me out of this and I will give up sparking forever!"

My first inclination was to get off that wagon and run for Rutherford Avenue, but the dropping fire was pushing smoke to the ground and visibility was reduced to near zero. Running the three hundred or so feet in boots and fire gear, and hampered by the increasing smoke and rising temperature of the fire probably would have been futile, if not fatal.

Thank God, and I mean this literally and sincerely, for a cool and experienced company officer. Captain Bob Ritchie calmly told one of the men to hop down to the driver's seat, put the wagon in reverse and back out without stopping. Forget disconnecting or shutting down the lines. The rest of us, including the captain, stood on the hose deck and rode out of the fire storm, while lines of hose burst and whipped about spewing water under great pressure in all directions. With the crew standing on that deck and Captain Ritchie, with his white hair, in the forefront, we may have looked like a retake of "Washington Crossing the Delaware" but in a sea of fire. Once safe, we regrouped, reconnected lines of hose, and took up new positions to continue the assault on the fire – Man's best friend, and worst enemy!

Anecdote:
That fire indelibly imprinted on my mind some facts that guided my career. First, a kid or a man, could get real hurt playing this game, and second, there is no substitute for experience, especially when you have other men's lives in your hands. On the first issue I learned to always be alert to conditions around me and to always think in terms of safety and escape for the men and myself. The second issue is far more important and probably deprived my family of some monetary return. Promotions in the fire department require a lot of book knowledge, but that will never take the place of going to lots of fires and learning something at almost everyone, which takes many years. Its called Experience!

Unfortunately, there is no way of testing an officer on the latter. That test comes when the "chips are down" and any lack of experience and judgment can result in serious injury or death to men entrusted to his care. It is unfortunate that the system has no real means of crediting practical experience - other than time, and so it is left to the individual as to whether his career will be dominated by the monetary principle, or the less selfish practical principle. None of this is meant to imply or even suggest that every injury or death of a fireman is due to lack of experience. On the contrary, firemen know that all the book knowledge in the world, coupled with all the experience in the world, cannot prevent some accidents. They just happen in God's Plan. Nothing man can do will alter it.

Following that fire I was determined that if I ever had a career in the fire service, it would be guided by the practical principle. It would be another manifestation of "having to live with myself and wanting to be fit for myself to know." The result was that it took me ten years to make lieutenant and fourteen more years before I donned the white coat and helmet of a chief. That is the bad news. The good news is that I was comfortable with my slow climb and confident of my abilities when going to the next rung of promotion. I can honestly say that I never felt uncertain of what decision to make as my experience and responsibilities grew, and my blood pressure never increased due to inner tension caused by any uncertainty of my decisions and actions. Again, this is not a reflection on any of my fellow officers, except, the excellent example set by the captain of Engine 42 that September night in Charlestown, when I developed my profound respect for Experience.

Anecdote:
By the grace of God, the most serious injury that occurred to any member under my command, while working at thousands of fires and other Incidents, was a broken back. It was suffered by a fireman, as he jumped to safety when a portion of a pier building collapsed at a four alarm waterfront fire I had while acting deputy. He returned to full duty in a few months.

On Sunday, December 7th, "a day that will live in infamy," Japan attacked the United States at Pearl Harbor and we were in

World War II. I was just past my eighteenth birthday and knew that before long I would be wearing Army O.D. or Navy blue. Everyone who was alive on that day can tell you exactly what they were doing when they heard the news. I was at Dot's house listening to the radio when they broke in with a news flash. Later, we went to the regular evening church service, following which the young people gathered around and soberly speculated on what effect the day's events would have on all our lives. My brother Richard and I both got home about midnight (Mom's curfew time). We sat around the kitchen drinking milk and eating cookies, and wondered how many more nights we would be able to do this together. Dick was a couple years older than me and joined the Eighth Air Force a couple weeks before I too donned the khaki. Incidentally, Dick had shared some of my early sparking interests, but wisely placed his music ahead of those smoky all-night stands.

More and more firemen were leaving to go on "Military Leave" and although some Military Substitutes were being appointed, they too were enlisting or being drafted. Not knowing what my future in the military might be, I was anxious to go to as many fires as possible then. The companies were always short of manpower so my presence to do watches and work at fires was doubly appreciated. There were lots of singles and multiples that I worked at, including several wool warehouse fires around A Street in South Boston. These were always very smoky fires and sabotage was often suspected or suggested.

Anecdote:
When permanent firemen entered military service, their vacancies were filled from the existing Civil Service list. These appointees were designated as Military Substitutes. If they entered the armed forces, men filling those vacancies from the list were appointed as Provisional Military Substitutes. Patrick Cady, who paid the supreme sacrifice on October 22, 1946, was a P.M.S.

In November 1942 I enlisted in the Army, hoping to see some of this country before being sent overseas. The Army was expanding so rapidly that it was difficult to provide barracks and training spaces fast enough. They assigned me to a specialty school in Boston for six months and told me to live at home. My mother was very happy and I had mixed feelings - but it meant six more months of sparking at night. The fires I connected with were so many and varied during those months that I feared my military service was going to have a dark ending and God was letting me have all this fun first.

The months of November and December were fun for me as I played soldier during the day and fireman at night, but they were tragic times for a lot of other people in Boston. On the night tour of Saturday, November 15th, there was a fire in Lyceum Hall in Maverick Square, East Boston (Box 6153). It came in just before two thirty in the morning and developed into a three alarm fire. The companies had advanced lines into the building and were making good progress when without reason or warning the building collapsed trapping many men inside. Fourth and fifth alarms were struck to bring in help to rescue and recover those noble men that hadn't gotten out.

When the final count was taken, six of Boston's Bravest had been killed and forty-three injured, most of them quite seriously. I had not bunked in that night but hearing it on the radio, I went with 42's Day Tour in the morning to relieve the Night Tour. Two or three men were still unaccounted for when we arrived. There were tons of debris to be moved and the day and night crews worked together in bucket brigade fashion as wood and stone were passed hand to hand to the street and piled up. By late morning a crane was brought in and the heavy granite blocks were removed. One by one the remaining bodies were uncovered and each time, a hush fell over the square as the iron men stood in honoring silence, with their leather helmets in hand and tears in their eyes, as the bodies of their fallen comrades went home from their "Last Alarm."

Anecdote:
Ladder 8 responded to this fire. The vehicle then assigned to it came under much discussion and became known as the "White Elephant." It was painted white, which was different, and had a one hundred twenty-five foot steel aerial ladder. It was originally purchased by a neighboring city, but when delivered it would not fit in any of their fire houses. Boston took it off their hands and assigned it to the Fort Hill Square house (Ladder 8). The main ladder was five sections and the sides were about twenty inches

high. Being of all metal, it had considerable weight and following the Lyceum Hall collapse there was "con" discussion as to whether the weight of the ladder against the building contributed to the tragedy. The "pro" side of the discussion came from firemen who were advancing a big line up the ladder when the collapse occurred. These members gave the ladder credit for saving their lives. When the collapse began, they hugged into the space between the twenty inch sides while granite blocks and other debris slid over them on the strong metal sides. They felt that without those high metal sides, they would have been knocked off the ladder.

The ladder was badly damaged and was reduced to one hundred feet before being placed back in service. The "White Elephant" was involved in several other incidents resulting in injuries and finally, maybe out of superstition, was repainted red - like all good fire engines.

Years later it was being test driven on the Strandway in South Boston following a major overhaul. Something went wrong and the tillerman was thrown from the tiller seat and killed when he struck the ground. The "White Elephant" was retired from service without honors, and scrapped.

Just two weeks later, on Saturday November 28th, tragedy again struck Boston and its fire department. Four hundred and ninety-six lives were snuffed out in the Cocoanut Grove Night Club (Box 1521) as fire raced through the interior. Engine 42's assignment was to cover Engine 33 and stay there. Young Cookie covered too, but didn't stay there. It wasn't far to the fire scene and they could use all the help they could get.

I don't recall all the companies that I helped, and in fact a lot was accomplished by a mixture of men, but those scenes have remained etched in my memory to this day. There was much fire to contend with and advancing lines was difficult. I remember assisting on lines going down the stairs and into the Melody Lounge, and coming upon an unbelievable sight. People sitting at the bar - some with glasses still in their hands. Natural instinct was to grab them and tell them to get out, but when touched, they fell to the floor - some with glasses still in their hands. There were people with every degree of burns. Some were charred beyond recognition, some were moaning or crying in agony because of burns, and others without visible marks, but rigor mortis had set in.

When the fire was under control, some companies continued with the overhauling to be certain there was no rekindle, but most men began the gruesome task of removing victims from the fire building and then from the area, either to hospitals or temporary morgues. I helped with both. Some bodies were piled up at the revolving doors and other exits, while other patrons never made it far from the location they were in when the tragedy struck. Flimsy evening finery that some of the ladies had been wearing was affected by the extreme heat and their gowns just melted away leaving them nearly nude. I remember grasping the hand of one woman, with the intention of carrying her out, but the skin from her wrist to the fingers peeled off like a glove.

Once out of the building, the victims were carried across Piedmont Street to a garage where a triage area was set up. In most cases it was just a matter of a doctor confirming death, but on occasion the examiner would detect a sign of life and there would be a rush to get medical attention and transportation. The garage wasn't large enough to hold all the bodies and soon military trucks began to arrive to help in the removal process. More doctors, including those from the military, arrived at the scene and triage stations were set up on the sidewalk. As victims were brought out, they were checked right there and the corpses piled into the back of army trucks, and when full, left for the morgues.

By daybreak the last of the Saturday night revelers of the Cocoanut Grove had been removed. I returned to Engine 33's quarters and this time I could tell the men of Engine 42 of what I had seen and taken part in and it was their turn to sit spellbound. The sight of so much death, first at Lyceum Hall and then the nightclub, took its toll on the firemen as well. Engine 33 returned from the fire with just the pump and its driver and he was so shaken that the company was put out of service until the Day Tour reported for duty.

One of Engine 33's men, Malachi Reddington, had been killed at the Maverick Square fire. Others, including my neighbor Tom Lydon, were still in the hospital in critical condition. Tom's back was crushed by one of the granite blocks and although he lived, he never went to another fire.

The Day Tour relieved us and I went home, cleaned up and went to church. I had been up all night and after dinner I laid down on the couch listening to the radio. Naturally all the news was about the fire and as identification of the victims became known, the new names were announced over the air. People who had not heard from loved ones and feared the worst, sat glued to their radios listening for new names – hoping for the best. It was like kids listening for "No School" announcements - - but there was no cheering. Each new name brought sorrow to a different family.

The activity of the night had not bothered me at the time. But later, as I lay half asleep on the couch, looking up at that charred mantle mentioned before, and the names of the nearly five hundred victims were read over and over again, the reality of what I had witnessed the night before started to sink in. The reading of each name brought back the horrible sights of those pitiful people and I couldn't sleep.

Sixteen nights later on December 15th I was again "bunking" in, and again a night passed without my head touching a pillow. Shortly before midnight, Box 1461 sounded for a fire in Salinger's apparel store at 493 - 507 Washington Street. On the third alarm we covered Engine 26 on Broadway and shortly after backing in, the fourth was struck and we went to the fire. We were ordered to take a big line into the lower level of the ladies dress shop. Smoke was getting thicker and we hugged the floor as we advanced the line down the stairs. Suddenly, as I was groping my way, my gloved hand touched an arm - and followed it up - over the shoulder - and to the head. Judging by the amount of hair, it had to be a woman, and I yelled out "There's a body here!" All the company headed in my direction and with their Wheat lights soon detected that it was only a store dummy that had fallen over. I expect I was still paranoid over my experiences of the past month, and the men were very understanding.

At the basement level it was getting hotter but no visible fire. We found stairs leading to the sub-cellar and forced our way down through the heat and smoke to the lower level. Through the smoke we could see what we were looking for - a red glow at the far interior end of this cavern. Guided by the glow, we advanced our line in that direction and as we reached it, visibility became clear. Fire was pushing out past a partially opened door and the captain called for the line to be charged. As air, followed by water snaked through our hose, the nozzle was aimed at the door.

The pressure of the water fully opened the door and the angry flames rushed toward us. The night's battle had begun! The room was overflowing with fire and again and again we beat it into submission, only to have it return with new vengeance and force us back. The see-saw war was waged for nearly an hour before the good guys gradually gained the upper hand and finally forced the fire back into its lair to stay. Cautiously we followed it, preceded by two hundred and fifty gallons of ice water a minute being expelled from our hose. Once inside that room we knew a battle had been won but the war was far from over. We were inside the elevator shaft room and looking up we could see tiers of fire impinging from every floor as companies above forced their fire to seek an avenue of escape as they advanced their lines.

Our stream was aimed up the shaft and some of the fire was darkened down, which meant the water was having an effect, but it also produced more smoke, which is the product of incomplete combustion. Captain Ritchie prepared for the battle by ordering the two All-Service masks brought in and arranged a schedule for their use. Since there was no more advancing to be made, the hose was secured with hose lines. In this way, only one or two men would be needed to direct it. His schedule called for two men, with the masks, on the play pipe in relays of ten to fifteen minutes and the rest outside breathing fresh air.

The way it worked was that the first two men started, and half way through the first period, another man went down and relieved one of the men - and took his mask. Thus the nightly cycle was begun and it continued until morning with all of us taking turns and resting in between. It should be remembered that the masks were only slightly more than filters and a certain amount of smoke got through as the filtering chemicals were weakened by use. Also the canisters only had a work life of two hours, but we nursed them through about five hours. This meant a lot of smoke got through. You can see why it was called a department of "iron men."

One of the men on Engine 42 that night was a "Man on Probation" who was detailed and early on the smoke got to him and he was removed to the hospital. That speeded up the relay cycle for the rest of us. Though the combined efforts of the five alarm response finally controlled the fire, we were never able to completely extinguish it in the elevator shaft. As night turned to day we learned why. The large ball of fire, which would not yield to our thousands of gallons of water during the night, was fed by a broken gas pipe. We were fortunate that it did not yield.

Seventy-three firemen were injured at that blaze. The rest of us who fought it were glad to be relieved there by the Day Tour who were fresh and could make up the thousands of feet of spaghetti that had been stretched during the night long battle. Although I was now nineteen and supposedly in prime physical condition, as a member of the Armed Forces, these were getting to be exhausting all-nighters.

It might appear that sparking took all my time, but in fact it was mostly at night and weekends. During the day I did work, first at Powers and Hall, but at the end of the 1941 I changed jobs and went to Merrimack Manufacturing Company whose office was at 53 State Street. There my title and duties and salary were slightly above "office boy," but it was only a stop over on my way to the Army.

On leaving Powers and Hall they gave me a little party, a little fire engine, another little gift, and a little note which read,

"Although he would rather fight a fire than run around to banks,
Our Paul is going to leave us now to join the State Street ranks.
At fifty-three he'll do his best to fill his brand new job,
Though forty-three might find him called to be a U.S. gob.
So please accept this gift from............."

I had a boyhood chum named Kolin Marsell who was looking for work and before leaving Powers and Hall, I convinced the Office Manager to hire her second non-college graduate - Kolin.

One of the things I learned best at the fire house was how to play cribbage. I taught the game to Kolin and together we became real cribbage addicts. Not only did we spend our lunch hours playing it in the basement of 30 Federal Street, but it so happened that both of us had to pick up mail for our employers twice a day at about the same time. We used to meet and go down the cellar to play a quick two out of three games, before returning to our respective offices. We thought no one knew of our clandestine meetings, except Mike the building superintendent, who let us use his office.

Kolin and I had talked of joining up together in the same branch of the service so we could look after one another - and play cribbage, but at the last minute I joined the Army and Kolin the Marines. Powers and Hall had a little party for Kolin and invited me, since we were such good friends. After the cake and ice cream, the Office Manager came out of her office and handed each of us a little wrapped gift. They came from London Harness Company and had our initials imprinted on them. They were folding leather cribbage boards - and we thought no one knew. In June of 1943 we both reported to our "boot camps" with our cribbage boards - and we never played cribbage together again.

Anecdote:
Kolin was with the Fourth Marine Division and survived the many bloody battles his unit was engaged in during the Pacific Island invasions. Our boyhood friendship, that had lasted for over a dozen years, just never did return, as our adult lives took different paths. During the eighties I visited him when he was a patient at the Spaulding Rehab Hospital. I took along my leather cribbage board and a deck of cards for old time sake, but it just wasn't the time to resume our old pastime. Kolin had been active in the New England Chapter of the Fourth Marine Division Association and following his death they changed the name to the "Kolin Marsell Chapter."

Anecdote, Second Alarm:
In the early eighties, when I was chief in District 3, we were stopped in traffic in front of 30 Federal Street where Powers and Hall still had their offices. I spotted a gentleman coming out the door and recognized him as one of the lawyers who was new with the firm when I had my first job there. I got out of my car and introduced myself. Somehow I recalled the row of about a dozen

offices and the names of each lawyer occupying the rooms at that time, also the names of many of the secretarial staff. He was amazed at my memory and filled me in on each one. Naturally, since forty years had passed, many had died. He was so pleased and excited with our meeting that he said he was going back in and tell everyone in the office. Then he paused, and soberly reflected, what would be the purpose since there was no one left who would possibly remember me.

Now I ask, could anyone really charge the city, or anyone else, for all that fun and experience? And how would one go about charging? ... By the hours spent in a fire house? ... By the number of times I responded? ... By how many nights I bunked in? ... By the number of fires worked? ... By the amount of dirty smoke inhaled? ... By the number of hydrants salted or shoveled out? ... By the number of watches I did - unofficially? ... By the number of entries in the Journal, in various handwritings? ... By the number of errands ran? ... By the Experience gained? ... By the number of jokes played? ... By the multitude of laughs? ... By the many tragedies witnessed? ... By the number of scoldings from Mom?

Today the circumstances are such that it could not be repeated, except possibly by a volunteer in a small town, but it was really something the first time around and I am grateful that it was my good fortune to have experienced it all.

Molasses Disaster, January 15, 1919.   Over 2 million gallons spilled out when tank broke apart. Flood of molasses was 15' high and over 150' wide.   Twenty-one people were killed, including one Boston fireman.

Pickwick Club Collapse, July 4, 1925.

War time Engine 39 with anti-aircraft gun mounted on hose bed. Standing at left is Fire Commissioner Riley and Deputy Chief Quigley.

Lyceum Hall fire, East Boston, November 15, 1942. Six fireman killed and 43 injured, many seriously causing them to retire. Note Ladder 8, the White Elephant.

Rescue 2, with Dalmatian "Neddo." Sparky Leonard driving.

Cocoanut Grove nightclub fire, November 28, 1942.   Four hundred and ninety-six patrons killed.

Rutherford Avenue, Charlestown, September 18, 1941. This one almost stopped my career before it started.

WAR DAYS AND THE BIG DAY

(or, Intermission From Boston Fires)

Starting June 4, 1943 and for the next nine hundred and ninety five days, my time was not my own as Uncle Sam was calling the shots and he had no consideration for sparking - unless you count the number of burning buildings caused by bombings and other war actions. To expound on my war time sojourn would take a volume of its own, but since this book is part biography at least a few pages should be devoted to those early dark days of World War II and the final triumph over the Axis powers.

From Pearl Harbor to Nagasaki in the Pacific and from London to Berlin in the European Theatre of Operations, there are tens of millions of stories that can be told by the millions of Americans who answered their country's call. We all ended up in the same places, and the enemy didn't know the difference, but it always gave me a bit of inward pride that my eight digit Army serial number began with a "one," which indicated voluntary enlistment, rather than "three" which indicated a draftee.

But regardless of dog-tag numbers, along with hundreds of others on that June day, I reported to Fort Devens, with my leather cribbage board and my Red Book to occupy any spare time Uncle Sam might give me. My assignment was to Camp Edison in New Jersey for basic training and then advanced schooling in the Signal Corps. At the start, our Advanced class numbered in the hundreds, but after weeks of strenuous weeding out there were forty of us left and we became the "DD Team" of a new Signal battalion. Our training had been most thorough and we were deemed capable of carrying out any Signal Corps assignment, whether in the field or a command center. With a lot of conscientious effort, our team earned a reputation, and became known as "Ali Laskin and his Forty Thieves" (Laskin was our Captain at the time). It was the most completely equipped unit in the battalion, in fact the whole camp, because of our concentrated application of the ingenuity for which our most recent schooling had trained us for both at home and overseas.

Following graduation from Advanced Training School, the entire Team was scheduled to report to City College of New York to be trained in government for the Army of Occupation. No way! The entire Team went to our superiors and requested immediate overseas assignment in place of CCNY. In a rare display of listening, our assignment was changed and we headed for England. I am sure our protesting had no real bearing on what happened but it made us all very pleased as we embarked on the "H.M.S. Aquatania" one Sunday night in February 1944 and sailed alone, without escort or convoy, across the North Atlantic to Scotland.

From Scotland we moved to Bury St. Edmunds, England, where by practicing our earlier training made ourselves quite comfortable among the units bivouacking there. One day during Mail Call of a neighboring unit, somehow the occupants of our pyramid tent accidentally moved the pot belly stove, complete with chimney and fire, from one of their tents to ours. Immediately following their Mail Call, and the discovery, there was a big camp investigation. Our tent was one suspected but since about half of the hundreds of tents had stoves in them, it was difficult to prove that ours hadn't been there all the time, especially in light of the fire that was roaring in it and the chimney pipe was securely in place. Other comforts somehow found their way into our barren barracks, which just proved that Laskin's Forty Thieves had paid attention in training and learned their lessons well.

From Bury St. Edmunds we moved to Plymouth in southern England to prepare for the invasion of Europe. Plymouth had the dubious distinction of being the "most bombed city in England" mainly because of the number of docks, which seemed to attract enemy bombers. Our unit was housed in Raglan Barracks, an old navy school.

The upper and lower bunks had chicken wire mesh stretched between two by four wood frames and mattresses were large cotton bags filled with straw. The straw was noisy and dirty and the wire mesh soon sagged. On my upper bunk, these were replaced in short time with a solid wood topping made from packing crates and somehow my two issued O.D. blankets were augmented with several more to cushion my carcass. It didn't take long for my buddies to realize that Cookie's bunk was a nice flat surface on which they could stand around and play cards or roll dice. I guess it was then that I learned to get along without much sleep. Speaking of sleep, we weren't there many nights before we were first awakened by the shrill shriek of the air raid sirens. Standing orders were for us to leave the barracks and go to the slit trenches that had been prepared.

Anecdote:
Up until the time the bombs began to fall, air raids were a dramatic and somewhat colorful sight to behold. When the Royal Air Force spotters had determined the direction in which the bombers were heading, the air raid sirens would sound to alert the public several minutes before there were any visible signs of activity.

Slowly, increasing numbers of huge searchlights would blink on and begin crisscrossing the skies as they scanned in search of the intruders. Their rays would pick up and reflect off the big barrage balloons as they rose into the skies on long cables in an attempt to force the enemy planes to go higher over the city and distort their bombing aim.

As the invaders came into view, the anti-aircraft guns would open up and the colored tracer shells would penetrate the growing lofty battle scene. Before long, Spitfires of the RAF would arrive at the stereoptic show and their machine guns, with every fifth bullet a different colored tracer, would be answered with tracers from the Luftwaffe planes as they fought to defend themselves and remain in the air to complete their mission. For added defense they would drop shredded tinfoil in an attempt to confuse the English ground radar. The brilliant beams of the searchlights would bounce off the shimmering pervading foil and magnify the smoke puffs produced by the ack-ack attack.

This magical display in God's firmament resembled a gigantic laser beam show - - before they were invented. Sometimes there would be a vivid explosion as anti-aircraft shells blasted a target and there would be a fiery trail as the plane dropped from the sky, and those watching wondered if it was one of theirs, or one of ours. Sometimes those searching beams would shine on dark dropping objects that came to a sudden halt when half round umbrellas opened above them. If multiple parachutes appeared, it was assumed the plane was one of their bombers and cheers would go up from those watching as the multi-member crew bailed out.

Before long some of that hardware which had most recently been a part of the heavenly show would begin to drop among the spectators - flak, pieces of shells and airplanes and sometimes flyers, and ribbons of foil draping over people and objects like paper streamers at a party. Before the sky show ended, the eerie whine of plummeting bombs and thunderous concussions would begin to rock the ground. The horizon would take on a red aura more spectacular than a brilliant sunrise and sunset combined, as the beginning fires demonstrated their mastery.

Most of those distant conflagrations were observed from a place of relative safety, but sometimes the enemy struck while I was in town and I had a front row seat to watch firemen of the British National Fire Service face the enemy undaunted - and often pay with their lives.

The role of our DD Team was to be a code unit for Armies or Corps, or be broken into smaller groups for detached service to Divisions or smaller units. We landed on Normandy's Utah Beach from an LCI (Landing Craft Infantry) and learned about hedgerow hopping first hand. Later we were assigned to Patton's Third Army and assembled in an apple orchard in preparation for the attack and break out of Avranches. It was my first assignment with an Armored unit and with all the noise those tanks were making it seemed to me this couldn't have been planned as a secret mission. The enemy was only a few hundred yards away but they could have heard us coming if they were a few miles away. Noise or no noise, General Patton had planned well, and we rolled out of the hedgerows and across France. Paris was liberated in August and our advance had been so swift that when we moved in on the German headquarters there, the switchboard was still intact, and we called direct to the Paperhanger in Berlin to tell him we were on our way.

In training we were taught not to drink any water without adding halazone tablets. Most of our chow since Normandy had been "C" or "K" rations washed down with questionable water, mixed with lemon powder or coffee for flavor and halazone tablets for health. In the basement of the German Paris HQ we found a wine cellar, loaded with cases of Gordon Rouge 1927 Champagne, plus other refreshing liquids. Before it was confiscated by the brass, we were able to liberate enough of it to allow the enlisted men, and non-coms, to stash their halazone tablets in the bottom of their knapsacks, and wash down the army rations with a safer medicinal liquid.

Paris is a beautiful city and I got to know it quite well. In its wisdom, the Army set up an Intelligence Center in Paris and I was among those intermittently stationed there. Because the intelligence work we performed was beneficial to both the U. S. and French Armies, on payday we were paid by both governments. Today we would probably be accused of double dipping, but in those days the extra Francs came in handy in the City of Light. When not on detached service, there was a room waiting for me in the Hotel D'Iena, which was our billet, not far from the Arc de Triomphe.

The Spring of 1945 found me on detached service with the First Allied Airborne Army, assigned to gliders with the 82nd Division. Plans called for us to be dropped at Templehoff Airport in Berlin when ground troops were twenty miles outside. But then, politics outranked military strategy and the Russians were allowed to take the German Capital. Following Victory in Europe on May 8th I was returned to my beloved Paris and wondered about being sent on to Japan. The atom bombs dropped on Hiroshima and Nagasaki helped to even the score for Pearl Harbor and the Peace Treaty was signed on September second, 1945 in Tokyo Bay. Plans for our battalion's deployment to Japan for the invasion were canceled and my reassignment order was issued.

Later in the autumn of 1945 I ended up in Berlin in the Intelligence Center there. Civil government was taking over from the military and the State Department asked me to take my discharge in Berlin and transfer to that branch of the government. I would be continuing my present army assignments but with a different hat and without going home. After almost two years overseas, I wanted to go stateside for a while, and reasoned that if my services were that much in demand, there should be no problem in my going home and then applying to come back. The person that interviewed me in Berlin agreed and so I waited for the Army to be through with me in Germany and take me home.

During my trip through five countries, there were plenty of fires and their aftermath to witness and that boyhood ambition to be a Boston fireman still burned deep within me and I was anxious to get back to it.

On January 21, 1946 I boarded the Liberty Ship "S. S. William Few" in Bremerhaven, Germany, for the ocean voyage home to New York. It wasn't an express trip. After passing through the North Sea, and the English Channel, still loaded with floating German mines, we sailed into the North Atlantic where we ran into a hurricane that turned our ship around, broke the steering apparatus and put a hole in the bow. During that turn around, the ship hit a forty-five degree list. One more degree and it would have kept going. The next day we made the best time of the whole trip - blown a few hundred miles backwards. We ended up in St. Miguel in the Azores for repairs and took on rations and fresh water. Again we headed for New York, but radar detected another storm and the Captain headed for Bermuda. That storm blew itself out and we finally sailed into New York harbor just as darkness was ending on the morning of February 19th.

Three or four of us had stayed up most of the night and as land was neared, we went up to the bridge and watched the approaching harbor on radar. As we peered ahead, the lights on the Statue of Liberty went out. One GI remarked that the least she could have done was to stay lit until we sailed by. One of the others, being a bit more philosophical, commented that the Lady had been waiting up for us for twenty-nine days and now that we were home she had every right to put out her light and go to bed. On February 23rd I was honorably discharged from the army, given my "Ruptured Duck" pin to wear as proof of service, and went home to pick up the pieces, and to spark.

Anecdote:
Guess one could still call it progress, but as noted earlier, my grandfather sailed from Bremerhaven on a two mast wooden vessel and in six weeks landed in New York City. Decades into the mechanical age, I sailed from Bremerhaven on a diesel fueled steel tub and landed in New York City in just over four weeks. Eighty-seven years of steady progress had shortened the trip that much.

An interesting note relative to BFD is that during World War II, most of the apparatus carried a white wooden plaque with a blue star on it for each member of that company who was on "Military Leave." Three of the companies included a gold star, denoting a member of that company had given his life in defense of our country.

While waiting for events to unfold, I joined the "920 Club." This was the name of a popular musical program on Radio Station WHDH, but returning GIs applied it to the program in Massachusetts whereby veterans could receive twenty dollars a week for nine months while they adapted to civilian life again and looked for work.

The next Fire Entrance Exam wouldn't be given until September so while waiting I applied to the State Department because traveling at someone else's expense appealed to me. It was my hope they were still anxious for me to join them in Berlin. I wrote them a letter one Sunday and mailed it Monday, figuring that since they sought me out in Europe, they really needed me and by the end of the week they would be knocking on my door. In another week it would be off to wherever my experience and training was most needed. It didn't work quite that way. About a month later they sent me an application, which I promptly filled out and rushed it back within twenty-four hours. More slow responses by the bureaucracy, and more prompt replies by the writer. Eventually came the interviews and more red tape and then word that I had been accepted and would be assigned shortly.

Meanwhile, the exam for Boston Fire was announced for September 19th. During the summer I had joined the Young Men's Christian Union on Boylston Street as they had an excellent reputation for training fire recruits for the strength test.

The Red Book that I purchased on Beacon Hill ten years earlier, and studied for three years plus in the Army, I knew word for word and cover to cover. My only wrong answer in the exam was including "Brookline" when they asked what other cities or towns were in Suffolk County, in addition to Boston. Two months later to the day, the marks came out. My mark was 92.85%. That was a composite of the written exam plus "Experience." My workouts at the YMCU became more frequent, and more strenuous.

The Firemen's campaign for a forty-eight hour week also became more strenuous and more promising. Voting day was the first Tuesday after the first Monday in November. If the outcome was ever in doubt, it was resolved at Box 1463 on the night of October 22, 1946 when Hoseman Barnard of Rescue 1 and Provisional Military Substitute Cady of Engine 39 lost their lives in the cellar of 70 Chauncy Street. A third member of the department survived the fire, but because his brain was deprived of oxygen for too long a period, he wandered aimlessly for nearly thirty years and died in 1974. It may have been more merciful if he had shared the immediate fatal fate of his two comrades that tragic night. The unselfish sacrifice, made by these two firemen, assured the shortened work week, and jobs for hundreds of returned veterans.

Following standard Civil Service protocol, our List would be established in six months, which would be March 19, 1947, but the people's mandate was for the hourly reduction to become effective in February. Most of us had taken our physical and strength tests and we were just waiting. The city received the potential list of candidates from Civil Service and mailed out "penny postcards" to the first few hundred names. Wording was to the effect that if you were interested in a job with the Boston Fire Department, report to Fire Headquarters at 60 Bristol Street at 8:00 A.M. January 22nd. My Big Day had arrived. After filling out the necessary forms and being sworn in, I reported to my assignment - Engine 42.

Anecdote:

My appointment to the Fire Department was about a week old when the doorbell at home rang at three o'clock in the morning. Western Union delivered telegrams at any hour in those days. Mine was from the State Department and read, "Advise earliest date you can report to Washington for overseas assignment." After all my patient waiting for nearly a year, now they were in a hurry. In the morning I called the one who had interviewed me several times and explained my position. I would like to finish my probation with the BFD and once permanent, I could apply for a Leave of Absence. Besides, Dot and I had set May third for our wedding day and although she was willing to change our plans, it didn't seem right to make her wait any longer after all her war time patience. The recruiter was understanding and said my name would be kept at the top of the active list until he heard from me. I hope my name is still at the top because I just may contact them when I retire, to see if they keep their word.

Every book should have some romance in it to keep the lady readers interested, so this one will follow suit. I met Dorothy in high school and later told our English teacher that Dot was all that I had gotten out of her class. Considering what I got, my diploma should have read "summa cum laude." Dot proved to be very patient, putting up with my sparking (at the fire house) and a lot of other inconveniences, but from the start we dreamed and planned for a future together. We hadn't planned on the war but took it in stride and when it was over we picked up the pieces where they had been laid down and went ahead with our lives. We were among the fortunate veterans, as we had a life to pick up. We had become engaged in September 1943 while I was home on a weekend pass - and I spent three months of my Army pay at Long's jewelry store for her diamond ring.

Dot wrote me long letters every day while I was in the Army keeping me fully informed of everything that was happening on the home front. Her descriptions of happenings were so complete that even today I sometimes have difficulty remembering if I was actually at an event or just the benefactor of her detailed descriptions.

Anecdote:
Since I didn't have a car when we were dating, we did a lot of walking and often passed by the big wooden coal storage building of the Metropolitan Coal and Ice Company at 3651 Washington Street in Forest Hills. Each time the thought ran through my mind that all that coal and wood would make a spectacular fire

especially at night. Dot's letter of Friday, May 11, 1945, was a masterpiece of fire reporting. She had the day off from work and was walking up to the store at Washington and Williams Streets, in the rain, when she heard fire engines. They were heading toward Forest Hills and she saw them stop in front of the Met Coal. Then she saw the smoke and forgot the store. Four alarms (Box 2463) were struck for the daytime bonfire and despite the rain and smoke Dot stayed till the All Out was sent. After drying out, she sat down and wrote me her daily letter which was extra long that day because she wanted me to know every detail of the fire that I had looked forward to - but missed.

To continue the romance, our forty plus years of marriage has been blessed with three sons, Bruce, Frank and Jonathan, and one daughter, Janna Leigh. Those were also Big days.

Liberation of Paris, August 1944.

Friday is Payday

(or, At Least We Hope So)

After being sworn in at Fire Headquarters by Fire Commissioner Russell Codman and Chief of Department Napeen Boutilier, they read off our assignments and we reported to our respective fire houses.

One of the men standing close by when assignments were announced asked no one in particular, "Where is Ladder 30?"
I replied, "Egleston Square, with Engine 42 - where I am going."
Since he had the car and I knew the way, we reported together to our new jobs. He was Provisional Fireman on Probation Morley J. Carter, and several years later he became my brother-in-law when he married Dot's sister.

Here it should be inserted that my Appointment was met with mixed feelings at home. In one way Mom was happy for me because she realized that it was the answer to an ancient ambition and a lot of my prayers but I don't think she ever really forgave me for taking a job that required working on Sundays. Sunday was the Sabbath and the Bible that Mom lived by, and brought her sons up to live by, taught that man was to work six days a week and the seventh was to rest and worship God. At the same time it didn't stop her from taking pride in each of her son's accomplishments, including my future promotions. On the other hand, Herb was delighted. It was a genuine gladness for his kid brother and not a fantasy of fulfilling his Depression stumped desire to be a fireman - but right from the start he harped on me to study for promotion. His reasoning was that the officers and men work the same schedule, so why not be an officer. And Friday is payday.

Reporting to the same Captain Ritchie, but now as a paid member, he greeted me with, "Welcome Young Cookie. You have the twelve to three watch and you're driving the wagon."

My apprenticeship had been recognized but I knew better than to pretend or expect my probation to be any different from that of the other men reporting for duty with me that day. I was content to start at the beginning with the others, play dumb and learn the ropes all over again - but sparking dies hard. Even though the work schedule was eighty-four hours a week, out of habit I still went sparking a couple nights a week - for a little while.

Not long after becoming a paid member, I ran into District Chief Ainsworth who had been both a lieutenant and a captain on Ladder 30, and a member of the department band during my pre-war sparking days. He congratulated me on my appointment and remarked that if I sat and did nothing for the next ten years, the city would still owe me money. It was nice of him to say it, but it was not my intention or my desire to sit and do nothing because I was still looking for action. He went on to say that he liked to see my brother Herb come sparking because the tapper usually died, but he dreaded it when "Young Cookie" dropped in, as more than likely it would be a busy night. He said that more than once he felt like telling me to go home, but there was no proof that I was the cause of the increased activity and besides, the help was welcome during those short handed early days of the war.

In February the permanent men started working the forty-eight hour schedule and we "provisional probationers," a sixty-eight hour week, by the addition of two-day tours of duty. For those who have only known a forty hour or less work week, it may be surprising to learn of anyone spending eighty-four hours in their work place, and without overtime pay. It should be pointed out that this 1947 hourly reduction was only another step in the long progression to a reasonable workweek.

Prior to December 1, 1889, the work schedule provided for two days off a month - and those could be taken away by the captain for disciplinary reasons. On that date the Day Off in Twelve became effective (the men only worked twelve twenty-four hour days and then had twenty-four hours off). In May of 1896 this was replaced by the Day Off in Eight, in December 1905 to the Day Off in Five and then to a Day Off in Three on February 1,

1918. This remained the schedule for six years to the day, when the Two Platoon (or eighty-four hour week) began in February 1924. So the reduction from eighty-four to forty-eight hours in 1947 was not the most drastic hourly change in the fire department. Two other less dramatic decreases took place during my career. In January 1970 the forty-six hour schedule and on July 1, 1971 we began the forty-two hour week. This is still the current work schedule.

I was assigned to one of the first drill classes and began my thirty days of training at the drill tower at Engine 2 in South Boston - my second stint at this learning process. When our list was officially established and the word "Provisional" was dropped, we were sent back to the drill tower at headquarters for a couple of weeks so we could experience the eight story "single pomp" and other lofty evolutions. And thus we became alumnus of the Thirty Day Department Drill School which first began at Bristol Street in 1889.

Anecdote:
In 1951 Fire Headquarters was moved to new buildings on Southampton Street. Later, the old headquarters buildings on Bristol Street was occupied by the Pine Street Inn. The eight story drill tower, which was built in 1889 and was copied after a bell tower in Florence, Italy, remains a land mark in the city today, but it has not been used by the fire department since 1952. As a result there are no more "eight story firemen" in Boston. Only those men who attended the 30 Day Drill School between 1889 and 1952 can claim this distinction.

Eventually all our elementary training was completed, the six months probation ended and we became permanent Hosemen and Laddermen and settled into the fire house routine that would last for the next forty plus years in my case.

It made a big difference in how you were broken in, because in most cases it also determined how you would fashion your own career. I was fortunate to be assigned to a house where the officers and most of the men were anxious, well willing, to drill daily and learn as much as possible about a profession that is both rewarding and dangerous. The daily house work was shared by all and usually assigned in pairs of one Hoseman and one Ladderman. In this way, if one company responded to a fire alone, the house work would still get done by the remaining member.

Some men believed in the theory, "If you sweep, don't swab; and if you swab, don't sweep." My first house work assignment was cleaning the third floor with a permanent Ladderman, Walter Maraghy, who would soon be promoted to lieutenant. Walter was a sincere dedicated fireman who believed and practiced that there was only one way to do anything - the right way. It didn't matter what others did. We would do it by the book. So we swept and swabbed every day. On "window day" we washed every window on our floor inside and out, summer and winter (using Bon Ami). On "brass day" we rubbed Noxon on everything that wasn't painted - and made it shine. It was an excellent breaking in and taught me that the city was paying for a specified number of hours of work, and I should expect to give them no less. And Friday would be payday.

Anecdote:
Walter later became a captain and then district chief, serving both ranks with distinction. He was my mentor when I was a MOP and an example as I rose in rank.

With regards to house work, brass spitoons were standard fixtures in those olden day fire houses. Many of the older men chewed tobacco and those "garboons" were a necessity if you didn't want slippery messes all over the floors. Further, most of the "chewers" developed a spitting aim that would rival Larry Bird's three-point field goal record and one of our officers was just such a marksman. A few of the young World War II Vets decided they were not going to be cleaning those filthy things any more so one day they washed and polished them and put them in the boot locker without saying a word.

The next morning, as our straight spitting officer sat at his desk doing his paper work, he let go with a wad over his shoulder, as was his custom. There was no "ping" and he paused for a moment. Without looking around he let go again and there was no "ping." He surmised what had happened to his practical brass vessel and with a loud voice remarked, "If they would rather clean the floor than the brass furnishing it's all right with me!" The next morning the shiny brass spitoons were back on their little black mats in their customary places.

By the time probationers become permanent and settle into the fire house routine, they realize that the work atmosphere in the fire department is different than any other job. It isn't just a case of working in close proximity with other men and sharing coffee and lunch. Rather, it is a close family relationship that develops. Spending a couple of ten hour day tours and fourteen hour night tours each week with the same group in a confined area brings you to the realization that you are not just working together, you are living together. Coupled with this is the excitement and danger of fighting fires, and depending on each other for teamwork and looking out for the safety of one another.

This work schedule never heard of the Gregorian Calendar so weekdays and weekends are the same. Public holidays and special family events are just consecutive days on the work calendar. Unless you can arrange a mutual swap for birthdays, anniversaries, graduations or other meaningful events, you spend them with your fire house family and get filled in on the event's details when you get home to your other family.

One problem is that everyone would like to be off Thanksgiving, Christmas, the Fourth of July, New Years Eve and the other holidays that normal people celebrate, but if your group is scheduled to work, chances are slim that you will find a willing swap. So your fire house family becomes even more closely knit and you begin to plan holiday celebrations around the dining table at the fire house. You don't forget that your loved ones are also celebrating alone but you learn to put that thought in the back of your mind and make the most of what you can't control.

Spending so much time in close confinement, the men often share their experiences - dating, engagements, weddings, babies who become children who have birthdays, first days at schools, Little League, Pop Warner, as well as other sports, and graduations and colleges. You know and share their family tragedies and deaths as well as rejoicing with them in the good times. Friday is payday and often times the wives stop by with the children to relieve dad of the burden of carrying money, and they get to meet one another and the fire house family grows some more. Names become faces, and acquaintances become lifelong friends. Most fire houses at least have a Christmas party for all the families and some extend their gatherings to summer picnics and other events that draw the extended families into a tighter unit. When tragedy strikes, it is felt and shared by all.

Prior to Christmas, the fire house becomes Santa's assembly line as the dads pool their knowledge and experience in putting "Tab A into Slot X," as they follow the simple printed instructions. But pooling knowledge goes far beyond the toy world. Men joining the department bring with them a variety of civilian trades and talents and this is a fringe benefit the tax payers get for nothing. As the fire department is called for almost everything, as well as fires, there is a good chance that the responding men will bring with them a varied background of experiences including plumbing, electricity, construction, diving, mechanics, cooking, medicine, and a collection of blue college knowledge as well. The result is that they never leave an incident without solving the problem or having called someone to the scene with the needed expertise.

This same sharing of abilities among the men has repaired thousands of autos, lawn mowers, toys, washing machines and other appliances of their extended family. It has fixed plumbing, wiring and roofs. It has built walks, walls, fireplaces and chimneys. It has cut down trees, put up fences, landscaped yards, painted ceilings and papered walls. It has built cottages, houses, garages, boats, electronic kits and financial fortunes. It has shared recipes, crafts, maternity clothes - and heartaches.

The list could go on and on but it all adds up to building a bond which exists in no other profession. When a member is seriously injured or pays the supreme sacrifice, it is that bond which makes the burden both harder and easier to bear. It is harder because of the closeness of the men, but it is easier because of the closeness of the families, as together we recognize that but for the Grace of God .... and we accept it.

It is every facet of every fireman and every fire house that makes up the total picture. The fire house is the focal point of the fire family, and although my favorite is the one I started out in, just as many stories could be told about any of the others. The names may be different but the varieties of men and their faithful contributions to the "tradition" are the same.

Egleston Square was the community commercial center for several hundreds of families as it provided a blend of stores that met most day to day needs. During prohibition it included a number of secret speakeasies whose locations were known to everyone familiar with the square. There were two drug stores, a couple of super markets of that day, several fruit stores and ice cream parlors, three barber shops (one of which included a matinee ticket to the Egleston Theatre with the twenty-five cent cost of a haircut), two hardware stores (one of which sold fireworks, which were legal then), a shoe store, a ladies beauty parlor, a toy store, two delicatessens and a diner, plus an assortment of other businesses.

Those other emporiums included two liquor stores and three drinking establishments, which had become legal in 1932. The latter were the "Quarter Deck," the "Plainsman" and the "JA Cafe." Collectively they added to the entertainment of the square. Friday and Saturday nights particularly were like "Fight Night on TV," only the screen was larger and the action was live.

There was also a second floor dentist who dropped his patients' extracted teeth on the floor, which after a while made his office look like someone had spilled a carton of dirty popcorn all over it, but he was a fine dentist. I don't think the Board of Health made many inspections in those days, but the firemen did. They get to see everything, and Friday is payday.

Two of the most popular buildings in the square were the fire house and the theatre, which were adjacent to each other, and both cost little or nothing to visit. Like most neighborhood theatres, the "Eggie" was filled every Saturday afternoon with a bunch of noisy little kids who brought along a bag full of penny candies and made about seven visits to the little boy's or girl's rooms during the two main features, cartoons, the weekly serial and the news, plus Pre-views of Coming Attractions. All of this was for your dime admission. Sunday afternoons were similar, but with fewer viewers as most kids couldn't get two dimes in the same week.

Wednesday was Dish Night, which meant all ladies attending received a piece of china with their admission price. Each time a dish slipped from a lap and smashed on the floor it was greeted with a round of applause from the audience. On Friday nights you could greet almost your entire high school class in the balcony. Other afternoon shows were faithfully attended by another group, which also produced no revenue for the theatre. Residents of the "old folks" home on Columbus Avenue (there were no Senior Citizens in those days) were admitted free, as were firemen.

Popcorn was popular even way back then and it was delivered about every couple weeks in large cartons, and then warmed and sold in small boxes for a dime. Management kept track of the profits by counting the number of small boxes that were sold over the counter during a performance. Most of the girls on the candy counter were friendly with the firemen and provided us with free popcorn by putting it in a paper bag or an empty candy box - which management didn't count. On the other side of the scale, the firemen did little odd jobs for the theatre, so the free popcorn balanced out and relations were good.

On a quiet afternoon or evening, the firemen sometimes stood up at the rear of the theatre, eating popcorn, and watching the movie. If there was a run, the man on watch sounded the siren outside of quarters and we ran for the apparatus. It only amounted to about a ten second delay, but was nerve racking when there was a noisy war film or if it was a "cops and robbers" picture with a lot of sirens during a chase - in which case the firemen would start out of the theatre several times.

With this in mind, we approached the manager for permission to install a little red bulb over the exit door closest to the fire house. All one Saturday afternoon was spent running wires from the fire house to the theatre and connections were made so that when the house gong went off, the little bulb in the theatre would light up. The first time it was used, it worked fine! The house gong rang in the fire house, the little red bulb lit up in the theatre, and one of the men yelled "fire." Not only did six firemen run out of the theatre, but all the paying customers went with them. The next day was spent diligently disassembling the fire house to theatre wiring because for some reason the manager withdrew his permission.

As suggested before, the other free building was the fire house. Kids came in for drinks of water, to get air for bike tires or with a broken toy for the firemen to fix. Simple cuts and bruises were treated and people caught in a rain shower on their way to or from the Egleston El station would duck in to keep dry. We had a couple of men in the neighborhood whose wives would not let them smoke in their homes, so each night they would sheepishly drop into the fire house to light up a cigar or puff a pipe full of tobacco in the "smoking room."

Radio broadcasts of sporting events attracted a certain clientele in the early days and when the men chipped in and bought a DuMont television set with a magnifying glass for the small screen, the fire house really became a popular place. In addition it was a safe place because there was usually a cop or two to maintain order - or study for promotion.

But everything in the fire house was not free. Down in the cellar of the Taj Mahal was the "Orange Crate Office." The office was open from about eleven in the morning until two in the afternoon and the Chief Executive Officer was Jock, a man who would have been in his third decade of Social Security checks if they had been in vogue then. His customers were drawn from Green Street to half way to Dudley Street, and from Blue Hill Avenue to Roxbury Crossing. His commodity was the opportunity to wager a bet on a horse, or play a number three ways.

In those days, oranges were shipped to the local fruit stores in wooden crates which measured about fifteen inches square and three feet long. The stores were happy to get rid of the empty boxes and a good many ended up in the fire house cellar. In spite of his eighty plus years, Jock patiently reassembled the crates. He turned some into chairs, a large desk for himself, library shelves holding an assortment of horse racing reference books, wastebaskets, an intricate file system and small tables displaying the latest "Green Sheets." There his customers could munch their lunch and ponder major decisions - all made from orange crate wood. Some of his customers sneaked in the back door while others boldly marched through the front door, but all went directly to the Orange Crate Office. When their business had been transacted, they left the same way they came in. No one saw anything.

When the day came that Jock went to meet his Maker, a large power struggle began to develop as several customers sought to become the new Chairman of the "Boards" and move into command of the Orange Crate Office. The captain of the house had other ideas. First, no one could take old Jock's place, and second, how long could luck hold out before the Taj Mahal would be raided. Following Jock's funeral, the captain included an Eliot Ness attack as part of the day's house work and Jock's furniture met its breaker too. It was disassembled with axes and flung into the furnace.

When Jock's faithful followers found the office closed, they clustered around outside the fire house in a daze, like a family of ants that returned to find their hole sealed off. For a couple weeks, out of habit, some continued to sneak in the back door or walk boldly through the front door, and then sadly leave by the way they came in - and still no one saw anything.

There are a certain number of memorable fires. They were memorable either to everyone, or just to a certain company or work group. Our first memorable one occurred in March of 1947 when a member of Rescue 2 lost his life on Brighton Avenue in a three alarm fire (Box 5123). It was the first loss of a department member since our appointment two months earlier, and it brought home the realization that we were in a business that played for keeps even if Friday was payday.

For those interested in statistics, or ancient history as the case may be, in 1947 - my first year on the job, Engine 42 had 963 runs making it the fifth busiest engine. We worked at 426 fires, which was more than the four leading engines did. Ladder 30 responded to 1019 alarms making it the fifth busiest truck. Rescue 2 was the busiest company in the city, and the country, with 2026 runs. Total alarms for the city was 15,189. The longest mutual aid response was to Biddeford, Maine.

Anecdote:
By comparison, in 1975, the busiest year in BFD to date, there were 63,775 Incidents. Engine 42 had 3,771 runs and Ladder 30 responded 4,223 times.

Just before our first anniversary on the job there was the memorable "Sleeper Street Fire." It was January 15th and a very cold day. It had already been a busy day for Groups 2 and 3 as there had been two two baggers, a three bagger and several other fires, as well as the usual stills and Automatic Alarms that accompany cold weather as sprinkler pipes freeze. Just before 1300 hours an Automatic Alarm came in for a leather company at 23-27 Sleeper Street in South Boston. As was the procedure at that time, city Box 7115 was struck following the Automatic and after the fire department arrived, five alarms were struck in quick succession. Engine 42 covered Engine 3 on the second alarm, but when we got there the third was in and off we went to the fire.

What a spectacular sight of fire met us as the apparatus turned from Congress into Sleeper Street and our wagon took up position in front of the fire building. We stretched three long lines of three inch hose from the fireboat, which had tied up in Fort Point Channel just beyond the Northern Avenue Bridge, and ran them into our deck gun and immediately began shooting a thousand gallons of water a minute into the upper floors. This would continue for the next few hours. But it doesn't take a full company to aim a deck gun and after a while, hand lines were started. By then water in the street was over our knees and it was very slippery underfoot because ice had coated everything. Just about every man fell at least once and since you became completely submerged in the two foot deep water, we just watched to make sure that everyone bobbed back up again. We stretched another long hand line up to the roof of the adjacent building and began aiming water down into the fire building.

Once the line was secured and operating, we took turns going below to empty the water out of our boots. We found rags in the building and stuffed some into our boots to hopefully give some warmth and also absorb some of the water. At 1630 hours they struck "Recall" and we knew we weren't going to be relieved at the fire for a long while, no matter how much cold and wet we had to endure.

Later in the evening we began to get the upper hand on the fire and at 0130 hours in the morning they released the Recall. Our pump was still supplying lines, so the Night Tour was left at the fire and we of the Day Tour rode back to Egleston Square on the wagon. Ice on the windshield was so thick that Roy had to drive standing up all the way. We were all soaked to the skin and frozen into our fire gear so it was a cold miserable ride back to quarters. I remember stepping off the back step and sliding my hands out of my wool mittens, which stayed frozen to the handrail in a horizontal position.

There was no overtime pay in those days and even though the Recall was over, we were ordered to remain on duty and respond with the wagon only for the rest of the night. After a hot shower and a few cups of hot coffee, we repacked the wagon, filled the booster tank and about 0500 hours laid down to rest and wait for the new Day Tour to report for duty and relieve us. Before going home, I freed my horizontal mittens from the rail and left them on a radiator to finish thawing out so they would be dry for my next tour. And Friday would be payday.

Anecdote:
The morning following the fire, my picture appeared in the paper for the first time as a paid fireman. The caption read, "Ice forms on the helmet of Hoseman Paul Cook of Engine 42." Over a half inch of ice had accumulated on it. There was also a picture of Hoseman John Abbot of Engine 26. He was a member of that first BFD Auxiliary drill class in 1940, from which I was aborted. Later John was a Line of Duty death.

Sooner or later, going to fires becomes a mechanical routine for all new men and little thought is given to what the next alarm may have in store. In the first chapter of this book it was pointed out that some "jakes" have spectacular moments in their careers, some with a lot of publicity and some with none. Probably no man enters the fire service with the intention of being a hero or filling his chest with medals, but from time to time a chain of events falls into place which thrusts some into a potential hero's role. To their credit, most men look upon these Incidents as just having happened to be at the right place at the right time - or perhaps the wrong place at the wrong time, as their names are added to those brave men who have answered their Last Alarm.

In the Spring of each year, the Boston Firemen's Relief Fund sponsors the Annual Firemen's Ball (in 1988 it was the 109th). The proceeds from the Ball are used to pay doctors' bills and for hospitalization of members injured in the performance of duty, and to assist dependents of deceased firefighters. At the Ball, recognition is given to those members cited for meritorious acts performed during the preceding year, as determined by the "Board of Merit," which is made up of all the deputy chiefs of the department. Dating back to the late thirties, I have attended most of the Balls, except when scheduled to work, and am still impressed with the recitation of the circumstances which precipitate the Board's selections. Since most of the medals are awarded in recognition of lives saved, an interesting follow up would be a study of what those lives have accomplished on their "borrowed time."

Anecdote:

Being aware of what is involved to be so honored at a Ball, it was only normal, after my appointment, to wonder when, or if ever, my call to duty would place me in that spotlight. A potential possibly arrived in the third year of my service. Groups 2 and 3 were again working and we were covering Engine 10 on a third alarm. We had just reported in when the phone rang and we were given a Still for a fire on Lime Street. Fire Alarm told us where the street was and we started down River Street only to be met by a civilian waving us down to report a fire on the next street - where we were headed anyhow.

As we turned into the street, smoke was pouring out the cellar windows and the open first floor door. A policeman met us and said there was a man down in the cellar. The captain ordered Marty and myself to put on All-Service masks and proceed into the cellar to search for the victim. We took the booster line with us for protection, and the rest of the company started to run a big line. We slowly made our way down the stairs as the smoke got thicker and the heat began to intensify. At the foot of the stairs we stumbled over a body and together we lugged him up the stairs, with a feeling of real accomplishment. As we brought him out on the sidewalk, the policeman that had met us on arrival said, "That isn't the man; that's my partner."

We turned him over to those on the street and Marty and I ventured back down into the dingy dungeon. Reaching the point of our first discovery, we groped around in the murky maelstrom of smoke and found a second stairway leading lower into the heated caldron. At the foot of those stairs visibility increased as the flames grew in intensity and by the increased light we saw our victim lying prostrate on the floor at the far end of the cellar. He wasn't a large man and didn't appear to be burned, so Marty suggested I carry him up to the street and he would begin attacking the fire with the booster line. We could hear the other men making their way down the stairs with the back-up big line so we knew the fire was the lesser of the problems.

Once on the sidewalk, the police relieved me of my burden and saw that he was rushed to the hospital - as evidenced by the newspaper pictures depicting the "heroic rescue" by the police.

With the fire knocked down and our lines made up, the captain reported to the district chief for orders. Spectators had told the chief of the "two" rescues and he was impressed. He dismissed our company and suggested the captain forward a report to headquarters on the two rescues so the Board of Merit could consider it. Good old Cap! He let go with a wad of tobacco splatter and with an empty mouth stated, "That's what firemen get paid for, saving lives and putting out fires. There will be no commendations from my company."

I have already expressed my respect and admiration for this experienced captain and the above sequence of events did not change my respect or admiration of him. It was just another lesson that the city was paying for a specified number of hours of work and I should expect to give them no less - and expect no more in return. The idea of being in the spotlight at the Ball never again entered my head and I just went ahead doing my job, and enjoying every minute of it. Anyhow, Friday would be payday.

It doesn't take many weeks of working forty-eight hours before you begin to accumulate experiences in various phases of being a fireman. Accidents provide a considerable amount of the runs. Many are real tragedies and some cannot be completely understood. One summer morning, early on in my paid career, we responded to Box 2157 at Washington and Valentine Streets for just such an accident. Two teenage boys were standing beside an El upright waiting for a street car to go to the beach for the day. A car coming up Washington Street, for some unknown reason, crossed over and pinned the two lads against the El upright -

removing three of their four legs just below the knees. We applied tourniquets and compresses and waited for the ambulances. Naturally the driver was very upset and could not explain how it happened. He insisted he was all right and tried to help, but in fact he was helpless in his distraught condition. We finally persuaded him to also go to the hospital to be checked up. The afternoon paper reported the accident and concluded with the report that the two boys were doing well, but the driver had succumbed to internal injuries.

Being present at a few such accidents, you begin to realize just how resilient the human body is and how amazing the recovery process is in some people. About nine o'clock one night in April 1948, a street car came down Columbus Avenue and into Egleston Station out of control. Apparently it had lost its brakes and the two quick turns in the station carried it off the tracks and tossed the motorman before it, and then ran over him. The heavy wheels severed his two legs and that is the condition we found on our arrival. Several passengers were less severely injured and were still on the street car.

There were no radios on the apparatus in those days so I was sent back across the square to the fire house to call Fire Alarm on the telephone and give a quick report on what we had. Rescue 2 responded with Lieutenant Charles Friberg in charge. He did an outstanding job in directing his crew in quickly placing jacks and raising the street car so the motorman could be removed and rushed to the hospital. When we got back to quarters, and after cleaning up, the firemen took up a collection and the next day a small check from the men of Engine 42 and Ladder 30 was delivered to the motorman's wife to help with her immediate needs. He survived his ordeal and was still alive at least a few years ago.

Experience at fires is also rapidly gained and paying attention to small details could be a big help for future days. I remember going to a three alarm fire on Blue Hill Avenue one winter morning. The fire was in the cellars of a block of "tax payers" and Engine 42 ended up with a Carey Cellar Pipe sending water into the lower region. Chief of Department John V. Stapleton, father of the present Fire Commissioner, was in charge of the fire and I recall him stopping at our operating point several times during the fire's progress. Each time he would kneel down on the sidewalk, remove his glove and thrust his hand into the cellar window and wave it around, and shake his head back and forth. Finally the time came when he repeated the ritual and this time he shook his head up and down. He said, "I think your getting to it."

What he had been doing as he waved his ungloved hand in the opening was getting a feel of the temperature and humidity inside the cellar. On the last thrust, he had sensed a drop in temperature and an increase in the wetness of the interior atmosphere. This indicated to him that the water was beginning to reach the fire and cool it down. The reduced heat was not absorbing so much of the water and so the moisture in the interior air would increase. He had us shut down our cellar pipe and advance a big line into the cellar, where we found the fire mostly extinguished. The chief had detected it all with a wave of his bare hand.

In describing the apparatus in the Taj Mahal, I only made mention of the "buckeyes." This is because they were a later innovation and added to the apparatus as attention-getters, or traffic stoppers, as the noise they produced was much louder than the air horns used on trucks today. Buckeyes were devices attached to the end of the tail pipe. A light weight chain to control it extended to the front seat area. The device contained a series of baffles that forced the engine exhaust through a small venturi when the chain was pulled. This resulted in the shrieking sound. The harder the chain was pulled, the smaller the exhaust opening became and the higher the noise level it produced. By throwing the clutch in and racing the engine, while pulling on the chain, the decibel could be raised to such a pitch that motorists would drive up on the sidewalk to get away from the nerve shattering sound.

They worked very well to clear traffic for the fire apparatus, but they had an adverse effect on the motors and they were later removed. Some of the men were so attached to these effective noise makers which stopped traffic, that when the devices were removed from service, the men had them chrome plated and mounted in their homes as a reminder of better days.

When not fighting fires, cleaning the house and equipment or drilling, the men found other ways to occupy their time. Back in the forties and fifties few firemen could afford new cars but they took good care of what they did have and spent much time polishing and repairing them.

One Summer, two of the men bought the same shade of blue Plymouth four door sedans and both cars had identical faded finishes. Gullible Jerry had his new (used) wheels parked at the end of the parking lane separating the fire house and the theatre. He was extolling the virtues of a new auto polish he discovered and egged on by the other men he proceeded to demonstrate it by applying some to a portion of the hood of his car. The polished area was a real contrast to the rest of the hood.

About that time Jerry had a phone call which turned out to be quite lengthy. Johnny Trickster, who had the companion car parked on the street, quickly swapped the places of his and Jerry's car. Using the same polish, he did an identical spot on his hood. When Jerry came back the men agreed that he had a fine polish and encouraged him to do his whole car, as one shiny spot was ridiculous. He worked all evening to complete the car and was justifiably proud of the new look appearance.

It was when he went to put the polish and rags away that he found his keys wouldn't open the trunk - or fit the ignition. Eventually someone laughed and Jerry realized he had spent the whole evening polishing the wrong Plymouth. The air was bluer than his car and Johnny Trickster just stood there with a grin from ear to ear. Then he put his shiny blue Plymouth back on the street, so Jerry could have his parking space back - for his dull blue Plymouth.

In the description of the fire house, mention should have been made that there were stairs, parallel with the right wall, leading to the second floor. There were about ten stairs and then a four foot landing with a metal fire door separating the apparatus floor from the upstairs living quarters. There was a metal hand rail on the stairs and landing but it was the landing that provided many hours of amusement and entertainment on quiet nights.

One of the men had a voice (enough said) and he enjoyed exercising it, in and out of the shower. It didn't take much prompting on a dull night to get a few choruses out of him and with a little more coaxing he could be inveigled into going to the stair landing for his vocalizing - because his voice projected much better from that height. Before long, someone would suggest the atmosphere didn't due him justice, so the house lights would be put out and the apparatus spotlights would be lit and aimed at the landing, which now took on the appearance of a balcony. For a microphone, someone would hand him the ten foot Fog Applicator and he would croon into it like an over-aged matinee idol, until something brought his concert to an abrupt ending.

It may be hard to believe this scenario could be repeated, but it was, time and time again as he was most gullible. Sometimes the sudden stop was caused by an alarm of fire. Sometimes "Elvis on the balcony" would notice his entire audience had sneaked away in the dark, and he was just singing to the Fog Applicator. Sometimes he would hit a sour note, which wasn't hard for him, and he would in turn be hit with a barrage of the salad fixings left over from supper. Sometimes it would be suggested that he sounded better in the shower, which was the cue for three or four streams of water from the brush fire extinguishers to cascade onto the "balcony" and the singer. And Friday was payday.

But work wasn't all fun and games. Two of our officer's favorite drill locations were Franklin Park for the Engine and the Egleston Theatre for the Ladder. At the park we connected to a hydrant and practiced with various hose and appliance connections and tried to figure out what the officers had done to the pump to cause trouble for us in trying to provide sufficient water or pressure. Whether hoseman or ladderman, everyone had their turn at all engine evolutions until they mastered them.

Then it was time to become more proficient in ladder truck operations: driving and tillering for everyone and then raising and maneuvering the stick. It was a seventy-five foot wooden ladder, spring mounted. It was raised, by removing a pin and stepping on a pedal. This released the spring and the ladder jumped from the bed. It was necessary to promptly grab the hand brake and control the rate of ascent so the ladder didn't go up too fast and snap. The fly was extended by two men cranking it up, and the higher it went, the heavier it got. We learned to count the clicks as the ladder climbed, as each one was a foot, and at night we would go out and drill, just to become familiar with estimating heights and placing ladders in the dark by counting clicks. If the drill was on the theatre, it always ended with every man climbing the seventy-five feet to the roof, with or without extra equipment, depending on how the officer felt that day.

Raising the aerial ladder to a building on Washington Street, which was the route of the Orange Line elevated structure, was tricky. It required placing the tiller section of the truck between two El uprights, removing the tiller seat and wheel, stepping on the pedal and grabbing the brake for sure, because if the stick was allowed to go up normally, it would hit the track structure. Once the ladder was out of the bed, it had to be rotated toward the building and then held in a slanted position while the truck was moved forward or backward in order for the ladder to reach the fire building. Once this position was attained, the placing of the ladder could be completed and the jacks set. It took a lot of practice to be able to do this quickly and perfectly, but whether Ladderman or Hoseman, everyone had their turn at all ladder evolutions, until they mastered them. All these drills had a good side benefit as the officers allowed us to swap between companies because we were all qualified for all duties.

If there was a spell of severely hot days in the summer, the officer would send a man out with a "shower bar" to be placed on a hydrant and give the neighborhood kids a couple hours to get wet and cool off. In those days hydrants were normally used only for fires and it might be years before a particular hydrant was opened.

My turn came for the "shower detail" and the officer sent me to Minton Street one hot humid afternoon. I didn't have a car so had to lug the shower bar (about five feet long and two inch diameter), the braces to hold it on the hydrant, a wrench, a maul and a "persuader pipe" to the location - a half mile or more from the fire house. While all the children stood around waiting for their shower, I removed the hydrant cap, secured the "shower bar" in place and with the "persuader pipe" tried to open the hydrant, which obviously hadn't been disturbed for a couple decades.

About that time a gentleman came out of a three decker, all dressed up in a white suit and a Panama Hat, which was the summer vogue for well dressed men at that time. Watching me struggle with the "persuader pipe" while the little darlings were becoming impatient, he came over and offered to help. We banged the operating nut to loosen it, pounded the wrench with the maul and strained with the "persuader pipe" as the little brats began taunting us. Finally the operating nut moved a little, then a little more and then it broke loose. Dirty black water came through the bonnet, squirted past the stem, spurted through leaking caps and out of the shower bar. My volunteer assistant, in the previously white spotless suit, now looked like a drowned Dalmation dog. He didn't look at me. He didn't look at the little urchins. He didn't say a word. He just turned around and disappeared, back into the three decker, from whence he came. I never saw or heard from him again - but I expect he never helped a fireman try to open a hydrant again either. And Friday is payday.

Speaking of showers, Herb continued to spend an occasional night bunking in at Engine 42. This mostly happened in the summer when his family was down the Cape and he stayed in the city during the week. He had a key to my locker and kept his toiletries in it. He usually got up earlier than I did because he would go home to change and go to work.

There was a strong family resemblance between Herb and myself and one morning at the fire house he got up about six o'clock, went to my locker, grabbed his soap and towel and took a shower. There was a cop, on his break, sitting on the bench by the black soapstone sink studying his law books. Herb finished his shower, closed our locker and went on his way. About seven o'clock I came down, went to the same locker, grabbed my soap and towel and took a shower. The cop was still sitting on the bench studying his law books. I finished, closed the locker door and was about to go to the kitchen for coffee, when the cop called me over. He had a perplexed look on his face and was scratching his head. He asked, "Didn't I see you go to that first locker and then take a shower about an hour ago?" In all honesty, I said "No."

As I went on my way, I heard him mumble to no one, "These books are really getting to me. I better give them up for a while." To his credit, he didn't give them up, and today he is a judge.

For some reason, water and firemen go together like salt and pepper. Any number of stories could be told about bags or other containers of water, that somehow empty in or out of fire houses. It isn't always the firemen who instigate the deluges but they usually get blamed for them. I will include just one story as illustration.

As mentioned before, there was just about enough room back of the fire house for an abbreviated horseshoe court and one summer evening some of the men were pitching a few games. In back of the fire house, on the other side of the fence, there was a house where several generations of a Greek family made their home. It included a porch on the second floor and on this particular warm night the children were playing with their new water pistols, and amusing themselves by taking pot shots at the men tossing quoits. Asking the kids to stop only prompted more aggression and the small amounts of water from the pistols were replaced with cups of water.

As the verbal warnings went unheeded, one of the men went to the fire house roof with a full pail of water. Just as he let go with the ten quarts of water, the grandmother, wearing her traditional long black dress, came out on the porch to see what all the noise was about. She was knocked down by the impact of the surprised shower and although not seriously hurt, other than her dignity, it took a lot of apologizing to keep it from being reported to headquarters.

I had my first accident driving fire apparatus on December 24, 1951 as we were returning from a small fire in Roxbury. Our return route was via Humbolt Avenue and as we approached Crawford Street, a car stopped at the STOP sign and then, just as we entered the intersection, it darted in front of me. The impact knocked the car back into Crawford Street where he belonged and added a small streak of black paint to the wagon bumper.

Damage to the old car was minimum, but on the day before Thanksgiving in 1952 I found a summons in my mailbox advising me that I was being sued for five thousand dollars, for personal injuries and property damages.

Shortly afterwards the city Law Department called me in to sign papers. They were settling the case for twelve hundred dollars. All that was needed was my signature, which would be an admission of fault and would involve "points" against my personal driver's license. Their reasoning was that the settlement was saving me (the city) thirty-eight hundred dollars, but to their consternation, I refused to sign because I didn't feel it was my fault. If the Registry was going to levy "points" against my license, it wasn't going to be that easy.

The case went to trial the same day President Eisenhower was inaugurated in 1953. I had looked forward to watching the ceremony, as it would be the first time televised, and the first Republican President sworn in since Hoover in 1929. The court date wasn't of my choice.

My witnesses were the men who were riding the back step and the officer. In typical rebel fireman fashion, the story told by one of the men made us all wonder if he was even with us that day. Despite the odd-ball testimony, the court found the auto driver negligent, partly because he had three other similar suits against public or utility companies then pending. He received nothing for his personal injuries or damage to his bucket of rusted bolts, but in the usual mystery of the court, his passenger was awarded two hundred dollars to tide her over while she waited settlement from the other three pending court cases. Keep tuned, we will go to court again and again.

When I went to the City Law Department to sign for the two hundred dollars, I asked if there was a commission on the additional one thousand dollars I had saved the city - but they just smiled. Friday would be payday anyhow.

As previously mentioned, the other fire house close neighbor was the JA Cafe. The two owners were as different as night and day as regards the fire house - in fact, as regards everything. One allegedly chose to become quite familiar with the garage at 600 Commercial Street in the North End and ignored the fire house. I am sure you have read about him in the newspapers or seen his escapades in several Hollywood versions. For the younger readers, I refer to the Brink's garage robbery that netted the largest crime haul of cash to that date.

The other owner frequented the station for shaves, showers and sociability. He was particularly fond of the men on Group 2 and most nights when our group was working, and after closing hours for his establishment, he would drive into Chinatown and return with a large platter of Oriental delicacies for us. He had a late model Cadillac, which we kept clean for him, and in return, he would let any of the Group 2 men borrow it if they had a special date or wanted to impress someone - just be back by his closing time. He was a bachelor without family and at Christmas we would chip in and buy him a nice present, which would bring tears to his eyes - and more platters from Chinatown to us. Later when the fire house was moved to Columbus Avenue, he was part of the Egleston Square that fell apart.

Another amusement which was practiced at the fire house was dropping a half-dollar. The fire house floor was cement and the apron outside was cement. With the doors closed, one could drop a half dollar inside and the sound would resonate outside. The coin would be dropped just as someone was passing the door and the search for the half dollar that followed was really a study in character. To wit, most people would stop on the spot and begin to search their pockets or pocketbooks. The men would systematically start with the pants and proceed through shirts, coats and vests, if they were wearing them, checking every pocket. Ladies would begin with their purses by making sure there wasn't a hole in it. Then they too would check all pockets in their attire. Once in a while one would kneel down and empty the contents of her bag on the sidewalk and then slowly replace the contents while, checking to see if a half dollar was missing.

At times there would be a scientific approach, probably by a guy who had an engineering background. After a quick look around he would reach in his pocket and produce another half dollar, which he would drop and watch where it rolled in hopes it would take the same path as the first and he would recover both. Sometimes they would end up losing their own coin as well.

On one occasion the coin happened to drop when a cop was passing by. As he took out his flash light and was searching the area, a more than slightly inebriated regular came out of the JA Cafe and slapping the bent over cop on the back, offered his services to help him look for whatever he had lost. He was sent on his staggering way with an even harder slap on the back and was lucky he wasn't bagged for disturbing the peace or interfering with the law.

On a Saturday night as the Egleston Theatre was emptying out, a paper boy was hurrying to the lobby with a load of Sunday papers piled about two feet high on his head. As he passed the fire house door the ring of a silver coin rang out and he made an abrupt stop. The problem was the pile of papers didn't stop, but shot several yards in front of him. On that one, the helpful firemen assisted him in putting his papers back together - and then even helped him look for his half dollar.

The city paid us for forty-eight hours a week, but many weeks they received back more than they paid for. There was no overtime and if you were working at a fire when the shifts were due to change, you just kept working until the on coming men showed up. By the time you got back to quarters and cleaned up, the city was getting an hour or more of free service from a number of men, plus the use of their personal cars for transportation. If there were a severe snowstorm, the city would hold men on duty. This worked so well for the city that they began calling men back when heavy snow was even predicted and many times there was a double crew for days at a time. I guess that could be considered a Friday payday for the city.

Halloween was one of the busier nights of the year as the goblins started fires in leaves and rubbish and pulled false alarms. The men couldn't be everywhere to stop the fires, but they could be somewhere to stop false alarms. The city accomplished this for a few years by ordering all off duty men to be stationed at fire boxes from dusk to about ten o'clock at night. There was no pay for it but it did cut down on false alarms, as the men didn't dare leave the box until the appointed time. It wasn't too bad for the men who had cars, as they could park beside the box and then try to keep from falling asleep. Without a car you just stood there. If you didn't have a watch you stood until long after you thought it was ten o'clock, to be sure. No one knew just what the punishment would be if someone pulled a false alarm from the box, you were assigned to watch.

Anecdote:

Speaking of details and the city's concern for the men's welfare, in March of 1952, Engine 23 had to be moved from their quarters because of a leaking gasoline storage tank. To guard the quarters twenty-four hours a day, a department detail was set up. The member detailed to the Northampton Street location was given a department car, without a battery, to sit in and a baseball bat to protect himself.

In front of the fire house on Washington Street there were two sets of street car tracks. The rule of thumb for the ladder driver was to start turning in the direction he wanted to go as soon as the front wheels went over the third track. The fire house was on an angle to the street and this combination made it tricky for covering trucks to get in and out without doing damage either to the fire house or the apparatus. Even the regular men had to keep their wits about them or the results could be disastrous.

One Monday night the "wits" must have been off duty. As the ladder truck was going out the door, the tillerman turned too soon and the end of the aerial ladder scraped along the wall snapping off the steam and water pipes going to the second floor, and knocking off the house door for good measure. It also broke the end of the wooden aerial ladder and the ends of a couple ground ladders on the right side of the truck. The broken pipes spewed hot and cold water all the way across the apparatus floor and the cracked steam lines filled the area with a hot mist.

The wagon driver was so intrigued by this chain of events, and so affected by the reduced visibility, that he drove right into his house door knocking it off the hinges and doing damage to the front end of the wagon. Needless to say the officers weren't too pleased with this series of events and it didn't help when the pump operator asked for a commendation because he was the only driver who got out of the house without doing damage.

For the first few years of our careers we were paid in cash. On Fridays the Paymaster arrived in a taxi with a suit case full of money and a policeman to guard him. He was a no-nonsense individual and quite unfriendly - except at Christmas time. As you signed on the dotted line he checked off the amount with a heavy black pencil. The men working would sign for and receive the pays for the men off duty and then be responsible for it. On many Fridays there would be fires and the men would get soaked, with the results that off duty men sometimes received their pay as a soggy assortment of stuck together bills and change.

There was no Christmas bonus and no extra pay for the extra hours the men gave the city, but the Paymaster felt he was entitled to a "Thank You Gift" from the men at Christmas for doing his job. If he didn't get it, it somehow affected the taxi that would arrive later in the day each Friday.

On the first Friday in 1948 we learned just how frugal the city can be with the tax payers dollars. It was payday and we received about fifteen cents less than the previous week. The explanation was that it was Leap Year and rather than not pay us for the extra day, they withheld a few cents each week to make up for the extra day.

While on one side Herb kept prodding me to study, there was another factor that also persuaded me to pursue the books. I have always been a light sleeper and anyone snoring would prevent my dozing off. We had one fellow who sounded like an army of tree saws and he could fall asleep while you were talking to him. When we came back from a night run and returned to the bunk room, he would sit on the edge of his bed to remove his hitch and then lay back. Before his head hit the pillow he was snoring with thunderous blasts.

It wasn't just me who was bothered by his nocturnal outbursts. In fact, the House Fund offered to pay to have his adenoids removed if it would end his annoying noises, but he would have no part of it. The other alternative was to get him out of the bunk room. Many nights his slumber couldn't be interrupted by thrown pillows, boots, pots, pans and anything else handy. Then we resorted to carrying him, bed and all, out to the smoking room and placing his four poster on top of the pool table, with his night hitch beside him on the floor. This made for a big first step when he got out of bed, but the trouble was he seldom made it. He would sleep through the house gong and miss the run. A few missed runs and the officer ordered us to stop our night maneuvers with the sleeping beauty. The alternative for me was to heed Herb's advice and study to get a room of my own.

To continue the biography portion of this book, our first child, son Bruce, was born on a Friday evening in July 1949. Being an important family event, naturally, Group 2 with Dad, was working the night tour. It really didn't matter because in those days child birth wasn't the occasion for a neighborhood reunion, with video cameras, in the Delivery Room. I dropped Dot off at the hospital on my way to work and the doctor called me about eleven o'clock to say we had a son and everyone was fine. Our second son, Frank, was born in February 1951 on a night I wasn't working so Bruce didn't have to stay home alone.

To keep things in proper sequence, our first daughter, Janna Leigh, was born after we had moved to the new fire house. It was in November 1954 and I was off duty that night. I had just come home from a lodge meeting and was wearing my tux, so the trip to the hospital was formal - and appropriate for our new daughter. Being off duty for two out of three births wasn't a bad average. The best news was that all were healthy children. We had much for which to be thankful.

Father had a longer period to rest and recover before our next offspring arrived in 1963, but the particulars of that night will come later in the book.

Eight story Drill Tower at Fire Headquarters on Bristol Street.

Members of Engine 42, circa 1950.
Cook is last from right, third row. Tommy Carroll is in center of
photo with head tilted.

Members of Ladder 30, circa 1950.
Second row: From left side, Morley Carter is first and Jim Doneghey is third.
Third row: John Campbell is second from left.

Sleeper Street, January 15, 1948.

Note hood cover on apparatus on left side of photo.

Sleeper Street, January 15, 1948.

Don't forget your boots!

CAMERA CATCHES ARCTIC

ICE FORMS on helmet of Paul Cook of Engine 42 as he takes a breather.

JOHN ABBOT of Engine 26 keeps apparatus moving to avoid becoming stuck.

Sleeper Street, January 15, 1948.

A NEW HOUSE FOR OLD AND NEW MEN

(or, All Good Things Must Come To An End)

Those of us who were assigned to Engine 42 and Ladder 30 found no fault with the old fire house and would have been happy to stay there for a few more years. It was first occupied in October 1892 and was still in excellent condition but the post-war apparatus was getting longer and wider. In 1947 we received a new Mack pump which was only about four inches narrower than the granite hub protectors at the doors. It was no easy task to speedily guide that new engine through the doorway, with only four inches of clearance, and still keep up with the old wagon which had plenty of room to spare. Even without the pressure of responding, it was no simple job to back it in. The problem was that the main floor of the fire house was on an angle and because of an El upright, you couldn't easily line up the apparatus with the door opening. As soon as the front of the piece cleared the opening you had to turn so the back step wouldn't hit the patrol desk. Those granite hubs had to go.

Anecdote:
The granite hubs were on each side of the apparatus doors. Their purpose dated back to the days of horse drawn apparatus and were intended to keep the wheel hubs from chipping away at the bricks, by allowing the wheels to scrape along the base of the granite if they came that close to the house. In the olden days the department had one stone mason and it became his job to remove the granite hubs. He wasn't the fastest workman this side of Naples but he was thorough.

For a couple days he studied the problem as to just where the pilot holes should be made and then with a star drill and maul began his work. He explained to us that by scientifically placing the right depth holes in the right places, he would be able with one blow of the sledge hammer to break that granite in a straight line parallel with the bricks. It didn't help that pennies kept falling into the holes he made, but after a week of penetrations with the star drill, Friday afternoon came and just before quitting time he raised his sledge for that mighty methodical wallop while the whole house turned out to watch. Like he predicted, the granite hub only required one blow, but instead of the expected smooth surface flush with the bricks, it looked like an outcropping of Roxbury pudding stone stuck to the bricks. The expert couldn't understand what went wrong but he would be back on Monday to figure it out. At this rate it would take weeks to remove all four hubs and the captain was getting disturbed over the scraped paint appearing on the fenders of his new Mack pump.

Over the weekend we all skipped the star drill and maul and practiced with the sledge hammer and other tools. When the mason from headquarters showed up on Monday morning his face fell to his soggy shoes when he saw the granite hubs had all disappeared over the weekend. It may not have been done scientifically but all that was left for the mason to do was to smooth out that Roxbury outcropping of his first attempt. This he did very nicely in briefly four weeks.

Around 1950 an architect was chosen to design a new fire house to replace Egleston Square and he visited us several times to learn what the men who would be occupying it would like in a fire house. Did he get suggestions! The chosen site was Columbus Avenue and Bragdon Street and it would be a single story building. The land belonged to a hospital and one story was that they sold it to the city because they were in need of funds. We don't know what they expected of a fire house, but from the start there were complaints of the noises made by the builders and then the occupants with their noisy house alarm and still noisier fire apparatus - not to mention the men.

Part of the cellar was to be an air raid shelter and since bowling was the current fad among the men he included a single bowling alley lane as part of the cellar. Naturally the men insisted that there be an automatic pin setter. Since the house was being designed for radiant heating in the floors the men figured it would add very little to the cost to extend those heated pipes right out to the apron and save a lot of work when it snowed. In the end economics prevailed and the finished house did not include heated apron, bowling alley or air raid shelter. It was built on a slab.

The move to 1870 Columbus Avenue was made on the afternoon of Friday, December 19, 1952. That morning we made several trips to the new house with the apparatus piled high with the beds, desks, chairs and other furniture. At the time I thought if it was ever my prerogative, a new fire house would start out with everything new. In the afternoon the Department Band led the way down Columbus Avenue followed by the members, on and off duty, marching in dress uniform and followed by the apparatus. At the new house the flag was raised and Arthur Fiedler of the Boston Pops led the Department Band in the National Anthem. Speeches were made, a collation was served and the public went home. It was then realized that no provisions had been made for closing the old house. It was decided to send Engine 42 back for the weekend, but first it was necessary to pile beds and other items back on the apparatus for the return trip.

Even though it had been vacant for only a few hours, the house to which we returned was even more barren than when we had left it. Souvenir seekers had removed many of the essentials like the brass house gong, poles and a relatively new Hardwick gas stove from the third floor.

Groups 2 and 3 reported Saturday morning for the Day Tour. There was no need to do house work, so the early morning was mostly spent reminiscing. The acting district chief stopped in for his daily visit and joined our conversation before asking if the coffee was ready. At this point he wasn't aware the stove had gone south.

About that time Jack Vehicle came down from upstairs carrying the big aluminum percolator and headed for the cellar. On his way he remarked, "coffee will be ready shortly. Get the doughnuts." The acting chief continued talking - and then he realized what he had seen and heard. He asked, "Why is Jack going to the cellar with the coffee pot?"

No one knew - so he headed for the cellar. What greeted him was a truly tranquil scene. There was Jack, nonchalantly leaning back in his chair in front of the furnace reading the morning paper. The furnace door was open and flames were lazily lapping up the outside. Jack had taken a mop stick, removed the mop and clamped the coffee pot handle to it. The six foot pole extended from the chair into the open furnace and the coffee was just starting to perk.

Jack may have been nonchalant, but the acting chief was non-understanding and immediately demanded an explanation. When he learned the stove too was missing, he really blew his top and made a lot of threats about going to headquarters Monday morning to get to the bottom of this! He left without having coffee.

When the acting chief was relieved by the on coming night chief, he filled him in on the grand larceny that had taken place at the old fire house. The chief came over to Egleston Square, sat down and asked for a cup of coffee - which was produced from the fiery furnace. He finished his coffee, washed his cup and on his way out, stopped and remarked, "I figure the stove should be back from vacation by Monday. Right?"

It was still a few days before Christmas but Santa Claus must have come early, because when "Morning Call" was sounded at 0700 hours on Monday morning, the stove was in place in the third floor kitchen and the blackened coffee pot was perking. Coincidentally, it was about the same time that the JA Cafe removed hot dinners from its daily menu and returned to cold sandwiches.

Engine 42 also returned - to the new house and on Christmas Day, Groups 1 and 2 enjoyed the first turkey dinner cooked up in the new Taj Mahal.

It wasn't long before we learned that the apron of the new fire house was a lot bigger than the wide sidewalk we shoveled at 3089 Washington Street. The first big snowstorm arrived on a day Groups 2 and 3 were working. The "old school" operated on the theory that snow must be removed from all fire house property to protect the City from law suits by people who might slip and fall. (Mayor Curley had a better theory - it was that the good Lord put the snow there and when He didn't want it there, He would remove it.)

The apron was close to fifty feet wide and about sixty feet long to the street. The wisdom of the men wanting the apron heated now became prophetic - but the reality was lacking. In addition, the sidewalk on Bragdon Street was a couple hundred feet long and six feet wide. The captain insisted the snow be removed from fence to curbing. The result was that we shoveled the whole tour, except the men who were lucky enough to be sent out to salt hydrants. When the apron and sidewalks were cleared we still had the parking lot, and the hundred foot driveway leading to it, to shovel, that is if you wanted to get your car out.

The summers in that house were more enjoyable and less work. There was a fenced in yard not only large enough for a full horseshoe court but big enough for the softball team to practice pitching and hitting - and there were no neighbors to shoot water from their porches onto the sun bums. Of course there was a good-sized yard to mow, which was a new experience for the city firemen. Thought was given to having the House Fund buy a goat to take care of the grass. It could also furnish fresh milk, but the idea was vetoed.

Mom had always tried to impress upon her sons that no good could possibly come from evil - and among the evils was gambling. A lot of men in the fire house did not hold to this belief, in fact they could prove that it was both good and profitable - provided they didn't count their losses. One of the men moonlighted by chauffeuring a semi-official of a local horse race track, and each year he would come in with a hot tip on a particular race. All the horse fans looked forward to this race and one year in their enthusiasm they tried to induce me to also invest. There was no interest on my part but they coaxed and cajoled and insisted that it was like throwing my money away not to join them. My warning was that if I did join them it would be throwing their money away, but their reply was "Impossible." In the end I threw in two bucks and at post time everyone gathered around the radio "while visions of sugar plums danced in their heads" and they made plans for how to spend their windfalls.

If the race was arranged, someone forgot to tell the horse. Although he wasn't the listed favorite, he broke from the gate and led the pack and was gaining at every turn. As he came into the home stretch he was leading by about twelve lengths and the cheering around the radio was deafening. Just before the finish line the nag must have spotted some filly he knew across the field, because he suddenly took a sharp left and went over the fence in hot pursuit - and took all of our money with him. Son of a gun, Mom was right again. For some reason the guys never again asked me to bet on their favorite fillies.

Through the fifties many of our residential fires were caused by so called space heaters. In its wisdom the state banned the sale and use of these time bombs from residential buildings, but in recent years there have been efforts made to re-allow them. Based on experience, fire departments will continue to oppose all such attempts. The fires caused by those heating devices were usually confined to the room of origin, but that depended on where it was placed. If it was near the doorway, the fire could spread in two directions, and sadly many times they were placed in a hall leading to several bedrooms. The resulting fires engulfed all the rooms and took its toll in lives of sleeping children.

Standard procedure for this type of fire was for the booster line man to begin attacking the fire with his three quarter inch hose while the officer and rest of the company backed him up with a big line. By a rapid, but frugal, dispersion of his forty gallons of tank water, the booster man could often put out the fire before the big line, with its two hundred and fifty gallons of water a minute, had to be brought into use. Due to the burning oil these fires were extremely hot and often quite smoky. The "booster man" was in there alone for the first couple minutes and usually without ventilation so it was an excellent way to learn basic firefighting, and the value of saving water and making every drop count. You also learned the value of ventilation for when it was done promptly and properly you could begin to breathe again.

Sometimes, when the heater had been placed outside the bedrooms, and the parents were screaming that their children were in them, you had to forget even the booster line and try to fight your way down a long hall to where the cries were coming from (if they were lucky). Meanwhile, the black toxic smoke and heat would be racing up the hallway to meet you and try to block your passage. It is repeated exposures like these that add up to firemen living ten years less than the population in general, which they seek to serve.

About noon one day, we responded to a fire in a three decker off Amory Street. The fire had started on the second floor and extended to the third. Our assignment was to take a big line to the second floor via the rear inside stairs and attack the fire. There was a report that the second floor occupant might be still in the apartment. As we stretched our line through the first floor flat and up the stairs to the second floor, there was a gentleman who had come home for lunch and was preparing his meal in his first floor kitchen. We asked if he had seen the second floor occupant and received only a grunt in reply. His only concern seemed to be getting something ready to eat.

When we forced the second floor door we were met by raging fire. It took several minutes to begin knocking down the flames and then start advancing the line into the apartment. As the flames were blackened down, we crawled into each room searching for any victims. This takes a while as closets have to be opened and a search has to be made in back of and under beds and other furniture. The smoke and steam makes it a slow difficult task.

As we fought our way into a final bedroom and knocked down the fire, we looked across the room and could see a man on the burning bed. Luke and I, who were on the play pipe, hugged the floor as we groped our way to the other side of the room. Reaching up to the bed I grabbed the man's leg to pull him to safety, but his knee came off in my hand like the cooked joint of a well done turkey. Looking on the bed he resembled an over done turkey with his toasted skin ready to burst. We called for a body bag. In a moment the room was filled with men and when the body bag arrived, it sailed over the heads of the assembled observers like a frisbie, and dropped at our feet. As quickly as the room had filled, it emptied. That is all except Luke and I. He said, "Since we found him Cookie, I guess we have to pack and remove him, especially since there is just the three of us in the room, and one is gonna be no help at all."

Even in tragedy, there is sometimes humor of sorts. As we carried the victim down the stairs and through the first floor kitchen, there was the man who had been so unconcerned when we arrived, eating his lunch and reading his paper. We had used so much water on the two upper floors that it had worked its way through the ceiling and was raining on his parade. He was sitting at the table with an umbrella over his head to keep his mess dry. He was still unconcerned about the events that were taking place over head but was quite disturbed that we couldn't remove our hoses running through his apartment so he could lock the door before he went back to work.

Another Incident that wasn't funny to the victim took place about three o'clock one morning in an apartment house in Roxbury. When we arrived a woman met us at the door and said her husband had been burned. Naturally we expected a fire and began to move in with a line of hose. She stopped us and said there was no fire, but please look after her husband. She led us to the bedroom where the man of the house was writhing in agony on the bed. His blistered buttocks were rosy red with second degree burns. It seems he had gotten up to go to the bathroom and while sitting on the hopper he reached around and pulled the chain. Instead of cold water to flush the toilet, it was scalding steam that gushed forth and he rose from the throne like he was jet propelled, but not before the damage had been done.

While some took care of his needs, the rest of us looked for the cause. Every water tap in the building passed live steam when opened, whether marked H or C. The problem was found at the hot water heater. Normally it receives cold water, heats it and sends it forth at hundred and forty or so degrees to the hot water pipes connected to it. In this case the water continued to heat as all safety features failed. The water in the tank became steam and eventually forced its way back into the cold water supply and out to the street. Of course the simple solution was to shut off the heater and open all the faucets to reduce the temperature. With all taps open in the building it took several minutes before steam stopped and hot water began to trickle. It took much longer for the burned bottom to recover from the sauna enema it had suffered.

The scheduled after midnight watches are twelve-to-two, two-to four and four-to-eight A.M. on a rotating basis. On the forty-eight hour week these were done on the group's first night back. Some of the men liked an uninterrupted night's rest, if there weren't any fires. So for a while we tried one man doing all the after midnight watches. By doing this you were able to "float" from watches for the next two weeks.

On the night tour of June 23, 1953 it was my turn for the all night watch. Soon after daybreak, Box 1532 was struck for a fire on Isabella Street in the South End. It developed into a four bagger and three occupants lost their lives. In the investigation that followed it was determined that the fire was caused by arson and that a possible suspect lived in the apartment building opposite our fire house. In an attempt to reconstruct the crime it was presumed that if the suspect left his home on Columbus Avenue and went directly to Isabella Street, and then returned home, he would have had to have left about four A.M. The police were seeking someone who may have seen him. Since our patrol desk faced the suspect's building, the investigating State Police figured it a logical step to check the fire house Journal to see who was on watch. Since my name appeared on the midnight to two watch only, they skipped me and questioned the men who supposedly did the next two watches. In the end it didn't matter because no one in the fire house saw the suspect come or go.

In spite of the fact I was completely happy with my role as wagon driver or being "Number One Pipeman," Herb continued to hound me to get in the books. Studying this subject came easy for me but promotions weren't plentiful. On my first exam I placed tenth on the list but only eight were promoted in the two years, so it was back to the drawing board.

One hot summer day I had worked the Day Tour for myself and was working the Night Tour for Tommy Carroll. We had finished eating and I was sitting in the yard reading the Red Book. Under "Construction Features" I had just read, "After a fire has burned uncontrolled for a few minutes in a building with frame walls, that building frequently becomes unsafe for both the fireman and the occupants."

Just then the house gong sounded. I drove the wagon to the fire, which was in the old Forest Hills Hospital on Orchard Hill Road. My wife had been born in that hospital, and before the night was over I thought I was going to die in it. It was a large vacant four story wooden building that was boarded up. There was a circular driveway in front and when we arrived, heavy fire was showing from the top floor and beginning to push through the roof. Dark smoke was mushrooming from most covered windows. It was obviously going to be a deck gun job and as the pump grabbed a hydrant, we dropped two big lines and I drove the wagon up the right leg of the driveway to the front of the building. Engine 53 had begun the same tactic using the left leg. Ladders 10 and 30 had already taken positions on the driveway and had raised their aerial ladders with the intention of roof venting, but this was unnecessary and impossible due to the growing magnitude of the fire.

Rather than allowing us to go ahead with deck gun operations, the chief first ordered the two engine companies to take big lines over the two aerial ladders and attack the fire from the raised ladders. He called for a couple additional engines and trucks for his one alarm fire. It was obvious the fire was working its way down into the wood building and our ladder lines were making no impression on it. We were ordered to move our lines into the building and work our way to the upper floor. The two engine companies simultaneously did just that in the heavy smoke. When we reached the top floor of the marble stairway, our company turned to the left and called for water. At that point, the roof over the stairs gave way and tons of heavy burning timber crashed down burying and collapsing our lines of hose.

Those of us on Engine 42 thought the men on Engine 53 were caught on the stairs so we rushed to that area. As it happened, they had turned right into a room on reaching the floor and they thought we were still on the stairs and they also came rushing to the stair area. We took a quick head count and all men were accounted for, but we were all trapped on the top floor without water. The stairs and most of the top floor were an inferno and the fire was now fully engulfing the floor under us. We had then been working for about an hour and my thoughts became academic, "After a fire has burned uncontrolled for a few minutes in a building with frame walls, that building frequently becomes unsafe for both the fireman and the occupants."

A couple of us were able to make our way to a burned out hole in the exterior wall. By throwing out my helmet, we attracted the attention of a man from Ladder 30. He quickly rounded up some men and they raised a fifty five-foot ground ladder to provide both engine companies with a means of escape. Once on the ground, both companies went into deck gun operations, which we should have done on arrival. Despite our efforts, we just watched as the fire which was now in full command, reduced the wooden building floor by floor till it got tired of playing and gave up with a floor and half still standing. As for the men on 42 and 53 there was no public confession, but I am sure each one gave a prayer of thanks to their Heavenly Father - I know I did!

Anecdote:
On June 17, 1972, four alarms (Box 1571) were struck for a fire in the old Hotel Vendome. It concluded with a portion of the building collapsing killing nine firemen. One of them was Tommy Carroll who was then a lieutenant on Engine 32. Life is strange! I often wonder if the "Grim Reaper" was stalking the Forest Hills Hospital fire that night looking for Tommy, and left empty handed when he found someone else was working for him!

A different but definite hero is the man who runs the House Fund in a fire barn. He is a fire brand hero in his own right for it is his thankless job to make certain there is always coffee, tea, cocoa, sugar, cream, crackers, peanut butter and marshmallow fluff in plentiful supply in the food locker. To pay for these he has to chase most of the men to collect their weekly assessment. It used to be a quarter, but now averages a dollar, or more. He takes a lot of abuse for not shopping bargains, clipping coupons or for substituting with generic brands. To their credit some House Funds are run so efficiently that they provide VCRs, TVs, microwave ovens, charcoal grills, ice cream makers, meat slicing machines and other kitchen equipment, as well as picnics for the men and their families. This is accomplished by a variety of profitable innovations like providing soft drink dispensers, plus candy, gum, peanuts, cigarette and other vending machines.

Back in the early fifties we had a man in charge of the House Fund at Engine 42 who was a pioneer in profiteering for this common cause. A lot of the men smoked in those days, and cigarettes could be purchased much cheaper in North Carolina. The one detracting feature of this mail order enterprise was that it by-passed Taxachusetts' profit. Nothing ventured; nothing gained, so every couple months a package from North Carolina arrived at 1870 Columbus Avenue addressed to "Joe Sparks."

After a half dozen of these CARE packages were delivered uneventfully, a State "revenooer" arrived at the fire house one morning and said he had the little store across the street at Columbus Avenue and Bragdon Street "under surveillance." He wanted to know if he could sit in the fire house and watch it? (Incidentally, back in the early part of this century, that little store was run by my grandmother). So for a couple weeks the "super spy" soaked up the fire house heat, drank our coffee, occupied one of our limited chairs, watched our television, played cards and eyed deliveries to the little store across the way.

One morning a mail truck pulled up in front of the fire house and delivered a box from North Carolina addressed to "Joe Sparks at 1870 Columbus Avenue." You'd think the "revenooer" had found the Hope Diamond! Right away the master detective figured the little "smartie" in the store had this box of goodies delivered to the even numbered side of the street so anyone watching would be thrown off the trail, but not this "revenooer." His additional stroke of genius was to have a fireman deliver the package to the store across the street. He would follow and catch them with the goods. Naturally the firemen were not enthused - or cooperative. After a long while, the "revenooer" put "Joe Sparks" and the box of cigarettes together - and smelled smoke!

Despite the hospitality he had received and accepted without paying any House Fund, he was all business and didn't believe in "giving a Jake a break." He confiscated the smokes and in the end "Joe Sparks was fined three hundred dollars (which the House Fund paid) and got some kind of a police record.

Anecdote:

A few years later "Joe Sparks" responded to a building fire. After the All Out was struck on the fire, Signal Ten Fifteen was struck for "Joe Sparks." He paid the supreme sacrifice and lost his life at that fire. Now it may be perchance that the "revenooer" is reading this book. If so, you now have the final act of that life in which you played a role. Or, as Paul Harvey says, "Now you know the rest of the story." You may have been proud of yourself and your accomplishment then, but as firemen, we didn't think much of you then - and we still don't!

It was at a good fire off Lamartine Street in Jamaica Plain that I almost had an ambulance ride to the hospital from a fire. It was a hot summer evening and on our arrival as the second engine on the first alarm, heavy fire was showing from the second and third floors of a four story brick building. We had run a big line via the front stairs to the third floor and had just begun to hit the fire when our line burst. The officer sent me back to have our line shut down and to get a replacement length of hose.

About the same time I reached the street, it was discovered that the fire had apparently started in the cellar and was making headway there. The chief had ordered a second alarm and was grabbing everyone in sight to get a big line into the cellar to attack the fire there while waiting for help to arrive. Despite my insisting that Engine 42 was waiting for a replacement length and wasn't able to resume the attack on the third floor fire until they got water, I ended up alone on the nozzle of the line going into the cellar.

At the foot of the stairs I lashed the line to the railing with a hose line and called for water. I could hear the second alarm apparatus arriving but no one came down the cellar stairs to assist me. As the two hundred and fifty gallons of water a minute from the play pipe knocked down the fire, the steam, smoke and carbon monoxide built up, and I began to get light headed and dizzy. When for some reason I began to see visions of lighted Christmas trees, I knew it was time to bail out. After aiming the open play pipe in the direction of where the fire had been the heaviest, I made my way up the stairs and out to fresh air.

Once in the open, I keeled over and was carried to the Red Cross truck. It so happens brother Herb was working with the Red Cross and saw to it that plenty of oxygen was administered to me in a hurry. I began to come around but was still pretty much out of the picture. About that time I heard the Medic say, "I can't get a pulse. Let's get this guy to the hospital, stat."

On hearing that I sat bolt upright and insisted I was OK. After a couple big glasses of cold Red Cross lemonade, things returned almost to normalcy and I refused that first ambulance trip and wanted to go back to work at the fire. The chief, in his wisdom, had his driver take me back to the fire house, and Herb came along to keep an eye on me. After a shower and dry clothes there was nothing to do but wait for the rest of the company to come back and then help change hose. Fortunately it was quiet the rest of the night and in a few days I felt as good as new.

It has always been my belief that we all have guardian angels. My many years of firefighting have proved it beyond a doubt in my own mind and life. One night we were working a two alarm fire in a commercial building. We were operating a big line in a large room on the top floor and did not have our All-Service masks on as the smoke was light. Suddenly extreme heat built up, the smoke banked down and breathing became difficult. A "Backdraft" was in the making. We shut down the line and moved back into the stairway to don masks. No sooner had we stepped into the hall when there was a flash and the roof came in burying our line and the place where we had been operating it. Some might consider this a coincidence - but they will have a hard time convincing me!

Life in the fire department is also a study in human nature. One New Year's Eve we were covering Engine 26 on Broadway and looking out the window we saw a motorist with a problem. His car had a flat tire and he was dressed in a tuxedo on this Holiday Eve. His lady companion was wearing a real fancy gown covered by a fur coat, so it would appear they weren't destitute. Since they were in work clothes anyway, two firemen went out to help. They jacked up the car, changed the tire and put the flat tire in the trunk. The New Year's Eve party bound people were so appreciative of the men that the gentleman reached in his pocket, took out a cigar, broke it in two and gave a piece to each man - and wished them a Happy New Year.

Along with the fun and the work, and to keep Herb happy, I continued studying for the next Lieutenant's Exam. That time my mark put me number nine. When the list was established there was one vacancy for lieutenant and the number one man, Leo D. Stapleton of Ladder 8 was promoted.

The Department started something new with that list. With the thought that new officers should have an idea of what goes on in the Fire Prevention Division, they began detailing the first seven men on the list to that Division so they could work and observe until there was a vacancy and they were promoted. The first seven were detailed to headquarters and when the next promotion from our list was made it was my turn to go to Fire Prevention.

This was just after Thanksgiving, 1956. The change from working day and night tours to a five day week didn't appeal to me at all, but for a promotion you will accept almost any inconvenience temporarily. Cheer up so things could get worse. At that time it was standard practice to assign some members of Fire Prevention to the department stores at Christmas time to enforce safety regulations. Two of us on the list were assigned to Jordan Marsh. It was for the two weeks prior to Christmas and the schedule was Monday through Saturday from nine in the morning until nine at night. There was no extra money for these seventy-two hour weeks but Jordan Marsh did allow us to eat in the employees' cafeteria at their supposedly reduced prices.

This arrangement did have a fringe benefit of sorts for me. We had to patrol all floors of both the main Jordan Marsh buildings and the Annex building. This included the customer's shopping areas as well as the back room storage and work areas. It was a real large complex to patrol and we didn't have radios so there was no way of really keeping track of our whereabouts, except that a captain from Fire Prevention kept making frequent and irregular visits.

Dot and I had taken the big plunge to buy a house and we were waiting to pass papers. We received the call to do this on Monday, December 17th, at a law office close to Jordan Marsh. Our savings were quite limited and we weren't sure just what our costs would be, so we had been very frugal and had done no Christmas shopping. Dot came in town and when I moved from inspecting Jordan's new building to the annex, we took a detour to the lawyer's office where we signed on the dotted line and became property owners. The seller was very nice to us and absorbed some of the costs we had expected to pay.

The result was that after returning to Jordan Marsh and surveying conditions for a while, we went over to the New Adams House, from where I could still watch Jordans, and we could celebrate our indebtedness to the Shawmut Bank Mortgage Department by dining out on the restaurant's "daily special." We then returned to the store and Dot accompanied me as I continued inspecting - and we did all of our Christmas shopping for our families, friends and our three children. Our present to each other was the house. That year our family's shopping was exclusive with Jordan Marsh, in spite of the fact that the best they could do for our seventy-two hour weeks was to let us use their cafeteria. Come to think of it, Jordans got all the fringe benefits that year.

After Christmas I returned to Fire Prevention and worked on Abatements and Service Orders for the next four months.

It is often remarked that firemen have a very morbid job - as they are either waiting for someone's house or business to catch fire so they can go to work; or waiting for an officer to die so they can get promoted. This isn't actually the case, but in fact the first events do trigger the second events. By April of 1957 I had moved up to number one on the list. On April 14th, Lieutenant Fred Ford of the Rescue died of smoke inhalation while at a fire in the West End, and the vacancy for my promotion to lieutenant was provided. It became effective May 1, 1957, after ten great years as a paid firefighter. I was happy and Herb was delighted.

Due to other officers seeking transfers, the actual vacancy was on Ladder 14 on Harvard Avenue in Allston. The Fire Commissioner at the time was, let us say, not the most popular man that ever held the office. For his own reasons, he had selected Ladder 14 and Engine 41, in the same house, to be his dumping ground for all the members which he considered misfits or whatever. Often there was no rhyme or reason to his transfers but he was boss.

When one is being promoted in the Fire Department it is required that he go to Fire Headquarters and sign "The Book." This is the term used, but in reality it is just a piece of paper you sign for Civil Service to indicate you have accepted the promotion and pay raise. It is a pleasant experience for those who get to do it one or more times.

I had a friend who was a "fixture" at headquarters and when he saw me in Signing the Book, he congratulated me and asked what company I was going to. When I told him the vacancy was on Ladder 14, he said, "You don't want to go to the 'dumping ground.' Let me go in and see my friend the Commissioner and have that changed."

My feeling was it would do no good, and for the promotion it didn't really matter to me where I was sent. But in he went - and I waited in the hall. After a few minutes the Commissioner's door opened and as my friend appeared in the doorway I heard the gruff inner voice say, "I said Cook is going to Ladder 14 and that is final. Now get out of my office!" And the door slammed.

My friend was very subdued as we walked down the hall, but he had done his best and I thanked him. Many of the first men promoted off our list began their officer careers in the "dumping grounds" - and all survived it.

Anecdote:
The origin of the "dumping ground" was strictly political. In the recent battle to be Mayor of Boston, John E. Powers had been pitted against John B. Hynes. Among a lot of firemen, Powers was the choice and in their enthusiasm for a victory (which didn't materialize), someone put a "Powers For Mayor" sticker on Ladder 14 and it was spotted while they were out doing In-Service Inspections. Of course it was wrong and the sticker was promptly removed but the damage had been done. In-Service Inspections were canceled until after the election, which Hynes won. He appointed a new Fire Commissioner who cleaned out the men of Ladder 14 and Engine 41, who may have been responsible for the sticker incident, and replaced them with men of his choosing.

On May 1, 1957 I changed from blue shirts to white shirts, and began a new phase of my hobby and career, at the "dumping ground."

Summer firefighting gear in olden days. Cook, wagon driver, is replacing booster hose following fire on Highland Avenue, Roxbury.

Ladder 30 with FWD truck at new house on Columbus Avenue. Jim Doneghey driving, Tommy Carroll tillering. Both men would later die in the Line of Duty.

VIEW FROM A PRIVATE ROOM

(or, No One Snores In This Room On Group 2)

The forty-eight hour schedule called for two and a half lieutenants on each company which meant that the junior officer assigned to one company divided his working tours between two companies, usually in the same house. When another vacancy occurred on his company he won the permanent berth and this I expected would be my immediate future. At the time the turnover of officers in that house was quite rapid but on reporting for my first tour of duty as an officer I was put on Group 2 which was a permanent berth on Ladder 14. Lieutenant Stapleton, who had been there a few months, wanted to continue working the split assignment to gain experience on an engine company. This was fine with me for after ten years on an engine company I was anxious to get some steady experience on a truck.

My first night as an officer was most interesting, as were many more nights and days that would follow in District 11. (Later, after nearly four years there, I had no reservations about where headquarters might send me because any other place would be anticlimactic). As previously stated, the house was known as the "dumping ground" and although there were a bunch of excellent firemen in the house, there was also the "Dirty Dozen" element who kept things interesting for a rookie officer.

That first night I reported to the district chief in his office and was briefed on my new assignment and what was expected of me. From there it was down to get acquainted with the men I would be working with on Groups 1 and 2 and to get familiar with the Four Wheel Drive ladder truck that would be my responsibility for forty-eight hours each week.

The running card was simple. Since there were only two ladder trucks in District 11 we went to all boxes starting with a five. Shortly after 2000 hours the tapper started striking and the first number was a five. Box 5238 - Cambridge and North Harvard Streets. As we turned out of the fire house and down Cambridge Street there was a big black pall of smoke developing to the left. I asked my new driver what was in the neighborhood where we were heading. He replied, "It's probably an automobile fire."

It was the first run and the first misinformation in my new position. It ended up being a three alarm fire in McNamara's Cement Company. There was no ladder work to be done as the buildings were already vented when we arrived. The chief ordered us to run a big line and operate on the bonfire - a role I was most familiar with.

We got back to quarters around midnight but an officer was needed for the fire detail that would last till morning. Being the junior officer in the whole department, guess who got it? Fire details in those days consisted of one or more men from each of the districts selected and usually an officer from the district where the fire occurred. I didn't mind the detail as here it was my first night with a white shirt (which had gotten black right away at the fire) and I would be in charge of a fire for the first time - an awesome responsibility!

By the time I got back to the fire with a clean white shirt the detailed men were beginning to appear on the scene and Engine 34, the first engine to arrive and the last to leave - also customary in those days, was returned to quarters. The spring night had turned a little cool and some kind-hearted neighbors provided a pot of hot coffee for the tired firemen - and also a bottle of something to take the chill off the night air.

I went about checking the buildings and then returned to the group of detailed men. It must have been a cooler night than I thought because the pot of coffee was mostly intact but the bottle of something was empty. News report of the fire should have included the notation that the new lieutenant poured hot coffee for all the detailed firemen about two o'clock in the morning, and then the happy little dwarfs went about their task of wetting down and overhauling the remains of the buildings. To this day when I see an orange McNamara Cement truck I am reminded of my first fire as an officer - and the detail that followed.

To digress for a moment, fire details are handled different today than they were in the olden days. Logic would indicate that with the abundance of automobiles now the old system would work better today, and vice versa. Today when a chief calls for a detail following a fire, he decides how many companies are needed. A common detail is one engine and one ladder and the Fire Alarm Office uses a roster of the fire companies to determine which ones to send and thus "share the wealth" so to speak. The men respond with the apparatus, work the detail and then return as a unit.

In olden days the chief determined how many men were needed to accomplish the task of overhauling and making sure the fire didn't rekindle - another mortal sin - - then - - - and now! The deputy chief of the division would make up the detail by selecting men from each of his districts. If a larger detail was needed it might be a department detail and men would be sent from all over the city. Many of the men didn't have cars then but it didn't excuse them from details.

Company officers assigned details on a rotation based on the company roster. If you were fortunate at night, one of the members might let you use his car. If not, it was public transportation - or walk. Fire details could occur at any hour of the day or night and you might be instructed to bring an axe, rake, fire extinguisher or other equipment. It was a common sight and sometimes an awkward experience on a fair day to get on a street car or bus dressed in rubber boots, rubber coat, helmet, wheat light belt and carrying a ten foot rake. Little kids would ask their Mommy what that funny looking man was doing dressed like that on a hot bus, but it was an accepted part of the job - and Friday was still payday.

My second night wasn't as spectacular but continued to be educational. Captain Mullen of Engine 41 would be working with me on my second Day and Night Tours. We had worked many of the same fires and incidents in Roxbury when he was captain of Engine 14 and I was on Engine 42. He congratulated me on my promotion and then gave me some advice which could be accepted or not, as I chose.

He said, "Paul, you are starting your career as an officer. Now you can either be a good officer or a good fellow, but you can't be both! And let me add, there are already too many good fellows." It was logical reasoning and I got the message. I had already made up my mind that even as I tried to be a good fireman, I would try to be a good officer - and at times it would be trying!

My second run as an officer came about 1900 hours on my second night and was also a learning experience. It was a false alarm and we were returning by way of Long Avenue to Glenville and cars were parked on both sides of the narrow streets. We got hung up at the corner and in trying to make the turn the motor stalled and wouldn't start. In those days it was a mortal sin to have a dead battery on the apparatus. Not wanting this revealing information to go over the department radios, I went to a store and called Fire Alarm on a pay phone to request the Motor Squad to bring us a new battery.

I thought I had handled the situation very nicely and returned to the street - and to the free-for-all going on there. It seems a citizen who had parked his car too close to the corner came out to move it so we could get around the bend, and one of my stalwarts had words with him. It ended up in a boxing match with my man winning, which didn't help in trying to placate the well-intended civilian. Finally the Motor Squad arrived with a battery and we were able to get out of there. Back in quarters I gave my first "father to son" lecture to my new crew of rebels. They never confronted me again by engaging in fisticuffs - but they unwittingly found other ways to test me and widen my experiences as an officer!

Chimney fires were very common incidents. These often took place in buildings that were once heated by coal furnaces and later converted to oil heat. Over the years, a build up of soot takes place in the flue, and this can become ignited by the extremely hot exhaust from the oil fire. Although they are routine fires, usually limited to the chimneys, there is always the possibility that there might be cracks in old flue liners or the confined heat might be conducted to wood framing touching the chimney and spread the fire to the building. Standard procedure is to extinguish the fire in the chimney and then check the area around the chimney for excess heat, from the cellar to the roof.

Brighton had an abundance of brick apartment houses along Beacon Street and Commonwealth Avenue, as well as a lot of other major and minor thoroughfares. These provided almost nightly experience in this type of firefighting during the heating season. On arriving at the given address, the truck would throw the stick to the roof at the front of the building and the engine would take the booster line over the ladder to the roof. Some of the chimneys extended quite high above the roof. Since water had to be sprayed down the flue to eliminate the flying sparks, it was necessary to somehow get to the top of the chimney.

One way to do this was for the laddermen to carry a baby bangor ladder up the eighty-five foot ladder to the roof. This was a slow process and hazardous if there was ice on the ladders. My new bevy of brilliant beauts had figured out a safer and quicker way to accomplish the same task.

Many of the apartment houses had elevators and most of them were of the vintage when the passenger cars were of open grill cage construction. The open cages allowed my Dirty Dozen to maneuver their ten foot wooden ladders into the cars where they protruded through the open-work ceiling of the car.

On my first incident of this type with them, I was still open for their input. We raised the aerial ladder to the roof so the engine company could run their booster, and we got on the elevator with the baby bangor ladder protruding through the open car ceiling. They should have pushed the button for the landing below the top floor, but why carry a ladder up an extra floor if mechanics can do it for you?

As we approached the top floor, the protruding ladder hit the top of the elevator shaft and brought the elevator to an abrupt halt along with the sound of splintering wood. It was stuck below the floor and the doors wouldn't open. It was impossible to budge the wedged ladder and I was concerned that if we did, the whole process might have damaged the controls and once freed, we might plummet to the bottom of the shaft. But we couldn't stay there all night and the chief would be looking for us to complete the chimney fire procedure so some action was needed. One solution was to apply an axe to the wooden ladder. In this way we were able to turn the two ten foot ladder sections into roughly four - five foot ladders. They turned out to be a useless length, but once they were shortened, the elevator was able to move to the top floor, the doors opened and we were home safe.

My versatile crew of calamity jakes could do tricks with big ladders as well as small ones. If the following episode needs a title, it might be "Let's throw the stick to the first floor."

One Saturday afternoon we received a Still Alarm for an automobile fire at the rear of a low number on Glenville Avenue. Engine 41 took a right turn into Glenville but my driver suggested that there was an alley off Harvard Avenue that ran parallel with Glenville and chances are the auto fire was there. It sounded logical so I agreed to his taking the alley. He was right and we came upon the burning vehicle. Meanwhile Engine 41 stopped on Glenville and ran their line between a couple of buildings and met us at the fire. It was a routine car fire. While Engine 41 extinguished the fire, the laddermen opened the hood, disconnected the battery, checked the trunk and overhauled the interior of the car. So far everything was routine and we chided the engine men for not knowing about the alley. They packed up their hose and went back to the fire house.

It was winter and there was snow on the ground as we headed for home by continuing up the alley to where it met Spofford Road. The driver intended to turn left onto Spofford, but parked cars lined both sides of that street and there was barely enough space for a baby carriage to drive out of the alley.

My driver did an outstanding job of maneuvering the front end of the truck out into Spofford Road between the rows of parked cars. To accomplish this it was necessary to drive the rear tractor wheels up onto a low wall adjacent to the inside of the sidewalk. The tillerman was helping all he could by staying close to the apartment house on the corner to help make the turn. The trailer was at a forty-five degree angle with the tractor and was proceeding cautiously. Suddenly the rear tractor wheels slipped off the six inch high wall, and with the resulting movement of the truck there was the sound of breaking glass. The end of the wooden aerial ladder had gone through the window of a first floor apartment. It went in very easily in a matter of seconds, but two hours later we were still trying to figure how to get it out and Fire Alarm was asking "Ladder 14, where are you?"

It would seem a simple matter to pull the truck forward and the ladder would come out of the opening where the glass was a few minutes before. The problem was the angle of the tractor and the trailer plus that blasted icy low wall that wouldn't let the tractor wheels remount it. Each time we tried a new movement with the tractor the ladder slipped further into the room. To the shattered glass was added a splintered window frame and eventually broken bricks. By the time we had made several attempts with the front end, we had about three feet of the ladder on the rear end sticking into the apartment and the whole truck was on a tilt.

After estimating how much of the ladder was in the warm building and how high the window was, we figured that if the aerial ladder was raised, it should clear the opening and we could be on our way home. We knew that once the pedal was tripped to release the spring raised ladder we would have to stop it and then control the speed of rise with the hand brake as we didn't want it to go up too quick lest it do more damage. What our calculations didn't include was the tilt of the truck. If I ever design fire apparatus there will be a "Tilt" light built into the dashboard, similar to that on pin-ball machines.

The release pedal was depressed and the brake was applied. The ladder slowly rose, but once it cleared the keepers the weight of the ladder along with the tilt of the truck caused it to stop rising and instead move in the direction of the tilt. The result was that more bricks were dislodged and the wooden ladder was bent and still living in the apartment. The tillerman had been standing beside the ladder with the intent of being helpful but when the ladder went sideways it almost knocked him off the truck and would have except it jammed his hand against the building. We had to use the battering ram to remove enough bricks to free his paw.

By placing wedges under the low side tiller tire and by releasing air from the high side tire we were able to pretty much un-tilt the truck. Then by manually cranking the ladder upright we were finally able to get it out of the building. The bad news was that the steel frame that the ladder normally rested on was still pressing against the structure. By then, some of the illegally parked cars had been moved by their owners and we had more room on Spofford Road to maneuver, but the low wall was still a stumbling block to our departure. Each move of the front end still caused scraping sounds at the rear. Finally in desperation I told the driver to put the truck in low low and just keep going. It worked and the umbilical cord between the building and the apparatus was finally severed.

This final lunge bent the steel frame still further. Once out on the street, we tried to lower the bent ladder into the truck's steel frame, which was bent in the opposite direction of the ladder. The results was that the rear of the truck took on the appearance of a V. The tiller seat couldn't be fastened shut and we rode back to quarters with the substitute tillerman steering from a standing position.

Once back home at the fire barn, we tried to assess the damage to the truck. We raised the stick without any trouble but we didn't dare try to extend the fly. Staring up the ladder from the turntable, it looked more like a spiral staircase than a straight way approach to upper floors.

Since the metal frame had been bent in one direction by scraping along a building, we theorized that it could be bent back to the original position by scraping it along another building in the opposite direction. Parked cars were cleared from the firehouse alley and the truck was backed in with the metal frame against the wall. Several attempts at pulling the truck forward with the tillerman forcing the frame against the wall proved futile. If the frame was bent at the apartment house due to metal fatigue, the ride back must have rejuvenated it, because it just wasn't going to be moved again in any direction. We ended up calling the Motor Squad and telling them we needed a spare truck.

Meanwhile the tillerman with the bruised hand began complaining of the pain. I sensed it was mostly his feelings that had been hurt and suspected he had already taken some pain killers. Since nothing appeared to be broken, even the skin, I tried to persuade him to just apply a cold compress, take a couple aspirins and see how it was in the morning. There were already enough papers that had to be made out before I went home without adding injury and hospital forms. He insisted he was in agony and was about to pass out. I doubted the first but expected the latter, and in disgust told him to go to Saint Elizabeth's Hospital.

The worst part was yet to come - explaining to the district chief why it took us two minutes to go to an automobile fire and two hours to come back. In those days any accident involving a motor vehicle and causing damage in excess of two hundred dollars had to be reported to the Registry. In explaining what happened I made light of the damages to spare my driver's license. Naturally no mention was made that a new eighty-five foot wood ladder would be needed, and that the tired metal would have to be woken up and straightened.

As for the building, a new window $25.00. Some wood trim another $20.00. A few bricks, some cement and the services of a mason for a couple hours - about $100. Add a couple dollars for paint and two more for a brush, plus $50.00 for labor and incidentals making a total of $199.00 so there was no need to report it to the Registry. The chief just sat there and shook his head in disbelief. Then he went to Spofford Road to take a look for himself - and I began the paper work.

Before he got back, the Motor Squad brought us a spare truck and I went down to assist in the change over and explain why they would have to drive it to the shop with the tillerman standing up. Once on the main floor, one of the men took me aside and said. "Lieutenant, you might want to know the man you sent to St. E's has not gone yet. He is up at 'Two Toms' ingesting more pain killers so he can make the trip to the hospital more comfortably." I asked him if he would please go and march, carry or drag him back, and lock him in the bunk room for the night.

About then the chief came back and called me to his office. He asked me again about my estimation of damages and again I repeated pretty much what had been said before. Again he sat shaking his head and asked if I had gone into the room where the ladder went in? I told him "No, but I had stood on the truck and looked into the room several times and it appeared OK."

He replied, "If you had gone in to examine the room you might have noticed the cracks in the wall and the fact the mantelpiece was moved about six inches. On the stone hearth there was twelve hundred dollars worth of 'arntique varses' which had previously sat on the mantelpiece." Some days you just can't win - but Friday would still be payday.

That same chief added an experience to my career that I would rather have skipped at the time. It was a Friday night and I was detailed to Engine 34 on Western Avenue. On his nightly visit he took me aside and explained that Station WBZ-TV on Soldiers Field Road was having a water diving act on their Rex Trailer show the next morning and they needed the tank filled. He suggested that I get the company up about six o'clock and be sure not to use the radio at the location. Fire Alarm knew of the arrangements but the grumpy Commissioner did not.

He added that there was a hydrant on the racetrack by the studio so there would be no need to run hose across the street. I had been in the district long enough to be familiar with water pressures in different sections and knew that hydrant wasn't much good. I told him we would have to hook up the pump, but he was against us doing this, as it would take too long to disconnect if we had a run. He also instructed me to be certain that none of the men got in view of the cameras, as he wanted no firemen on TV.

I left orders for the man on patrol to give a long ring at five fifteen because we would need the extra time if we couldn't use the pump. We arrived "on location" about five thirty. Five hundred feet of two and a half inch hose was stretched and connected to the hydrant and the operating nut opened. As expected, with that length of line the water just dribbled out of the butt end and into the tank. We connected the pump to the hydrant and increased the flow of water. The pool wasn't filling fast enough to satisfy the needs so we ran a second five hundred foot line to speed up the process. About quarter past seven the chief stopped by to see how things were going. On seeing, he got back in his car and left - after warning me again that the men were not to get in view of the cameras.

The diving act had been planned as the show opener at seven o'clock, but no diver in her right mind would attempt a two and a half gainer in eight inches of water. As we continued to pour water from our two big lines into the pool the director kept moving the diving act to a later spot on the program. Wooden bleacher seats had been set up next to the pool for the hundred or so kids in attendance despite the early hour.

The round pool comprised of a well-padded plastic liner stretched over a metal frame that was made of chain-link fence type material. Where the two ends met to form a circle they were connected by a number of "C" shaped links that were held in place by the outward exertion of the water against the frame. Slowly the water in the tank rose - one foot - two foot - three foot – and was approaching four. We estimated it was approaching ten thousand gallons and the dive act manager wanted one of his girls to make a trial dive. Actually it was a simple jump into the tank. For some reason the "C" shaped links that held it together came undone like a zipper. The ten thousand gallons of water broke free from the dam that had been holding it and firemen with their gear bobbed along with the fast moving flood. In an instant the cameramen forgot all about Rex Trailer and Pablo (and their instructions not to show firemen) and zoomed in on the unfolding deluge.

On coming to the surface, my first thought was the water would topple the bleachers where the kids were. The same thought entered the other men's heads and as we gained footing all raced in the direction of the little spectators. The cameramen covered our every movement with dedicated tenacity. Fortunately, the thousands of gallons of water quickly spread in all directions, and the bleachers withstood the watery onslaught.

Needless to say there was no more diving that day and right through the eleven o'clock news that night, WBZ-TV played up the heroic wet firemen that their cameramen captured. It made good publicity for the fire department, but I am sure the district chief shuddered and shivered every time he heard the news that day. If the grumpy Commissioner saw it, he said nothing. At least I wasn't called into headquarters that week to explain.

Meanwhile back at the ranch on Harvard Avenue more exciting adventures were anxiously waiting to unfold. If you must have a fire, what better place to have it than in your friendly neighborhood fire house? It seems one of the men, before going home, hung his pants in his locker with his pipe in a pocket. Apparently it still containing smoldering tobacco. After a reasonable time the Yellow Bole heated up the pocket it was in -

and then the entire wood locker and then other lockers. The sweet smell of pipe tobacco soon mixed with the more pungent odor of burning clothes and charring wood before it was discovered that the locker room was on fire. Quick work by the men with a booster line, backed up with a big line, confined the fire to the single room and a still alarm assignment.

When word of the blaze reached headquarters, Grumpy came out to see what damage his "dumping ground" had sustained. He wasn't a happy camper that day either and wasn't at all impressed by the good stop made by the men on duty. Nor was he receptive when Captain Mullen took advantage of the Commissioner's rare visit to that fire station to ask for a P. A. system for the house. The captain's timing must have been off because we never did get the P. A. system. In fact we were fortunate to get replacement lockers, and the men had to clean up and paint the place themselves. It wasn't the first, or last, fire house in Boston to have a fire in it, but it did make the local newspapers and was the subject of local conversation for a few days.

A couple weeks later we had a run to an apartment house about two o'clock in the morning. Light smoke was showing from the open front door so the men set the jacks and began to throw the stick to the roof while I reported to the chief for orders. As I approached the front of the building there was the unmistakable smell of burnt food. The chief dismissed the engine companies and held the two trucks, with resuscitators. He said matter of factly that there was a couple in the back bedroom who needed oxygen.

The facts were that the lady and gentleman had been out celebrating something till "last call" and had come home happy and hungry. They put some pork chops on to fry in the kitchen and since it was a warm night they took off all their clothes and laid down on the bed - probably to rest and wait for the chops to get well done because everyone knows you shouldn't eat rare pork. When we got there the chops were well done and looked like two pieces of coal. In fact they were burning like two lumps of coal. The bed mates were completely out of it and on doing the "Primary Survey," my men must have determined the gentleman was the least seriously affected by the smoke because practically all the observation and attention were being directed to the young lady in her birthday suit. Their dedication to service with the resuscitator paid off, for after a few liters of oxygen the young lady stirred and opened her eyes. Compared to her, the half dozen or so men in her bedroom were over-dressed, but ignoring her own appearance, she looked up at her helmeted visitors and asked with a giggle, "Are you firemen from the fire house that had a fire in it? I thought that was the funniest thing I ever heard. A fire in a fire house!" To be sociable the men laughed with her.

By then the ambulance was on scene. The gentleman and the shapely laughing lady were breathing on their own and the medics wrapped them in blankets and transported them to St. Elizabeth's. I made a note to order some blankets for the truck so we too could cover laughing ladies - but somehow the note got lost on the way back to quarters.

Anecdote:
Of all the smokes encountered at fires, burnt food is probably the most pungent and least liked by firemen. It not only burns the eyes and penetrates the lungs, it permeates everything you are wearing right down to your socks. It stays with you until you have breathed fresh air for about an hour and showered and shampooed from head to toe for about an hour. All clothing you were wearing has to be washed with a strong detergent - unless you want every hungry dog in town to follow you home.

Two contrasting events that took place give indication of the variety of life around a fire house. Shortly after my promotion and assignment to Ladder 14, a Boy Scout came into the station and asked about getting a Merit Badge for "Firemanship." It immediately took my thoughts back to when I was twelve years old and went to a lieutenant at Engine 28 for the same reason. We went up to my office and I reviewed his requirements and after he proved his knowledge on the subject I signed his paper. He left the fire house a very happy camper - the same as I had over twenty years before. In the past, the scouts in Allston apparently had trouble finding a fire officer to examine them and sign their paper signifying their qualification for the "Firemanship" Merit Badge, because for a while there was a steady stream of scouts coming to the fire house on Group 2. It was most gratifying to see so many young nervous boys coming into my office and so many smiling satisfied scouts leaving with their "Firemanship Merit Badge." I wonder if any of them ever became firemen?

The other illustration is on the seedy side of life. There was a gentleman - no he was a "loan shark" who had several of the men in his little black book. He stopped in every Friday and would loan anyone ninety dollars with a repayment plan of ten dollars a week for ten weeks. Always being interested in good investments, I jokingly remarked one day that I could loan money at a better rate and still would be happy with the return. Somehow my remark reached the "shark" and on the next Friday we worked, he called me aside and said if I wanted to be a banker I should quit the fire department and go to the First National. Not wanting to be intimidated by him, I told him that was fine, but the fire house wasn't a bank either, and at least when Group 2 was working he wasn't to come in this fire house for his customer's withdrawals and deposits. If he did I would have him arrested for trespassing. In the future his customers would have to go outside to deal with him.

One night a few months later we were returning from a run by way of Cambridge Street and someone spotted a body under a parked car. We stopped to investigate and about the same time the police arrived. The body had met with foul play. It was the "shark" whose fire house transactions I had foreclosed on. The police wouldn't let anyone near him - and all the men wondered, hopefully, if someone had gotten to his little black book and destroyed it.

Studying books is basically time well spent, but some times, events happen that make you wonder if you read the right books, or if you read the books right.

One humid summer evening several of us were standing in front of the fire house when a car stopped to report smoke coming out of the railroad yards on Cambridge Street. One of the men ran to the corner to take a look, and about the same time the telephone rang as Fire Alarm was sending both companies to that location. As we turned the corner onto Cambridge Street we could see a sky full of orange and brown smoke and a vapor cloud building up over the freight yards. On arrival a yardman told me there was a tank car leaking nitric acid. As the liquid fell to the ground it ignited the grass and wood rail ties.

At times like these you try to remember what the old Red Book has taught you about the substance. I thought, Nitric Acid - its a corrosive liquid, noncombustible but dangerously reactive with many materials. It won't burn but will cause ignition of some organic materials. This is what was happening now. Fumes are toxic and it rang a bell that the acid vapors will mix with the moisture under the arms, and other sweat areas, and cause burns. Self-contained breathing apparatus should be worn but we have All-Service masks. It mixes with water so it is OK to run a line to extinguish the fire, but men must be kept upwind. Also call Fire Alarm to have them strike the box so you can turn the whole problem over to the chief.

The railroad men in the yard were most cooperative. They produced bags of soda ash that was spread on the spilled acid to neutralize it. A tank truck arrived to begin emptying the rail car. While we remained upwind and maintained a safe distance, the driver of the tank truck climbed up on the rail tank car to make the necessary connections to begin the transfer. Before climbing up he put on heavy rubber gloves as his only protection and remarked he wouldn't go anywhere without them because that stuff burns. No mask, no breathing protection. So who's book was right?

As more empty tank trucks arrived and the liquid level was lowered below the crack, the leaking stopped. The grass and debris fires were put out and the vapor-smoke cloud dissipated. The chief ordered the All Out and we went back to quarters - and I took another look at the books. This isn't the way such an incident would be handled in today's hazardous material world of the DEQE and EPA, but in those days we were lucky, in our ignorance - many times over.

Anecdote:
Lieutenant Solomon Russell of Chemical 1 died on April 1, 1902 after inhaling Nitric Acid fumes from a broken carboy at an incident on Sudbury Street.

Some firemen are real entrepreneurs. We had one in that house who ran a lawn mower repair business, although his mechanical ability was limited to screwing and unscrewing tooth paste caps, and then he was likely to cross thread them. This lack of mechanical talent did not stop him from bringing a load of broken mowers to work in his station wagon. He knew there was talent among the men he worked with and he would con them into restoring the units to a working condition, while he did the bookkeeping and laughed all the way to the bank. His business was testimony to the esprit de corps among firemen and their willingness to assist one another.

We are all better off when accidents don't happen, but for some reason they do occur from time to time. Fire engines of the fifties still had open cabs and no seat belts. Shortly after 0800 hours one morning just before Christmas in 1959 we were responding to a fire near Chestnut Hill Avenue. Our route to the box was via Commonwealth Avenue and shortly before we reached the Washington Street intersection the traffic light turned green for us. Our bell and siren were sounding and we could see the cars to our right on Washington Street had come to a stop, but just as we entered the intersection a tractor trailer truck entered from our left. At this point, Washington Street is an up grade and for whatever reason the truck driver continued through the red light.

When he saw the approaching ladder truck he stepped on his gas pedal and my driver stood up on our brake pedal. For a moment I thought these dual actions were going to succeed, but the trailer truck couldn't get enough momentum going and at the last moment we hit the rear end of it, knocking it over on top of three automobiles. My driver, who was already standing on the brakes, was catapulted out of the cab and came down on the pavement breaking his pelvis. Sitting beside him, I expected to take the same trajectory route, but the impact jammed the motor back through the firewall and pinned my legs to the seat. As I worked my way free I heard someone say, "There is a man under there."

I thought the truck driver must have fallen out of his cab and the truck had landed on top of him. Once free from my entrapment, I grabbed the radio and told Fire Alarm we had a Code 9 (accident) at Commonwealth and Washington, that there were some injuries, including department members, and to send ambulances, the police, the Motor Squad with the department wreckers to lift vehicles, and the department photographer.

On hearing my message, the district chief (the same one who discovered the "arntique varses") got on his radio and told Fire Alarm that if Ladder 14 wasn't going to make the run, then send him another ladder truck. I didn't know how serious his fire was, but I knew he wasn't going to show at my serious accident.

After getting help on the way, I scurried around sizing up the situation. The truck had not landed on the driver but there was a man in the first crushed car. Surprisingly, he said he was all right, but begged us to please get him out. In removing him from his now compact car, his hand was cut by broken glass, but that was the only injury he suffered. The other two cars were less seriously compressed and the occupants weren't compressed at all - but that isn't the way it was put when we went to court many months later.

About this time, a man came up to me and said he was from the trucking company, and did I want their big wrecker. I assumed he was speaking of the trucking company involved in the accident so I said "yes." My thinking also was that the fire department wreckers may not be capable of lifting the loaded trailer truck. He went off to make the call.

Various helps began to arrive and the first ambulance took my driver to St. Elizabeth's. Of all the participants, he was the only one that needed immediate medical attention, although the second ambulance took the ladies from the second and third cars - as we would hear many months later.

At this point it became pretty much routine. Police arrived and cordoned off the area. More ambulances reached or returned to the scene and the department photographer took pictures. With the help of department and private wreckers, the trailer truck was up-righted and towed away. Smaller tow cars removed the three autos and the department wrecker prepared to tow another Group 2 damaged Ladder 14 to the shop. The district chief never made it to the location but the deputy chief and the Acting Chief of Department did respond. The deputy asked for the details and was concerned about my driver going to St. E's with a busted pelvis.

The paper work for an accident of this magnitude took the rest of the day to complete. The reports included which department members were present and the actions they performed. Mention was made that the deputy and Acting Chief of Department responded and investigated the accident. This was routine. By the time the paper work was finished my legs which were jammed in the accident began to stiffen up and become sore. Before going home, I went to St. E's where they took x-rays and diagnosed that nothing was broken, but there were severe internal contusions of the leg and knee areas. Instructions were to stay off them for a week to ten days. They warned me that these bruises may come back to haunt me in future years. They did.

A few days later the district chief called me at home and asked if I could come in to the fire house - something about the paper work. When I got there he showed me my lengthy written report which had been labored over so long. Across it in red pencil was written, "I did not investigate this accident. I merely responded to expedite department matters. signed, Acting Chief of Department." I got the message - no one wanted to be involved with this one! So I spent a couple more hours making out new accident reports and indicated the highest ranked member of the department present was Lieutenant Cook. This made most everyone happy and able to inhale a deep relaxing breath.

Just as I was leaving the chief asked, "By the way lieutenant, did you order a private wrecker at the accident?" I replied, "Yes. Why?" "Well it seems the city got a bill for seventy-five dollars from a private wrecking company, and they want to know who was responsible for it." In disgust I said, "Tell them to put it on my tab. If I have to pay for a new ladder truck, a tractor trailer and three automobiles, what's seventy-five more dollars for a wrecker?"

Many months later we went to court for about a week. Most frustrating! The staff of lawyers the trucking company sent, plus a lawyer or two for each of the occupants of the other vehicles involved, made an impressive array against the single attorney the City Law Department provided, at the last minute. In spite of his late assignment he did a very respectable job defending the fire department and the city.

Strange, but during the intervening months the tractor-trailer must have doubled or tripled in length, judging by the number of plaintiffs who claimed it fell on their cars. Most of them were dismissed in the beginning when the true length of the truck was taken into consideration.

Like most court trials, it was very annoying to an honest citizen who might think he is in a "Hall of Justice." Objections flew fast and furious like a flock of frightened finches, with the justified ones being denied and the frivolous ones being sustained.

At one point when I was on the stand the judge threatened to hold me in contempt because I said I wouldn't answer a question "yes" or "no." The question was, "Since you were sitting beside the driver, did you try to stop the fire truck?" I wanted to explain that the driver was already standing on the foot brake pedal and the emergency brake is located on the floor to the left of his seat. It was completely out of my reach, unless I knocked the driver off his feet. Our city lawyer told me to answer the question one way or the other, and then on cross-examination he would bring out the logical explanation. This seemed logical, so I answered. When he tried to raise the point again, it was objected to as being irrelevant - and was sustained by his honor.

The trial dragged on for a few days and was settled really in no one's favor, which I guess was a moral victory, and probably normal for "Justice."

Everyone, except the firemen, got a little something and the city paid for the private wrecker. Also getting nothing was the man with the cut hand that we pulled out of his crushed car. It seems his car was registered in another state, and he had a local address for seven months. Massachusetts' law says you have six months to register your car in the state, so the court denied his personal injury and property damage claims and fined him for driving an unregistered vehicle.

Hoooooooray for Justice ! ! !

TIME FOR A CHANGE

(or, Variety Adds New Smokes To Life)

In the Fall of 1960 a vacancy for lieutenant opened on Engine 30 in West Roxbury. By then I could be considered some sort of a veteran officer being well into four years on Ladder 14, which in those days was some kind of a record for a lieutenant in the "dumping ground." Although every workday was still a challenge, the idea of transferring to a company closer to home did have some appeal.

At the same time there was a vacancy for captain on Ladder 25 in the same house. Captain Mullen was considering a transfer there himself. He liked working with men he knew and that helped him to convince me it would be a sensible move. His reasoning was that it would be a quiet place to study, since there were just too many other interesting facets that took up most of the time on Harvard Avenue. Believe me, those other facets, though demanding at times, had more appeal than studying. Herb was noncommittal but championed anything that motivated me to get in the books. Being a lieutenant was satisfying enough for me - but not for Herb. Besides no one snored in my room now, so that incentive was missing.

We each submitted a request for transfer, and on November second we both moved to West Roxbury. Captain Mullen was one of the Famous "96" and after nearly twenty-five years on busy companies he was satisfied with a slower pace, but right from the first tour worked I knew it was a mistake for me.

Anecdote:
*When I came home from work Bruce and Frank would always ask,
"Any runs?" Being interested in baseball they would jokingly add,
"Any hits?" This meant any fires. On this day one of them added,
"Any errors?" My reply was, "Yes, going to Engine 30."*

It took well over a year before another vacancy that interested
me opened up. Although Dot knew better than to attempt
influencing any decisions in regards to my work, she was pleased
with the transfer. Using loving wifely logic she reasoned to herself
that it would be less driving for me, especially in the winter, and
with fewer runs and fewer building fires there should be less
chance of injury. That logic is not necessarily true, as the
following suggests:

Joseph B. Sullivan of Ladder 19 was killed on December 3,
1947 when a ladder truck turned over while on a brake test.

Arthur Gately of Engine 30 was taken from a dump fire on
October 19, 1953 and died at about the time he reached the
hospital.

Arthur Spacone of Engine 2 was thrown from the apparatus
and killed on December 25, 1959 while responding to a False
Alarm.

James Sexton of Ladder 4 was thrown from the truck and
killed on December 7, 1962. He also had been a young spark at
Engine 53.

Lieutenant Joseph Downing of Engine 2 was burned at an
automobile fire on September 19, 1970 and died October 16th
from those injuries.

Edwin Foley of Engine 30 slipped off the apparatus and into a
snow bank on December 30, 1970 as the company responded to a
False Alarm. He was run over by the same piece of apparatus and
killed.

Jeremiah Collins of Engine 45 was killed at a small fire in Mt.
Hope Cemetery on July 4, 1971 when the small building partially
collapsed.

James Doneghey fell from Ladder 30 and died on November 5,
1971. He was a veteran of the old Egleston Square fire house.

Bernard Tully of Engine 30 was killed on January 22, 1974
when the apparatus was involved in an accident due to icy road
conditions.

   Although not a minor fire, Lieutenant George Gottwald of the Rescue-Pumper Unit died March 3, 1970 from injuries received at a three alarm Roxbury fire. His grandfather, also named George and also a lieutenant, of Engine 38-39, was killed on February 5, 1898, along with five firemen when a floor collapsed at a three alarm fire on Merrimac Street. The others killed were the captain and three men from Engine 38-39 and the chief of District 3.

Anecdote:

Engines 38 and Engine 39 were two companies housed in the same fire barn on Congress Street and were usually referred to as a unit. The railroad industry had considerable property in that section of the city and they were concerned about fire protection. To make certain there would always be fire apparatus available to respond to their buildings, they built the fire house, purchased half of the apparatus and donated them both to Boston, with the proviso that one of the companies would always remain in quarters to be available for response to their property. Following our entry into World War II and with the fear of air attacks on the East Coast an anti-aircraft gun was mounted on Engine 39's pump and publicity was given to the fact that the Boston Fire Department was prepared to do battle with any enemy.

Anecdote, Second Alarm:

That Congress Street fire house is now the Boston Sparks Association Fire Museum.

   The fact that I didn't find contentment on a less urban company is no reflection on the men who do. God in his wisdom did not make us all alike, and because of this fact it is easier to fill vacancies in every fire house. Besides, prior to going to so-called quiet companies, many men spent a lot of years on so-called busy companies and earned a little slower pace if they wanted it.

   Just because I wasn't happy with my Engine 30 assignment doesn't mean it was a total waste because some knowledge and experience can be gained anywhere in firefighting. First, distances between fire houses is greater than in the more congested neighborhoods - which means a longer wait for help. Second, there is greater distance between hydrants - which means longer lines of hose have to be laid which results in delays getting water on a fire. Third, firefighting is like any other job in that one tends to get a little rusty when the action isn't frequent. Fourth, a quiet fire house isn't always conducive to studying because human nature being what it is, one tends to put off the unpleasant task figuring there is plenty of time to get to it. Statistics bear this out as the majority of men promoted are from so called busy companies.

The list of reasons could go on for a while but I will cut it short with mention of dump fires. Prior to the DEQE and EPA stepping in and making a lot of rules and regulations relative to contamination of land, sea and air, the accepted practice was to dump all rubbish and waste products into large open areas. Either by design or accident these dumps frequently caught fire and reduction in the mass of dumped materials made room for more trash. Through the sixties, the three locations in the city that gave firemen the biggest dump headaches were Hallet Street in Dorchester, Barry's Ledge in Roslindale and Gardner Street in West Roxbury. There were many smaller locations in other sections of the city, but once fire started in any of these three major sites, they were likely to burn for days - and nights.

Nearby residents, and motorists using adjacent streets, were annoyed by the prodigious amounts of smelly smoke that flowed from the source and permeated their homes and reduced driving visibility to near zero. They were usually hundreds of feet or perhaps a mile away from the fire and found the conditions most annoying. They probably gave no thought to the firemen who were at that moment, and for hours before and after, working on top of the contaminated burning piles.

When a dump fire is large enough it can be attacked with deck guns and portable guns, but once the volume of fire is knocked down the only way to finish putting it out is by persistent use of hand lines. The fire will burrow deep down into the debris which may be twenty or more feet below the surface. As an area of the underground garbage is consumed by the fire, it creates a void which is likely to collapse by the sheer weight of the trash above it or by the movement of the water and firemen working on it.

Long lines of hose are needed to reach the fire and high pressures are required at the nozzles to force water into the dense mass. SOP is to locate a hot spot as evidenced by extreme heat and smoke belching forth, then forcing the nozzle into the fire at that point and flooding it until the smoke subsides. The line is then advanced to the next obvious hot spot and the ritual repeated. In the case of an extensive dump fire there may be a dozen or more fire companies tied up at that location for days just doing just this. In such cases back-hoes and front end loaders would be brought in either to uncover the fire or blanket it with dirt or other noncombustible solids.

A side attraction to dump fires is the wild life that is forced from their domiciles. No matter how hot the weather the men know they must keep their hip boots pulled up to the maximum height lest a rat mistake his leg for a tree trunk and decide to take refuge at a higher level. Some of those four-legged beasts with long tails were bigger than cats and on occasion the police would stand by with their guns. Unofficially, some companies that regularly responded to dump fires would bring along a twenty-two caliber rifle and assign a member to ward off the refuge seeking frightened rodents.

An added hazard was operating in the dark on uneven terrain. The nature of the battle involved advancing hose lines well into the dump and beyond areas recently uncovered and extinguished. Often the underground fire would flare up again and break through the surface. Then it was not uncommon to have the fire burn through the hose and the men would lose the water. That was like being caught behind enemy lines without ammunition. Many firemen have suffered broken limbs by falling into holes caused by collapsed fire tunnels. Often times they were burned before being rescued by their comrades. Spouses take note that quiet companies do have their moments and are not always the safest companies.

Hopefully, this is a better picture of what is taking place a long way from that street where motorists grumble because there was little visibility. The hundreds of trucks that daily pick up all kinds of refuse from every imaginable source in the city and deposit it all at one location so firemen can spend hours inhaling the toxic smokes are doing these firemen no favor. Much of the smoke contains multiple carcinogens that add up to a time bomb in the men's lungs, but they do the job without complaining. There should be no wonders why these men can face the paymaster with a clear conscience on Fridays, even if it was slow that particular week. This should also help to give a better understanding of why firemen die ten years before their time. The rules and regulations of the EPA and the DEQE came too late for too many firemen.

By June of 1962 I had enough of being assigned close to home and going to the Gardner Street dump too frequently. There came a vacancy for lieutenant at Engine 28 in Jamaica Plain and I applied for it. The transfer was effective June 26 and I was back in the same district with my beloved Engine 42.

When you voluntarily seek a transfer you wonder for a while if it was the right move, and although later years would prove my transfer to Engine 28 was a stroke of genius, I had serious doubts the first few weeks. Being the junior lieutenant again, I would spend my first day and night on Engine 28 (Groups 1 and 2) and the second day and night on Ladder 10 (Groups 2 and 3), but due to vacations my first few weeks were on the engine all the time.

That first Night before the Fourth tour a week later I should have been on Ladder 10 - where I belonged. The evening started out just fine. I was back in the district where I had responded to so many bonfires over the Fourths in my sparking years and the first ten years they paid me. It was good to be back in familiar territory and having a busy evening.

Shortly after midnight Fire Alarm sent Engine 55 to Henshaw Terrace off Corey Street in West Roxbury. The location was closer to Engine 30's house but they were at another fire. The thought went through my mind that if it was a building fire, it would have a good start while Engine 55 was traveling the extra distance - but they don't have building fires in West Roxbury. I knew that from being there for a year and a half!

When Engine 55 arrived on scene the officer reported fire showing and minutes later ordered a Working Fire on Box 2821. It was 0031 hours and Ladder 10 left for the fire. I wished I was with them - and would have been too except for vacations. A minute and a half later a second alarm was struck and Engine 28 was on the way. In the Red Book was a section designated,

"Points to Be Considered by Officer Personnel While Responding to Multiple Alarms" and point 6 in the sub-section marked "Relative to Surrounding Neighborhood" listed "Accessibility of buildings." From my time spent in West Roxbury I knew Henshaw Terrace was a dead end off Corey Street. I figured most of the apparatus would approach the fire by way of Centre and Corey Streets. I knew Hastings Street was the next street running parallel with Corey and that there was a hydrant a short way up on the left. As we proceeded to the fire my strategy was clear. We would bypass the fire and take the hydrant on Hastings Street, run a big line through a yard and over the fence to arrive right in front of the fire building, ready to go to work as soon as we ordered water for our line.

Everything went as planned and the deputy chief in charge was surprised and delighted to see Engine 28 come over the fence with the big line as the fire was taking off and presenting a major exposure problem. I ordered the line charged and as the water arrived we began knocking down the exposure fire. Our line was very effective at that point and the deputy expressed high praise for my ingenuity in sneaking in the back way. But then the sparking "gremlins" must have arrived. We had run one side, or five hundred feet of hose, which was enough to get the line into the house and at that point we would reduce it to inch and a half hose. Just as things were going well, the first length of our hose burst - wetting the deputy. I sent a man back to get another length of two and a half inch hose and the Hose Clamp. The deputy said, "Forget the hose and Hose Clamp. Get a Burst Hose Jacket."

I ordered the man to get the Burst Hose Jacket - - and also the hose clamp and a length of hose. I sent a second man with him. When they came back, I wanted to clamp the hose and replace the burst length, but the deputy said it would take too long, so use the Burst Jacket. I knew it was hopeless because the things only work in Drill School - never at fires when they are needed!

One of the men tried to apply the jacket but the pressure was so great coming from the hole that all he succeeded in doing was getting himself soaked. A second man tried it with the same results. I knew I could do no better, but with the deputy watching I at least had to give it a try, and that is how I too got soaked.

We were the ones who were hot and wet but the deputy was the one who was boiling. Without our line passing water, the overlapping fire had taken off in the two and a half story wooden duplex, and to further complicate the situation, there was a report that a female occupant in the right side unit was unaccounted for. Other engine companies were bringing in lines from the Corey Street end (not the clever approach we used) and the trucks were laddering the building using ground ladders. The fire had extended from the right to the left side unit in the cockloft.

After watching our fruitless efforts with the jacket, the deputy yelled that he would show us how to use the appliance. He too got watered down as the burst hole continued to grow without its "jacket," but it didn't stop him from boiling.

While the chief was talking to some neighbors about the missing occupant, I took the opportunity to tell my company to quickly clamp the hose and replace the burst length. Just as we removed the burst length, but before it could be replaced, the deputy spotted our actions and ordered us not to replace the length as it would take too long. Instead we were to put the nozzle on the shortened line and advance the line up a ladder to the attic of the left unit. I protested that we didn't have enough hose but at that point the chief wasn't interested in facts. One of the companies had just reported to him by radio that they had found the body of the lady occupant.

With regards to "time," I have learned that "too long" spent at the right time, somehow saves time in the long run. In this case we were able to get about half way up the ladder when we ran out of hose, as was to be expected. The deputy was yelling for us to "Get in there!" and I was yelling back that we didn't have enough hose! We couldn't go up, and the deputy chief wouldn't let us go down for more hose. Some might say we had reached an impasse, but that wasn't the case because right or wrong, the chief is always right!

There was a young spark that I had come to know when I was on Engine 30. He was watching the incident unfold and as the deputy and I engaged in a shouting match (which a news photographer caught on film and graced the morning edition with) he had the presence of mind and initiative to bail me out of the mess. On his own he went to an engine and brought back a fifty foot length of inch and a half hose and a play pipe. He passed it up the ladder and we quickly attached it to our shortened line and were able to get up and into the attic - out of sight and ear-shot of the deputy. Once in position, we opened the ceiling and then did a respectable job of driving the cock loft fire back into the right unit - but the deputy didn't see any thing good we did that night. There was one more episode to the story that night, but it is one of those stories mentioned in the beginning that is better left untold.

Anecdote:
That young spark took the Entrance Exam when he was old enough and when I went to Engine 25 as captain in 1967 he was one of the members of my company. He was a good student and today he is District Chief Edmund Maiorana of District 5. Thanks Ted for that timely assist long ago - when it was most needed - and most appreciated.

The five years spent in Jamaica Plain were not as spectacular as the years in Brighton/Allston, or maybe I had just gotten used to being an officer. There were plenty of fires. Some went well and some were snafu, like the one above, but it all added up to experience, for which there is no substitute!

It was while I was at Engine 28 that our fourth child, son Jonathan, put in his appearance. The importance of manpower to run lines and raise ladders has already been indicated. To let a man leave the station while on duty usually involves a serious situation at home because the shortage of even one man makes the work load heavier for those remaining. I was working the Night Tour of December 11, 1963 on Engine 28 and Captain Jim Finn was on Ladder 10. Captain McLaughlin was acting chief in District 9. I had seen Captain Finn at Roll Call but not since then. Shortly before 2000 hours Dot called to say I better get home quick because things were happening.

I knocked on the chief's door and when admitted explained that my wife was in labor and asked permission to go and take her to the hospital. He stared at me for a few seconds and then in his flowery articulation said, "Come on lieutenant. Can't you think up an original excuse to get out of work? Captain Finn just gave me the same cock and bull story and I let him go." Needless to add, he sent me on my way to the hospital.

I paused just long enough at the house to pick up Dot, which was somewhat essential. She was most uncomfortable as the desk clerk insisted she needed her Blue Cross, Social Security, telephone and a lot of other numbers before she could be admitted. Between a couple of contractions, which were then about ten seconds apart, Dot asked, "What numbers does the baby have to give before it can be admitted - - or expelled?"

Matter of factly the admittance clerk said, "Well if you are that uncomfortable dearie, I suppose your husband can give me the information - if he knows it." I did know it and Dot, matter of factly, gave birth to our fourth child, just as they wheeled her into the Delivery Room.

Stopping at home again just long enough to tell the kids they had a baby brother, I was back in the fire house shortly after 2130 hours. Captain Finn's wife wasn't as prompt in presenting him with a son (later that night) so he got to stay out longer - or maybe it is just that rank does have its privilege.

When Jonathan was on the way, we realized we needed more space at home to accommodate a new baby. The solution was to either move to a bigger house or add on to the present one. The latter seemed more to our financial ability and so I drew up plans for a twenty-four by twenty-four foot addition. It included two large bedrooms with large closets, a bathroom with double sinks and a small hall with a closet. Underneath was a two-car garage.

In due time a building permit was obtained, but the estimates given by two contractors were out of the question so we decided to build it ourselves - with the help of a few firemen. The job was tackled with fear and trepidation, but the foundation was dug on October 31, 1963 and then we had to go through with it.

I had hopes of getting the roof on and the sides closed in before winter but didn't quite make it as the snow season arrived with Jonathan on December eleventh. I worked on the roof during the day before going in to work the Night Tour, and planned to finish it the next day. Although it was snowing when our tour ended, I rushed home and went to work on the roof. After slipping a couple times, common sense prevailed. It was stupid to risk getting hurt with Dot in the hospital tending our new family. So tools were put away for the winter. In the spring, work resumed. One fireman delivered the lumber and windows, another the insulation, a third did the electrical work and a fourth provided the plumbing. In the end it cost us less than half of the contractors' bids, and their estimates did not include carpeting and a few other extras we put in. The fire house family is really something!

Back at the paying job, the Jamaica Plain fire barn had been built in the nineteenth century and was three stories high. Somewhere in the mid sixties it was decided to take off the third floor and modernize the rest of the house. The alterations specified new lockers, toilets, ceramic showers, tiled floors, painting, outside lettering and a new side entrance, as well as removing the top floor.

Neither the firemen nor the tax payers were consulted on the project and the designers must have been fans of Sesame Street. Although the original house was probably red brick Federalist, the front facade was covered with baked enamel green metal panels. On the new lowered roof were placed three dimensional stainless steel block letters a foot high, indicating it was the home of LADDER 10 and ENGINE 28.

To complete the modernized monstrosity, the plans called for an L shaped entrance partition connected to the fire house wall adjacent to the existing door. It was made of cement blocks about six feet high with about a twelve inch opening before it was capped with a rounded sloping green fiber glass roof which gave it a pagoda like appearance. The twelve inch opening defeated any intention to provide protection from the weather as rain or snow poured in as one waited for the door to open. All this entry did was eliminate two parking spaces. The men referred to it as the Chinese Outhouse because many nights it was mistaken for that type of a facility by patrons of the local pubs who felt the call of nature and feared they couldn't make it home in time.

When the project began it was discovered that the fire barn had been built with a hung third floor, which meant that the floor was suspended from the roof supports by means of pipes. It was a tricky process, or so they said, to remove this hung floor and it would cost a lot more than budgeted. The result was that there was enough money for the ugly appurtenances to be added to the visible outside, but not enough to provide the unseen inside alterations which would have made it easier to maintain and more comfortable for the men. They did remove the black soapstone sinks and replace them with white china but there were no new lockers or showers. In place of ceramic tile, a new coat of cheap paint was applied and the wooden, mop catching, floors remained.

One evening we received a shipment of diesel fuel. The fill pipe was on the same side of the barn as the Chinese Outhouse. The regular driver, who was familiar with the delivery location, had been out sick for several months and it was his first trip to the fire house since his return to work. It was during his extended absence that the Outhouse had been added. He pulled his truck up in front of the fire house as of old, put it in reverse and whipped the truck back to the fill pipe, as he had done countless times before.

Oops !   C-R-A-S-H !   The Chinese Outhouse had new ventilation!

With the noise and the shaking of the house I went down to investigate the obvious. The men thought it quite humorous but the driver was very upset as it spoiled his driving record and there would be heck to pay for the accident.

"What accident?" I asked, seizing on the opportunity to get our parking spaces back.

"The building addition. I never even saw it," he apologized.

"And neither did we" I answered. "Deliver the fuel and get on your way."

He went away happy with his driving record still in tact and as soon as he left there was a long ring for all men to report to the main floor for a drill. Tonight's subject would be "Use of the battering ram and other wrecking tools." It was a cool night and the men were very attentive. Within an hour the drill was over - and there was a neat pile of building blocks stacked in back of the barn, along with some useless fiberglass panels.

Shortly after 2300 hours the district chief returned to quarters, and shortly after that I was called to his room.

"One question. What happened to the Outhouse?"

"What Outhouse?" I answered with a question.

"Dismissed! - - And leave room for my car."

We had our two parking spaces back and everyone lived happily ever after - except maybe not the architect from Sesame Street.

The fire department constantly monitors conditions in the city that might effect the ability of apparatus to respond promptly and safely. In 1963 several bridges in the South End and Back Bay were closed during the construction of the extension to the Massachusetts Turnpike. To assure quick response in those areas, during the period from April to November, the department established a temporary Engine 6, to be located at the Fire Alarm Office in the Fenway. It was fully equipped and manned by a detailed crew of one lieutenant and three firemen.

Being a department wide detail I won it twice. The first was a Day Tour and the second a Night Tour. Although all the detailed men were trained and capable firefighters, it does take a little practice to function as an efficient team and one tour of duty together is not long enough to perfect it. The operators at Fire Alarm tried to reassure us by pointing out that Engine 6 was just an extra engine, and usually the last to arrive, so most duty was just assisting those already on scene.

Guess what! The first run on my Day Tour was about noontime and we went to Beacon Street at Audubon Circle (Box 232). Even before we pulled in, first, there was the distinct smell of wood smoke as we moved down Park Drive. Coming into the Circle we were met by heavy dirty brown smoke pushing from the second and third floors of a building on the far side of Beacon Street. Where were all the companies we were supposed to assist when we arrived last? Makeshift company or not, we got a big line into the second floor and went to work. When we got back to Fire Alarm I chided the operators for their reassurances and they assured me it was the first and probably last time it would ever happen.

Some weeks later was my second Engine 6 detail and it happened again. The crew was different but even the Box location was the same, Beacon Street at Audubon Circle. As soon as we left Fire Alarm, about two in the morning, there was the aromatic smell of burning wood in the air and we knew we were going to work again. This time, fire was coming out the second floor front windows of a brick apartment house on the near corner of Beacon and Park Drive - and for the second time Engine 6 was the first company to arrive. Detailed or not, we again got a big line into the second floor and went to work. When we got back to Fire Alarm there were no further assurances from the operators and they accused me of being the jinx. They sounded like District Chief Ainsworth, as previously reported. Oh well, Friday would be payday.

In those days Engine 28 was considered a "Home Guard" which meant it seldom left the district. Since Proposition 2-1/2 and the loss of nearly a third of the City's fire companies, there are no more "Home Guards."

On May 22, 1964 there occurred the "Bellflower Street Conflagration" (Box 7251). This fire involved nineteen buildings, mostly wooden three deckers, on Bellflower, Dorset, Howell and Boston Streets. Engine 28 was one of the fifty-five Engine Companies and ten ladder Companies that responded and I was glad the "Home Guard" connotation had been broken. We were closer to the last than the first to arrive, but that didn't matter, as there was plenty of fire for everyone. I would have hated to miss the biggest fire in Boston in a long time. It was almost unbelievable to see so many buildings burning in a major city, but the fire service is full of surprises and there is no room for complacency.

Fortunately, fires of this magnitude are rare and while they are a catastrophe to the owners and occupants, they are a dream come true for the news media who can look sharp and on the ball as they have plenty of time to record the happenings. For the firefighters doing the work, and the chiefs in charge, the early stages are a nightmare. As the fire intensifies and grows, the radiated heat produced by it reaches out and involves additional buildings. The advancing heat dries out the wood and raises its temperature to the ignition point where the entire exterior of the structure suddenly erupts in flames. The heat is so intense that within minutes the fire enters the building and consumes the interior as well.

First requirement is to cut off the fire's extension by use of heavy stream appliances, deck guns and ladder pipes. Large volumes of water are needed fast to cool down the fire and break up the radiated and convection heat.

Sometimes the strategy has to be to give up an additional building, or more, to give the fire department enough time to take a stand at a workable distance from the main fire. Wind speed and direction are important factors that have to be considered at all fires by the chief in charge. It is exciting to watch the firemen's devotion to duty as they unselfishly and without thought to their own safety rush to place in motion those actions which will eventually allow them to triumph over the enemy. The only good feature about conflagrations, from the firemen's point of view, is that there is little overhauling to do. This is because the super heated flames consume about everything flammable, and leaves little - neither building nor contents. The thousands of times I have left a fire and returned to quarters, and then to a home intact, my heart has gone out to the victims who have just lost something - or perhaps everything.

On the night of October 1, 1964 one of those too frequent disasters struck the Boston Fire Department. Box 1671 was struck for a fire on Trumbull Street in the South End and in a matter of minutes there were five alarms on it and five firemen dead. In this fire it was only a matter of minutes between the time the two lieutenants and three firefighters left their three respective fire houses, arrived at the fire scene and began working, and a wall collapsed snuffing out their lives. Also killed by the crashing wall was a spark who was taking pictures. It all happened so quickly that there was no time for Deputy Chief Fred Clauss, or anyone else, to observe "Factors or Conditions Which May Indicate or Influence the Possibility of Partial or Total Collapse of a Building" (Red Book, page 185). There were none!

We now know that in buildings erected in the South End around the turn of the century, the mortar used to hold the bricks was of a consistency that is affected by heat. For some reason, and fortunately, it was only used in the South End. That fire was a traumatic event for Deputy Chief Clauss and one he never really got over. Shortly afterwards he came down with cancer and died. Today some doctors suspect that a traumatic incident can trigger cancer in some individuals. It would appear that Fred's case was a classic example of this. Freddy Clauss began his career on Ladder 30 in my sparking days, so I had a special attachment to him and empathized with him through it all.

On March 29, 1966 I ordered a multiple alarm struck for the first time in my career. It had been a busy warm spring day with a lot of brush fires for the Day Tour. I had just relieved the officer on Ladder 10 when Box 2541 was struck. We were the first company in and as we turned from Green into Washington Street there was a three decker well involved in fire and spreading to a second one at the corner of Woodside Avenue. I called Fire Alarm on the radio and ordered them to "Strike a Second Alarm on Box 2541."

All we carried on the truck was three hundred feet of inch and a half hose. We quickly connected this directly to a hydrant and began hitting the overlapping fire as best we could in our attempt to stop the fire from spreading further. As mentioned before, it was a busy day and available apparatus was scarce. As the fire spread to another three decker and I was looking for an engine company to supply water in volume, the second company to arrive was Ladder 3 from Harrison Avenue. Lieutenant John Campbell was in charge and they too ran an inch and half line and we ordered the Third Alarm. Eventually the engine companies started to arrive, but before it was over five buildings were involved and four alarms were struck.

In early 1967 we had a series of fires in the Roslindale Square section of the city. One of them was in a wallpaper and paint store on Washington Street just beyond Bexley (Box 2631). The fire started in the rear of the long store and Engine 28's first assignment was to take a big line to the second floor in the front to cut off any fire extension to the upper floor. There was none so we moved our line back to the street. The fire was aggressively advancing toward the front of the store and engine companies were setting up lines on the sidewalk to hold it. Engine 28 had reason to prove itself and this seemed like the opportune time. While the companies on the sidewalk opened their lines to protect us, we took our line through the broken out display window and began advancing it toward the rear of the store where the fire was roaring. Heated paint cans were popping their covers and adding their contents to the several inches of water accumulating on the floor.

About half way into the store we ran out of hose and yelled back for "more line." Ordinarily, when this call goes out there is a little scurrying out on the street and about four more feet of hose is advanced. On this night there must have been a small army that got on our line in the street, because suddenly the stiff hose moved forward and continued its advance for about twenty-five feet. We who were on the play pipe and hanging onto the line were knocked to the floor and pushed the distance submerged in the water and paint blend that was then nearly knee deep. We were wearing All-Service masks that became soaked and thus useless.

Once the line stopped moving, we picked ourselves out of the water. We were twenty-five feet deeper into the building and twenty-five feet closer to the advancing fire. All we could do was hold the gained ground and direct our line ahead into the fire while taking a beating without our masks. Paint cans continued popping around and over us but slowly we began to win the battle. This was with the help of a couple engine companies that were advancing their lines from the rear of the store. They had been pushing the fire toward us. It so happens the paint we had been showered with was exterior green oil base paint. We were green from the top of our helmets to the bottom of our fire coats and boots. With the fire knocked down I reported out to the deputy. He took one look and said, "You did a great job - for a green lieutenant."

Before leaving the fire scene, the store owner gave us several gallons of paint thinner so we could wash the green paint out of our hair before second and third washes with conventional soap shampoo. Some men used the thinner to cut the paint on their fire gear making sure to wash it well with soap and water before hanging it up to dry.

When we came back to work the next night, our captain who had worked the Day Tour, had new helmets and fire coats waiting for those of us who had worked the night before. He may not have been the most popular officer but he was experienced and knew the solvent saturated gear would be a hazard when exposed to heat again. I still have that old helmet as a reminder of when I was a green lieutenant.

Anecdote:

On February 23, a few nights after the above fire, there was a fire on Dennis Street in Roxbury. Firefighter John Reilly, then of Engine 13, had been at the paint store fire and had washed his gear with solvent before cleaning it with soap and water. As his company advanced a big line up a ground ladder and through a window into a room that was charged with fire, his fire coat burst into flames and he was burned severely. It was later determined that the heat of the fire vaporized the solvent residue on his fire coat raising it to the ignition point.

The fact that Firefighter Reilly was spared from paying the supreme sacrifice that night was undoubtedly due to the quick action of a new man, FFOP Joseph Gaffney of the same company. Joe pulled him from the room and slid down the ladder with him. He was highly commended in General Order 10, series of 1967, and was given the John E. Fitzgerald Medal for the Most Meritorious Act of the year.

As pointed out earlier, some men serve their whole career without being so honored and Joe was thrust into a hero's role while still wet behind the ears. Those who know Joe would agree with the paraphrased words of the immortal Winston Churchill when he said, "This was his finest hour!"

Years later Joe frequently filled in as my Aide in District 3. He later paid the supreme sacrifice himself, dying of cancer while still an active member. "Greater love hath no man........."

I was still enjoying being a lieutenant and Herb was still nagging me to be a captain. It is strange how obscure events in life can have a major effect in changing the course of one's history. A series of just such arcane events were about to begin in my life and Herb would be ecstatic, in his reserved demeanor.

Bellflower Street Conflagration, May 22, 1964.

Trumbull Street, October 1, 1964.
Five firemen killed when building collapsed shortly after their
arrival.

TIE, NOAH, MA

(or, You Can't Get Promoted Unless You Are On A List)

Through the Depression years and into the forties, the pay scale in the Boston Fire Department remained pretty much stagnant. A Man On Probation started at sixteen hundred dollars a year and on each of his first five anniversaries he received a hundred dollar increase so that starting his sixth year he was full paid at twenty-one hundred dollars a year. A lieutenant was paid twenty-five hundred and captain twenty-seven hundred. The big jump was to district chief which paid thirty-seven hundred dollars and a deputy received forty-two hundred. All worked the same eighty-four hour week.

When the cost of living began to escalate, the city fathers opened the treasury chest barely enough to let light in and doled out raises of one or two hundred dollars. These were "across the board" raises which meant that all ranks received the same amount and those in City Hall made sure the increases didn't become a yearly ritual. When repeated requests for raises fell on deaf ears at City Hall, the Firefighter's Union on several occasions went to the public for a raise via the ballot box. Each time an appreciative electorate responded with a resounding affirmative vote. These voted raises were also "across the board" which meant the four hundred dollars a year raise to make lieutenant and two hundred more to make captain ceased to be an incentive to study. A few months of moonlighting could produce a better financial return and often included Social Security as a fringe benefit.

In spite of this logical long range reasoning, the truism still held that if you wanted bugles you had to be on a list. By 1966 I was approaching ten years as a lieutenant and Herb was approaching twenty years of nagging. If the same pattern of ten years in each rank was maintained, I would have forty years on the job before studying for deputy. That would be great for experience but at that point it wouldn't matter.

Due to normal attrition, promotions were happening a little more frequently. In September 1965 Captain Finn was promoted to district chief and left Ladder 10. The vacancy wasn't filled until August 1966 when Captain John Campbell was transferred to the company. John was a Ladder 30 man from the old Egleston Square days and I had worked with his wife at Canada Dry Ginger Ale before I knew John. He had made captain in June - in fact his entire list of twenty-two lieutenants were promoted between June and November of 1966. This never happened before and it got me thinking a little, and Herb pestering a lot.

Getting prepared to take a fire promotional exam is not an overnight adventure. In those days, between the Promotional Red Book, the Crosby-Fiske (now the NFPA Handbook), Shepard's Book of Hydraulics, Massachusetts Fire Prevention Regulations, Laws, the 300 plus Underwriter's Bulletins, past exams and an assortment of other pertinent publications, it took a couple months just to line up the study materials. Most students then figured a minimum of six to nine months, or more, of studying ten to fourteen hours a day to consider themselves almost prepared. In the matter of laws, regulations and the Red Book lists in particular, your answer didn't have to be word for word, but, if it was you were sure of a hundred percent on the question. Most of the students could recite hundreds of pages word for word - and those were the men who topped lists.

At that time the Captain's Exam consisted of writing a Report on a given subject and then ten questions, essay type, which included the fire problem. Your mark was based on the Report being worth 2, the Practical Questions 10 and Experience 3, for a total of 15. The Report mark was based on writing, content, grammar and spelling.

The next Captain's Exam should have been in June 1967. As we worked together one night in November 1966 John asked if I was going to take the exam - and why not, because you can't get promoted unless you are on the list! He went on to say, and then demonstrate, that he could teach me in fifteen minutes to memorize and repeat word for word the twenty "Precautions to Be Taken Concerning Operations to Be Performed on a Roof." I had strong reservations about his boast, but he was right and went on to prove it. To further demonstrate, we did the twenty-one points of "Advantages of Inch and a Half Hose" in another fifteen minutes. When I got up in the morning and could still recite the twenty and twenty-one point lists word for word - I was convinced and curiously enthusiastic.

It was all done with word association, by using a list of a hundred words starting with TIE, NOAH, MA. I couldn't wait for the next tour to work with John. He had told me to review the two lists and when I gave them back to him the next tour we worked, he was convinced of my sincerity and taught me a couple more lists. This was great and I started giving serious thought to studying. It would be close, but if I spent the rest of 1966 lining up material and then gave it my all till June, with John's help - well maybe there was hope. John wasn't so enthusiastic. He wasn't going to commit himself for seven or eight months, even for old time sake, but he would get me started.

Things were progressing nicely until we worked the Night Tour of December 23. I arrived at work first and read the General Orders. It announced the Captain's Examination would be February 18, 1967. Minimum Weekly Salary, $148.50. Maximum, $188.50. Less than two months away! No way Jose!

When John came in I was watching the news. "Come on, you will never make captain watching TV," he said.
"Forget it, read tonight's Orders," I replied in disgust.
He disappeared into his room to read the Orders, and then called me.
"It's a tough break, but it's a surprise to everyone and you are all in the same boat. I think you can do it in two months. I said I didn't want to get tied up for seven months but for seven weeks I'll help - if you do your part."

There were serious doubts in my mind but we stepped up the pace to several lists every tour we worked together. I reviewed, read and listened to taped lessons for sixteen to eighteen hours a day while I ate or worked around the house. Despite my long hours and longer efforts, February 17 arrived at least ahead of my schedule. The night before an exam one is supposed to relax, go to a movie. Do anything but study or look at books. Instead I learned another couple lists and some more law and went to bed late and thus was totally unprepared to take an examination.

Saturday morning, February 18, 1967 arrived and shortly after seven, as I was eating breakfast, my scanner beeped out downtown Box 1441. Within six minutes five alarms were struck for the "Crawford-Hollidge" department store fire. I was tempted to forget the exam and go to the fire, but common sense prevailed.

We took our places in the exam room at the High School of Commerce on Warren Street in Roxbury and filled out the necessary forms that proved our attendance. The monitor then said he had an announcement to make. "All of those in the room who are here to take the Captain's Exam for Boston are excused. Seems there is a big fire in Boston and some of the men who were planning to take this exam are at the fire and cannot get off in time to get here. The exam is canceled for Boston and you will be notified by mail of a new date for your exam." Prayers that I hadn't even dared to pray were answered!

There was a loud cheer by the lieutenants from Boston and we all went to the Crawford-Hollidge fire. To this day I still tip my hat when I pass the corner of Tremont Street and Temple Place, site of the Crawford-Hollidge parking lot.

I hoped our exam would now be put off until June where it belonged, but Civil Service rescheduled it for three weeks later on March 11th. During those twenty-one days I maintained and then increased my rigid studying schedule. The only difference was that this time I closed the books at noon on Friday and went to the movies the night before the exam. While eating breakfast the morning of the exam I didn't put on my fire radio - lightning isn't likely to strike twice.

Back in the now familiar exam room we completed writing our Reports and they were collected. After a ten minute break for nervous visits to the men's room, the Question Booklets were placed on our desks and on the given signal, we were allowed to open them. A quick scan of the questions and I knew Herb's nagging, and our joint prayers had been answered. Three of the questions had two parts and these plus four of the other questions fell into the TIE, NOAH, MA category. I could answer seven of the questions word for word, or close to it, and the other two were reasonably familiar. The fire problem likewise held no real surprises and in relaxed confidence I put my answers in writing and went home to wait the official results.

In those days, Civil Service followed a set pattern. Two months from the exam date the marks would be mailed out and you then had seventeen days to visit the State House to see your exam and how it was marked. If you thought you had good reason to appeal any questions it had to be done in writing within those seventeen days - and there were no exceptions. You could bank on the List being established six months from the exam date and only then were the official standings made known. The List was good for two years.

In the fire department, the day the marks on any exam arrive in the mail the telephones, both within the department and among the exam takers at home, begin to ring off the wall. The purpose of all the dialing is to establish an unofficial but usually accurate standing of the students. It took a couple days and the suspense could be nerve wracking as participants inched ahead, or fell behind, as new marks became known.

In the case of my Captain's Exam, the marks arrived in the mail on Saturday, May 13. I was scheduled to work the Night Tour and picked up my mail on the way to the fire house. As I pulled into the parking lot, Captain Campbell and most of the men were waiting for me - or rather for my mark. They had about every mark except mine and on their list Lieutenant Frank Sullivan of Ladder 16 was number one with a mark of 90.55%.

Captain Campbell anxiously asked.
"What is your mark?"
"I don't know."
"Didn't you get it in the mail today?"
"Yes."
"Well what is it then?"
"I don't know."
"What do you mean you don't know?"
"I just picked it up at the house and since you did all the work for me, I figured you should get the mark."

I handed him the unopened envelope. John was dumbfounded for a change, but he proceeded to make a big production out of opening the news while nearly a dozen men anxiously watched. He carefully tore off the end of the envelope and slipped out the white piece of paper and said, "First you look in the upper right hand corner to see if you passed."

Doing so, he added, "Well you passed. Then you cast your eyes a little lower on the paper for the actual mark." He stared for a moment and then yelped! "You're number one! You're number one! You son-of-gun (not quite the exact words), you got a 91.33%."

The confidence, and thanks to God, that I felt in the exam room was born out. My mark on the Report was 91. Of the nine questions I had three 100s, one 96, one 95, and two 90s. The other two were a 75 and a 70. On the fire problem the mark was 92. With Experience it all added up to the 91.33 %. Hooray for TIE, NOAH, MA!

Then the phone calls began all over again, and in a short time everyone who cared about the list knew Cook had topped it and they adjusted their lists.

In my euphoria that followed, Box 2435 at Brookside Avenue and Cornwall Street was struck and both companies responded. It was a False Alarm. After we had checked the area, Captain Campbell got on the apparatus radio and called the Fire Alarm Office. "On orders of Captain Cook, send the All Out on Box 2435."

I figured everyone in the department would be thinking the same thing! What an egotistical guy this Cook is! Here he is, probably number one, but already he has himself promoted and referring to himself on the air as a captain. John and the rest of the men thought it a big joke.

When we got back from the run I called Herb and told him the marks were out - - "and a guy named Cook is number one on the list." In the department I was egotistical; but Herb was ecstatic, and I am sure a little proud of his kid brother.

By October rumors were rampant that some more promotions were going to be made but rumors are always plentiful in the fire department - something like the military. When I drove into the parking lot for the Night Tour on October 25, some of the men were standing at the door and waved me away. On going into the fire house, they told me I had been promoted. I told them I hadn't signed "The Book" yet, but they showed me General Order 44, series 1967, that came out that day announcing promotions that took effect at 8 A.M. that morning.

That was the good news. The bad news was that I was detailed to Engine 14 for the night. I went in to see the district chief and jokingly protested that it was not department policy, or tradition, to detail a captain to another company. He studied the Orders and said, "You're right captain. I see Vinnie Kane made lieutenant today and he is working tonight. So as captain, you detail him to Engine 14." Hurrah for tradition and policy, as I had to begin cleaning out my locker.

The next General Order that came out listed our new assignments, which would take effect a week from Wednesday on November 1st. Mine was to Engine 25 on Oliver Street downtown. Bob MacInnes went to Engine 10 also in District 3.

Anecdote:
Lieutenant Dennis Sullivan, also of Engine 28 was likewise promoted to captain that day. A bit of trivia is that for a week there were three captains assigned to Engine 28 - Raymond Favret, Paul Cook and Dennis Sullivan.

On November 1, 1967 I took over as Company Commander of Engine 25 and began to learn an altogether different aspect of firefighting. It was a two piece Engine company and one of the few "foam" companies, which meant there was extra equipment carried on the pump so that a heavy blanket of foam could be applied on flammable liquid fires either by a regular nozzle or by a bazooka. The wagon was a High Pressure unit which had two large long chrome guns mounted on the deck. Six big lines could be connected to feed water into each gun, so together they could throw nearly three thousand gallons or more of water a minute - an impressive sight and a potent power. They were capable of raising roof tiles or knocking down walls, not to mention breaking windows or pushing over anything not well secured. A third gun could deliver an additional seven hundred gallons a minute.

While I was captain of the company the department added another piece of apparatus known as "Special Unit 1" and assigned it to Engine 25. It carried two 300 pound tanks of dry chemical powder, and the propelling equipment, for use primarily on electric and manhole fires. Between the three specialized pieces of equipment we picked up a few additional runs that we might otherwise have missed - and I still hated to miss runs.

Now I was also in the High Pressure District. Throughout the downtown area there are just over five hundred hydrants that are on separate water mains and there is nothing but hydrants on the mains - no domestic connections. At that time the system could be supplied with water from one of the two High Pressure Stations. The HP Station on Kneeland Street supplied pressure by steam pumps. The other HP Station on Atlantic Avenue supplied pressure by means of electric pumps. When installed in 1921 the system was also capable of taking sea water from the harbor and passing it through the special pumps and mains.

Pumps are not connected to these special hydrants but four big lines can be directly connected to the four independent outlets and controlled individually. Static pressure in the system is about fifty pounds but once a box was struck in the High Pressure District the pumps were put into operation with an initial pressure of one hundred and fifty pounds. By the time men and apparatus arrived at the box location this high pressure was waiting for them at the five hundred plus hydrants. For this reason the pumps on the apparatus were not needed at these hydrants. As a back up, the apparatus pumps would connect to a regular post hydrant or a Lowry hydrant.

Anecdote:
The reason the high pressure pumps were started at a hundred and fifty pounds pressure was that we still had Water Towers that had been in service since the late nineteenth century. Some of these were spring raised and some hydraulic or water pressure raised. The latter required a hundred and twenty five pounds water pressure to raise them so the station pumps were started at

twenty five pounds higher to allow for any friction loss in the system. If needed, the station pressures could be increased to a maximum of three hundred pounds and this was usually done in twenty five pound increments. Today they are started at a hundred pounds and are seldom raised higher than two hundred and twenty-five pounds due to the age of the system. The pumps are now located in a single story new building on Kneeland Street and are operated by telemetry from the Fire Alarm Office. Prior to this arrangement two men were on duty at the pumping station at all times working the regular fire department schedule.

The transition from Division Two to Division One also involved learning new fire tactics. No longer were spectacular fires the routine three deckers, which are basically all alike, and the block of tax payers (rows of connected stores that produce tax revenue for the city) at which the laddermen do the forcible entry and throw ladders to the roof for ventilating. This is accomplished by removing skylights while the hosemen advance big lines into the store, and usually end up fighting their way into the cellars (taking a beating as they go) where these fires usually originate. This doesn't mean that the frequent repeat makes them simple or carefree because fires are full of surprises. In reality there is no such thing as a routine fire.

First of all, some of the downtown buildings are so large that you can have a good fire in progress and there will be nothing showing. In these cases you first have to find the fire and then begin your attack. Instead of buildings forty to fifty feet high you are faced with buildings forty to fifty (or more) stories high and instead of a single cellar you might have five or six floors below ground. These interesting facts present a real challenge to firefighters, and to the chief in charge.

All the things you studied about sprinkler systems, standpipes and fire pumps were rather vague then. Now they became reality and daily tools of the trade. Fires and accidents in the subways add a new dimension and cap log fires on the waterfront were something never seen in Franklin Park or at Jamaica Pond. Because four engines, two ladders and the Rescue responded on most boxes there always seemed to be plenty of manpower, but when you begin moving a big line up eight or nine stories in buildings without standpipes, there is never enough help.

It was while I was on Engine 25 that I thought the calendar had turned back to the war years. There had been some riots in the Roxbury and Dorchester sections of the city, and the fire department adjusted by changing response patterns considerably. During one busy evening we were returning to our covering assignment by way of Quincy Street. As we passed under the railroad bridge, shots rang out and the windshield in front of us shattered. No one was injured, but that wasn't the fault of the shooter. It was the Grace of God, and I thank Him.

While the rioting in Boston may not have been as spectacular as that in Detroit, Newark or Watts, the city had its share of deliberate fires, false alarm and harassing. The changes in response patterns involved establishing Task Forces that were made up of two engines, one ladder and a chief. All responded with police escorts. Chiefs went back to wearing black helmets and black firecoats to make them less conspicuous, and fire apparatus refrained from using their flashing red lights and sirens in order to reduce tension and limit attention. All men were issued special helmet extensions to protect them from thrown or shot missiles and apparatus was moved out of fire houses to safer locations.

Following the shooting of a lieutenant on Ladder 4 and the burning of Engine 42 by a Molotov Cocktail, the fire department had to take expensive measures to protect the firefighters. The back steps on the engines were enclosed with plexi-glass and closed boxes were designed and fabricated for placement on ladder trucks to protect tillermen. Clear, thick, plastic panels were installed in front of all windshields to provide an additional measure of protection for drivers, and roofs were installed on all apparatus not already having them.

Although firefighters took the brunt of the pent-up emotions, the events of that hot summer also had an effect on the tax payers and city residents due to the expenditure of city funds for measures already mentioned. In addition, there was the cost of repairing damaged apparatus and the medical expenses for the injured firefighters. All residents of the city were deprived of the normal, full, quick response of the fire department during those periods of uncertainty. The news media conveniently forgot to call the tax payer's attention to this costly aspect of the "unrest" - and they still neglect to mention the sporadic harassment of firemen that continues to this day.

It should be pointed out that in spite of the fact that the fire department was the target of many of the attacks, not once did the men refuse to respond out of fear of being injured or killed.

Anecdote:
On many occasions when the Task Forces responded to the incendiary Incidents, they were greeted by a host of angry spectators who were lying in wait for them. From rooftops, or from behind fences or other shelter, they pushed or threw everything from refrigerators to smaller missiles at the firemen, as they fought to control blazes. After viewing a couple such events, many sparks, including our son Bruce, gave up going to fires in areas of unrest.

Perhaps it was because my tenure on Engine 25 was relatively short that there arc not too many outstanding events to report. We went to a lot of fires in all sections of the city either by the running cards or by special call because of our unique capabilities. At some I used experience learned at previous fires but at most I learned something new that would help me in the future. Sometimes everything went well, and sometimes there were snafus - not always of our doing.

Two of the latter occurred just after daybreak on two separate Sunday mornings, and both were three baggers. The first was in a building on Tremont Street on a snowy Sunday morning. Engine 25 was special called because our dual deck guns were needed. At the time we didn't know it was our guns the chief was waiting for and we slipped and slid all the way to the South End as fast as we dared. When we arrived at the fire the chief had a clear space in front of the building waiting for us and already had big lines laid in place and ready to be connected to our gun outlets. When he saw we had a spare wagon, without guns, he was ready to kill. It wasn't our fault we had a spare piece but it might as well have been because after facing his full fury, he sent us slipping and sliding back to Oliver Street.

The other three bagger was at the Fish Pier, and also on a cold winter morning. The building was pretty well gutted and the attack had been reduced to outside big lines. The TV media had just arrived and the cameramen were focusing on the winter wonderland scene of ice covered firemen and equipment and the torrents of thundering water escaping from the hoses. Suddenly our line went flat as we lost water. Not wanting the publicity of being on TV and standing there empty handed I told the men to turn around quick and put their backs to the cameramen so no one would know it was Engine 25 that had lost their water. They did - just in time.

With each promotion there was a fringe benefit, that I never gave thought to before getting it. As a fireman, I never minded doing night watches. In fact I enjoyed the quietness of the nerve center of the fire house and the responsibility it involved. It provided a great opportunity to catch up on reading and if you were studying it made additional waking hours to learn and review. When I was promoted to lieutenant, the thing I enjoyed most was not being called for an after midnight watch. Being detailed from one company to another, both as a firefighter and a lieutenant, was an accepted part of the job and it never bothered me, especially after I owned an automobile and no longer had to depend on public transportation when going to a detail. The fringe benefit most appreciated as a captain was that there were no more details to other companies.

I had again settled into the happiness of my new rank and probably would have been content to remain a Company Commander until the paymaster crossed my name off his list, except I guess I was beginning to grow up. Although the city had been paying me for doing the work for over twenty years, I still felt like a little boy playing his favorite game and who was some day going to grow up and have to put away childish things. Herb continued urging me to stay in the books and other factors were starting to make practical sense to me.

First there was the "Officer's Contract" that made it all worth while. Second, once a captain, there are times when you are detailed to acting district chief and once I got a taste of that added responsibility of the rank, my appetite was whetted for more. Third, there were a couple lieutenants in the house who wanted to study for the next Captain's Exam and they were looking for a tutor - unpaid. Helping them study, and teaching them TIE, NOAH, MA, kept me in practice and prepared me for the next District Chief's Examination which was in May of 1970.

Fires are full of surprises as already suggested. We always held our breath when Box 1251 at Richmond and Commercial Streets came in, because it usually meant work. Throughout my years, and even going back before, this box has had more than its share of working fires and multiples. One evening when we responded to it for a vacant building on Richmond Street it ended up a three bagger. There had been several previous fires in the building and these had left it with weakened floors and burned through stairways. For safety reasons the attack had been mostly from the outside with ladder pipes, deck guns and hand lines supplying the water. Fire had been pushing from most of the windows of the four story building at the start, but one by one they had been blackened down and many of the heavy stream appliances had been shut down.

The building was fully illuminated by the department's Lighting Plant, when suddenly a hand appeared over the sill of a fourth floor window. Slowly, a second hand made its way to the window and even more slowly, a soaked head appeared above the hands, and then the neck and soggy chest of a man filled most of the burned out window. A ladder was quickly raised to that window and a couple firemen scampered up to bring the water logged gentleman to safety. Once on the ground the vagrant was quite nonplus about the whole incident and murmured something about having to find a new room where the roof didn't leak. That man had missed his vocation. With his ability to endure that much heat, smoke and water all alone in a burning building for that long, well he should have been a firefighter and I was ready to sign him up for my company. He didn't want to go to the hospital, but since it was an early fall evening and the air a bit nippy, he finally agreed to go when he was promised some dry clothes and a shower - and this time with warm water.

One of the most spectacular fires that I went to as captain of Engine 25 was one that had the potential for even more serious consequences. It was a five alarm fire on Salem Street in the North End (Box 1224) on the extremely cold night of February 1, 1971. The box came in just after supper time and was quickly followed with a second alarm on which we responded. The third alarm was struck before we arrived at the location and as we turned from Cross Street into Salem the fire had engulfed several buildings on the left side of street. It was reaching across the full width of Salem Street and lapping up the sides of the buildings opposite those already burning.

At the time there were no post hydrants on Salem Street, so Lowry hydrants were the first line of defense. The good news was that all the men knew this and made it a standard practice to quickly remove the street plates and put the Lowry chucks in place even if nothing was showing. As a result there was a minimum amount of time lost. In a matter of minutes we had our portable gun set up on the street between the burning and smoldering buildings and two big lines run from the pump so we could begin putting up a water curtain to break up the radiated heat. The team work of the five alarm response was successful in stopping the fire from jumping Salem Street, although it did extend to a couple buildings on Baldwin Place. Fortunately no lives were lost although this did not look possible when we first arrived.

Once the fire was knocked down and under control, the miserably cold task of wetting down and overhauling the burned shells of homes began. On this near zero temperature night it was going to be a particularly distressing and a tediously long task. The Red Cross and the Salvation Army were on hand to serve hot coffee and bouillon, but it was the good Italian people of the North End who opened their stores and homes and hearts to invite the firemen in to warm their bones and allow some of the ice to melt from their gear. As a substitute for the coffee and bouillon they offered homemade hot soup – minestrone, of course. I was one of the many snowmen who took advantage of this hospitality and stood too close for too long near a pot belly stove in a store and allowed the pleasant heat to warm my hands and feet too fast. The painful effect of the too rapid transition from the extreme cold to extreme heat caused frostbitten fingers, which could not be sensed at the time, but which lingered with me for several days and provided much discomfort. As distressful as that night was, Friday was still pay day. Better still, I was number three on the District Chief's List.

This chapter started out by reporting that pay raises from the early forties through my first twenty plus years on the job were "across the board." It was while I was a captain that the union negotiations for a salary adjustment ended up with an arbitrator and this learned gentleman from Harvard determined early on that the "across the board" raises had put the officers at a distinct salary disadvantage. To correct this "injustice" he proposed to establish a percentage pay difference between ranks and then determine what was the proper salary for a firefighter.

At the election held at the Hotel Bradford on a Sunday afternoon and evening its acceptance was voted. It became known as the "Officer's Contract" because supposedly they had benefited the most. This may or may not have been true, but it did cause a lot of firefighters and officers to begin thinking that perhaps the most profitable moonlighting they could engage in was studying. The result was that examinations became even more competitive for all ranks, and a lot of private businesses had to begin looking for new reliable part time help.

With the help of TIE, NOAH, MA, one of my downtown students made captain in August 1970 and the other one in January 1973. The District Chief's Exam was held in May and I again left the school room with confidence. The composition of the Chief's Exam was quite different from that of the Captain's Exam. There were ten essay type questions and a Fire Problem that was much more involved and complicated. These represented 80% of the mark. Experience counted for 20%.

On the ten questions I received four 100s, one 92 and five 90s. The Fire Problem earned me a 97. Hooray again for TIE, NOAH, MA. My mark was 92.76% and Captain Frank Sullivan, whom I had nudged out of first place on our Captain's Exam, nudged me into third place on the list by a fraction of a point, due to his higher Experience mark which was aided by his couple college degrees. As for the captain who topped the list, he was the brother of one of my "students" and I jokingly accused that future captain and chief of giving his older brother all my answers so he could beat me - - grateful appreciation!

After I was promoted to captain and before I made district chief a new practice was begun relative to men on lists. Due to a change in the Union contract, henceforth, when there was a temporary vacancy for an officer because of injury, vacation or other reason, the highest man on the List for promotion to that rank would be detailed to the company, or district, in an acting capacity. He would assume the duties of the vacant position and be paid the salary of the rank. When my Chief's List was established in November of 1970, I was included in the acting assignments, and being number three, these details were quite constant.

My first night as a certified acting district chief, in District 4, was a busy one and provided evidence of the loneliness of command. In the early evening we responded to Beacon Street and Massachusetts Avenue (Box 1583) for a top floor fire in an apartment house on the corner of these two streets. I took my proper position in the front of the building and gave orders for the basic attack for this type of building. The first truck took position in the front of the building and raised their stick to the roof to begin ventilating. The second truck raised its aerial to a top floor window where light smoke was visible. The first engine took an inch and a half line through the front door and up the stairs to the fire floor. The second engine took their big line over the stick to the top floor while the third engine stood by with a big line waiting to be placed. Both engine companies called for water for their lines so I knew there was fire in progress.

I could hear windows being broken and the men with axes cutting holes in the roof, but there was still not much visible from the street. Neither my driver of the night nor the officers with radios working the top floor were giving me information about the fire despite my radio calls to them. Either we were having radio problems or they were too busy to answer. In either case I had the uncommitted engine take their line to the fire floor via the ladder and they shortly called to have their line charged. I was a lonely voice of authority on the street and was about to call it a Working Fire so the deputy would come in and keep me company.

While this was happening there was a fire in Jamaica Plain that turned into two alarms, and a box was struck for a fire in South Boston. As I took my radio to give the order, the chief in District 6 beat me to it and ordered a Working Fire for his problem. Now both working deputies were committed and there was none to come to my party. Just then my driver came down the ladder to report that they had the fire knocked down. It had involved three rooms and had gotten into the area between the ceilings and the roof but they had caught it.

"By the way chief," he added, "you know this side of Mass. Ave. is District 5 - and the chief working hates to miss fires." I had Fire Alarm notify District 5 that the fire was on his side and when he came on scene, I quickly filled him on the particulars, and left before he could berate me for waiting so long before notifying him.

Shortly before 0700 hours on a Saturday morning, and again in District 4, we responded to a smoke condition on Upton Street. It was about the time when the former rooming houses in the South End were starting to become owner occupied and being converted into quite luxurious town houses. As we entered the building, there was the obvious strong smell of new varnish, fresh wall paper and recently installed carpeting. There was also the smell of light wood smoke.

Two brothers and their wives who had bought the house and added their labors of love to make it a home, told us there was a smell of smoke coming from the area of the third floor fireplace. It had been used the night before they admitted. I had a booster line run to the third floor and sent officers to investigate the other floors. One of them reported that the second floor wall under the upper fire place was quite warm and I had an inch and a half line brought there. One look at the hose and the brothers and their wives begged us to do no more damage than was necessary.

They began rolling up the new rugs in that room. I explained that the heat could either be a carry over from using the fireplace the night before or the repeated warming of the hearth could have started a smoldering fire in the supporting rafters. Since the upper wall was starting to darken it was obvious there was hidden fire and we would have to open up the wall. We would begin close to the ceiling and do as little damage as possible but it had to be opened up. The line was charged and the wives ran to get towels and anything else that would absorb water. With the first penetration, smoke poured out and charred wood lathes were exposed. More of the newly papered wall had to be removed and the residents began to cry. As the laddermen with rakes began pulling off the wooden lathes the extent of the fire became clearer and a brick wall began to take form.

Through their tears the brothers saw this, and all of a sudden they became interior decorators again. It was a beautiful brick wall that was being exposed. "Why not remove all the wood lathes and new wallpaper and put oak book shelves against the brick wall! It would be dramatic and charming." The wives forgot their towels and the floor and joined their husbands in planning the new rustic room.

We had lost our spectators and their restraining admonitions which made the job of opening up the wall around the second floor fireplace much easier. They were so engrossed in redecorating that they didn't even notice that we also exposed some ceiling rafters for them before we found all the fire. You can't put oak shelves against ceiling rafters, but we finished our job, rolled up the hose and went home. There wasn't even a "Thank You" for our demolition contribution to their new remodeling project.

First, second, or third, it didn't matter where I was on the Chief's List because a reduction in the hours of our workweek was drawing closer. Under the most recently negotiated contract the work week would be reduced to forty two hours on July 1, 1971. History repeated itself in that City Hall delayed promoting the needed six district chiefs and other officers until July 28, but that didn't matter because I had been acting district chief much of the time since our list was established - and getting the pay on Fridays.

I was covering Chief McLaughlin, the same one who had given me time off to welcome our new son Jonathan years before. He was then assigned to District 3 but had been injured in a fur store fire on Tremont Street and wouldn't be returning to active duty. When natural furs burn they give off hydrogen cyanide gas. Frank and a few other men who were at that fire inhaled too much of the poison. The result was that the tax payers lost the service of several dedicated firefighters much too prematurely. It again demonstrated the morbidity of our profession as we wait for someone's property to catch fire or a brother of higher rank to get injured and retire.

The equalizing factor is that as you revel in your climb up the ladder of promotions, all too soon, someone else who is number one on another list will be anxiously waiting for you to end your career so he can get promoted.

This is the ever-continuing cycle that becomes the history of the fire service, as men enter, maybe advance through the ranks, and then all too soon become a "Who."

"Spaghetti" at the Crawford-Hollidge Fire, February 18, 1967. The delay in the Captain's Exam caused by this fire allowed me the extra time needed to top the list.

Captain Cook at South Boston fire, February 1968.

FROM SILVER TO GOLD BUGLES
(or, There Will Be A Few More Gray Hairs On The Roof Now)

The only ritual that took place when I was promoted to lieutenant and then captain was "Signing The Book," and in the case of making captain that was even after the fact. By the time my gold bugles came along on July 28, 1971, the department had begun a little recognition ceremony at which time you were sworn into your new rank by the Fire Commissioner and pictures were taken as your family and invited friends proudly watched. This was a significant step in the right direction. It gave a bit more meaning to the family, for the many hours you had deprived them of your companionship. All of a sudden it all became worthwhile.

Today a cold cut collation has been added to the promotion ceremonies that are still held in Memorial Hall at Fire Headquarters. Each time it gets more impressive as the families of the promoted men beam with justifiable pride and joy, as they sit in that hallowed hall with the pictures of many firefighters who paid the supreme sacrifice look down on their living brother being honored with promotions.

As memorable as that special event is, it only lasts a little while and then it is back to the fire house routine. This generally involves transfer to another house and district and probably on a different group. You have to begin all over again getting acquainted with new faces, personalities, names and idiosyncrasies. When you become a chief, it is easier, the men have to get used to you!

After the surrogate student who was number one on our list had been promoted, Frank Sullivan, yours truly, and the next four captains were sworn in and presented with gold badges on that July afternoon. It was a rewarding and happy day. Along with Dot and our three sons (Janna was away at summer camp), Mom and Herb joined the assembled families at our swearing in ceremony. The pastor of my church, Rev. Arnold Olsen, also attended and offered prayer for the men being promoted.

I am sure Mom was proud of the "runt of her litter" even though I would still be working on the Lord's Day when Group 2 was scheduled. As for Herb, he was probably the happiest of all the family spectators although he didn't show it. His nagging had paid off for me again, but I suspect that for at least a few seconds nostalgic thoughts must have crept into his head and he might have imagined himself getting a gold badge - if only things had been different back in the Depression days. In my triumph, I watched Herb and sensed this - and inwardly vowed to be a chief worthy of his ambition - and his nagging.

One of the first things you must realize when you put on the Gold is that you are in charge and your decisions can have far reaching effects. One of my first evening runs as a chief was one of those pesky "odor of smoke" Incidents. This is when there is usually no fire or heat, just a faint smell of smoke. Quite often the reported smoke dissipates between the time a person calls and the fire department arrives, but you still have to search everywhere looking for even a wisp of the elusive stuff. You must keep in mind that you are tying up a considerable amount of equipment and manpower that is now not available for an actual fire. For this Incident, FAO had struck a box and the deputy had responded, which meant my role was to direct operations inside the building.

The deputy's aide, who acts as his remote eyes and ears - and sometimes his voice, was with me. He was experienced and once in a while quite forceful and domineering, when he could get away with it. Still getting my feet wet in my new position I made the mistake of asking the aide what he thought about this suspected smoke condition - hoping to get a confirmation of my own thoughts. He must have been uncertain too and replied, "It doesn't matter what I think. You are the chief and you make the decisions."

For a moment I was surprised - and a bit perturbed at his comment, for many times in the past I had seen him quite outspoken and domineering with company officers. Then I realized that in spite of his attitude at this time, he was absolutely right. I was fortunate to have been reminded of my proper place so early in my new rank. I immediately ordered the "All Out" and sent all companies back to quarters - - and kept my fingers crossed until morning.

Along with the gold bugles when you are promoted to chief you are issued a white fire coat and a white leather helmet. These are so you can be conspicuous at a fire as the man in charge both to the firemen and to any citizens who are looking for someone in the fire department with whom to find fault. Now that the implements had been issued to me I was anxious for my first fire where my white coat and helmet would stand out as the point of authority.

It happened about six o'clock one morning with a fire in the basement press room of the *Record-American* newspaper in Winthrop Square. When the deputy arrived I proceeded to the fire location to direct inside operations. It was a typical pressroom fire like I had been to many times before and would go to several times more - but this time I was in charge. The vast amount of liquid ink used in the printing presses sprays and saturates everything and permeates all soluble surfaces. As the heat of this fire increased and reached the ceiling it released the dissolved pigments there which quickly mixed with the water spray from the automatic sprinklers that were operating on the fire. We advanced our lines on the fire in this shower of diluted black ink. When the fire was extinguished and I returned to the fresh air, my new previously white fire coat and leather helmet were as black as the ones I had been wearing for the previous twenty-four years. So much for the white coated figure of authority.

Since I inherited Chief McLaughlin's berth in District 3, I also, by choice, inherited his Aide, Joe. He was a good fireman, a good aide and a popular guy. He knew the district and how to find his way around the city. He was a savvy jake and if he reported to me on the radio that we needed a big line, or it was a working fire, or whatever, I knew his judgment could be trusted. He knew everybody, or everybody knew him. He had lots of connections and was always willing to use them for other firemen.

Listening to the fire radio for so many years I had often heard messages for car so-and-so to call Fire Alarm, or some other designation and wondered what emergency was taking place, or what important message was waiting to involve the particular chief. Now that I was a chief I would be getting those vital calls also.

It wasn't long before the first one came, "Car 3, call Engine 8 right away." My imagination ran rampant. What earth shattering emergency had taken place in my district that required the District Commander's immediate attention? I told Joe to go to the nearest fire house so I could make the directed call. Using my most authoritative voice I instructed the Fire Alarm operator to give me Engine 8. When the phone was answered I identified myself - but before I could ask for the officer, the voice on the other end said, "Oh, I am sorry chief. I wanted Joe."

This happened so regularly that it finally reached the point that when such messages were received on the radio, we went to the nearest fire house and I sat in the car and let Joe tend to his business. Once in a very great while he would yell out, "Its for you chief," but those times were few and far between.

Anecdote:
After being my aide for five years, Joe retired. Shortly afterwards he came down with the Big C and died ten years before his time - another dedicated firefighter who gave more to the citizens of Boston than he received back.

June 17, 1972 was another tragic day for the Boston Fire Department. That day there was a multiple alarm fire in the vacant Hotel Vendome and as it was being brought under control a large part of the old structure suddenly collapsed. Group 2 was working but the early afternoon fire was in District 4. When my relief came in I walked over to view the fire before catching my bus home. The whole building was still standing at that point and from all outward appearances the fire was at the routine point of mopping up operations.

I continued on to the Greyhound terminal and home. It was shortly after my leaving that the collapse took place for when I got home, Dot told me of the news flash telling of the tragedy that had befallen the Boston Fire Department. When a roll call was taken of the men present, and tons of debris was removed by the zealous firefighters seeking their brothers, the death count was nine valiant firemen. Nine brave unselfish men, who died too many years before their anticipated, "ten years before their contemporaries." They too gave more to the tax payers of Boston than they received in return.

One thing about being the chief in a district is that you get to respond to everything in the district and the variety of happenings never ceases to amaze. About 0300 hours one morning we responded to a reported accident in the north bound lane of Dewey Tunnel near the South Station. Our normal response route was by way of the south bound lane where we would stop and pass through one of the dividing doors between the two roadways.

When we arrived in the tunnel that night we saw a few Rhode Island Red hens strutting in the roadway, apparently looking for corn. As we passed through the dividing door, there were feathers and chickens all over the place. Many of them had obviously been run over by surprised late motorists who in the early morning hours might have expected to see pink elephants but not red roosters. A truck carrying about nine thousand live chickens to market had tipped over and broken wooden crates and flying giblet makers had taken over the tunnel roadway. Halted drivers were blinking their eyes in disbelief of what they were seeing.

In due time tow trucks arrived at the scene to upright the turned over vehicle and another truck from the poultry farm arrived to salvage what they could of the feathery fugitives. I later learned that some of the frightened fowl found their way back to the Oliver Street fire house for refuge. When Group 3 reported for duty in the morning, and the men opened their lockers, they were greeted with a closet full of cooped up cutlets, seeking to flee their captivity.

Even though there were close to two thousand men in the fire department back in the fifties, you knew about all of them. There were several reasons for this. The forty-eight hour schedule involved a mixing of the work groups so that you had opportunity to work with more men in the district. Since there were more fires of longer duration all over the city, you ran into otherwise would be strangers more often. In addition, group changes were much more frequent to cover vacations and injuries. As you shared Red Cross, Morgan Memorial, Boston's Spark Club or Salvation Army coffee after the big ones were knocked down, old acquaintances were renewed and new introductions made.

The old Navy Fire School in South Boston was in full swing drilling men on ship fires. BFD inherited this excellent training center from the U S Navy following the war. Firemen were detailed there a week at a time on a department wide basis. Other reasons included the fact the Russell Club and the Union were rivals and with interest in both of these associations at fever pitch, attendance at meetings and the fellowship that followed afterwards strengthened the bonds of friendship.

The Officer's Club and the Chief's Association were joined almost immediately by those who were eligible and rivalry to become a leader was keen. Fire and funeral details were on a department wide roster and interest in the Softball League and other sports attracted many participants and brother spectators. Of course TV was still a novelty and had not yet begun to glue families to the tube so fire department activities made up a large part of the social life. For example, the Firemen's American Legion Post 94 had over five hundred department members and meetings were mobbed. The combined interest and efforts of these members succeeded in getting one of their own, District Chief J. Herbert White (formerly a lieutenant on Engine 42 in my sparking days) elected to the high office of State Commander in 1952.

The "Dandy Drillers" were another group that brought together firemen from all over the city. It is the name given to the team of about thirty firemen who went to different neighborhoods of the city, as well as Boston Common, putting on demonstrations of the evolutions learned in Drill School. It was most active during Fire Prevention Week in October of each year and usually made up of recent graduates of Drill School. It gave the tax payers an opportunity to see their firemen doing the pomps, sliding the rope and jumping into the net, as well as other activities that are routine in the department. The faces of the men doing these tasks were constantly changing but their performances probably inspired some young men to seek the job. Because of all these activities and opportunities to join together, there were few strangers among all the personnel of the department.

For better or worse the forty-two hour schedule divided the men into four groups. Each group works one fourth of the one hundred and sixty-eight hours in a week. One advantage is that you always work with the same men and a strong team effort can be developed. You still get to know most of the men on your group throughout the city but not so many men of the other groups. Many of the elements sited above which provided opportunity for a get-together, are now missing. In a sense the one department has become four, but fortunately for the citizens, the enthusiasm to save lives and protect property has not diminished among the dedicated servants, regardless of which group they are working on. Actually there is a friendly rival between groups as to who does the most work or makes the most rescues.

When the four groups were set up in July of 1971 there was an attempt to equally distribute the experience and talents available. I was assigned to Group 2 in District 3 and would be working with Deputy Chief John O'Mara who would be the Division Commander. This relationship would continue for fourteen years and I have always felt fortunate to be part of his team. The company officers on our day included Captain Bob MacInnes on Engine 10 and Lieutenant Phil O'Farrell on Ladder 8. Phil had been a fixture on that truck for most of his life and knew the hundreds of sprinklered buildings in the district like the back of his hand. He was invaluable on the hundreds of automatic alarms to which we responded each year. He stayed on Ladder 8 until he reached mandatory retirement, and died a few months later.

Many of the other Group 2 firefighters had spent many years downtown and their combined experience and knowledge of the area made my job a lot easier. Most of them are now "Who"s but if you are reading this book, thanks again for the professional job you did. You frequently made me look good.

If Engine 42 was my first fire department love, District 3 had to be a close second. For me the variety of structures and ethnic neighborhoods presented challenges that can't be paralleled in any other district in the city. I could never understand why more district chiefs, especially those aspiring to be deputy, did not want to spend more time in this district. It can provide a wide range of experience that could later benefit not only their own careers, but also the lives of men they are entrusted with, as well as the tax payers. It was my good fortune to spend fourteen interesting years there. During that time seventeen other district chiefs passed through on the other groups and another thirteen have passed through it in the three years since I left to go to headquarters.

Many of the occupancies of the buildings in District 3 have been continually changing since I was first assigned there in 1967. Some that were then occupied are now vacant, like the Washington Street theatres, and some that were vacant or sparsely occupied have been replaced with high rise office buildings, apartments or condos. Included in the district are parts of Chinatown and the Combat Zone and in contrast is the Brahman Beacon Hill. The major retail stores of Downtown Crossing and the high value financial district that is still spreading are part of it. The old West End, and the ever, and always, delightful Italian North End, add a picturesque flavor to an already demanding responsibility. In addition there is Boston Harbor and the many inner islands to which the Marine Units respond. The Orange, Red, Green and Blue Line MBTA subway tunnels as well as the Sumner and Callahan vehicular tunnels going to and from East Boston are included. The Southeast Expressway, otherwise known as the longest parking lot in the world, winds through the district with Dewey Tunnel on one end and the Tobin, or Mystic River Bridge, on the other end.

Under Proposition 2-1/2, District 2 was deactivated and the territory of Charlestown was added to District 3. This possibly made it the largest big city fire district in the country, as it encompassed seven fire barns housing 5 engines, 3 ladders, an Aerial Tower and Squirt Company, the Safety Unit, one Rescue and two fire boats plus the High Pressure Pumping Station. Later the Haz-Mat Unit was added. Manpower averaged two hundred and thirty officers and men - which is a lot of men to maintain records for, balance strengths, arrange vacations, keep track of detail lists, as well as doing your own paperwork and overseeing that of the company officers. It was a challenge I thrived on.

One of the buildings in the district is the Aquarius Theatre. Originally it was Loew's Orpheum Theatre, where in 1940 I took Dot on our first date to see "Little Nellie Kelly" with Judy Garland - her choice. On changing names it became a home for Rock Shows and soon fell into disrepair. When I reported for work one

Saturday night, the chief I relieved advised that there had a been a problem at the Aquarius the night before and that he had been there during the day to address the situation. There would be a Rock concert there again that night.

It turned out to be a busy evening but shortly after the theatre opened for the show I was there to inspect it. There were several violations. Chained doors, blocked fire escapes, unlit Exit signs and a few others that I pointed out to the manager. I ordered that they be corrected before the concert could begin. While talking with him, my aide called on the portable radio to report we had a run. I told the manager I would be back to check on his progress before he could start the show, and left to go to the fire.

We responded to a good fire in the North End which was obviously arson caused and had suspected racial overtones. The extinguishing of the fire and overhauling, determining the cause, taking part with the Arson Squad in the investigation that followed and waiting for the police and photographers to arrive and do their particular jobs, took several hours. As soon as I was free, I returned to the theatre, but the concert was over and the theatre locked up.

No reports had been forwarded from the district relative to the Friday night, or the Saturday day time participation by the department, so as I waited for my relief on Sunday morning I typed out a report of what had transpired. It included my visit on the night before that had to be abruptly terminated because of the North End fire. I listed the violations pointed out to the theatre manager. I reasoned that my report would reach headquarters Monday morning and be forwarded to the Fire Prevention Division and official action by them could begin. My relief came in and I briefed him on what had taken place. I went home and forgot about the Aquarius Theatre.

Monday morning I was back for the Day Tour and at about 1330 hours, as we were going about our business, the car radio broke the squelch and called, "Car 3. Report to the Fire Commissioner's Office immediately." Now what! Somehow I knew this call wasn't for my aide.

Ten minutes later I was in headquarters facing a disturbed Fire Commissioner in his office. It was about the Aquarius

Theatre and my report, and why I hadn't resolved the matter Saturday night. If I couldn't resolve it on sight, the theatre should have been "abated" or closed. My report meant nothing! My alibi and explanation was that according to the Rule Book, "Fire Duty" takes precedence over everything else and I couldn't be expected to be in two places at one time, but my reasoning fell on deaf ears.

His unreasonable comment was that he expected me to know what was going on in every building in my district at every hour of the day and night. That would be most helpful - but quite unrealistic. Impractical as the advice was, it nevertheless was an excellent suggestion to become familiar with as many buildings as possible in the district before being faced with a problem or fire in them. As the Commissioner dismissed me, and we shook hands for old time sake, I told him he had caught me once but he never would again.

The first thing I did, on returning to work for the Tuesday Night Tour, was to visit the Aquarius and inspect it with the manager. A report was forwarded to the Commissioner that all violations found on the previous Saturday night had been corrected. This was true. The slate on the Aquarius Theatre was clean once again. Maybe not for long, but it was clean then.

It didn't take long to learn what went on in at least some buildings in my district. On a rainy night we were sent to a building on Beacon Hill with a report of smoke in it. There was no doubt about this fact when we opened the lower entry door. The immediate problem was to determine where it was coming from. Engine 4 ran a line to the front door and I sent the two trucks to look for the source. It soon narrowed down to a third floor apartment, which was locked. The engine's line was advanced up the stairs and charged and then forced entry was made.

As the door was swung open much smoke poured out into the hall but it did not have a pungent odor. The truckies opened some windows and as the smoke cleared a bit it was obvious that the point of origin was the kitchen. On closer checking it was observed the smoke was coming from the oven, but it didn't have the annoying burnt food smell. On opening the oven door two blackened lumps on the rack were emitting all the smoke. If those lumps were potatoes baking, they had to be the largest spuds in the hub.

Just then an embarrassed woman came into her apartment and explained. She had been grocery shopping in the rain and her bundles had gotten wet as she walked up the hill. The top items were two rolls of toilet paper which were soaked. It seemed logical to her to put the oven on low heat and place the wet rolls in the oven to dry out while she went next door to visit a friend. All the confusion we caused in the neighborhood brought her home to her smoky apartment. She was all apologies as my men removed the two wads from the oven and soaked them with water in her sink - which brought her back to her original problem.

Another night we responded to an "unknown condition" on the fourth floor of a Chauncy Street building. It turned out to be an artist's studio and the condition soon became as "known" to us as it was to the poor victim. The male model had a physique that reminded me of Michelangelo's statue of David that we had seen in Florence, Italy. The artist thought well of it too as he was making a plaster cast of it that would later be used for a bronze reproduction. The problem came when they tried to remove the cast. The model was a hairy individual and apparently he had been slathered with an insufficient amount of grease before the wet plaster was applied. When it dried, most of the hairs over his whole body set in the plaster. Before we arrived someone had used a hammer and broke much of the plaster into small pieces in an attempt to remove it. The model was in agony as every time he moved the hairs were strained beyond his endurance and he yelled out in pain.

Our first attempt was to hold a piece of the plaster and with surgical scissors reach under and cut away the hairs. No matter how careful we were, every movement brought more cries of agony and tears to the model's eyes. It would have been a long tedious and painful process to continue removing it in this fashion so an alternative had to be found. In the end we took rolls of "cling" bandage and wrapped our plaster covered model as tightly as we could. He looked like an Egyptian mummy but the movement of plaster was reduced enough to keep him from yelling out, but any motion still caused him much pain. We strapped him into a Stokes basket and carried him to the elevator. Here there was another problem. The elevator was too small to accommodate the basket. We ended up carrying him down the four flights of narrow winding stairs to the street, with each bend creating new torture for him. Once down, he was taken to New England Medical Center where they could medicate him and give him a shave.

A sub-cellar fire in Court Square ruined an entire evening for us as it confronted us with a night of near total frustration. We responded shortly after six p.m. and before we had eaten dinner - which was probably a good thing. A real heavy smoke was billowing up the cellar stairs and to locate the fire the men had to grope their way down in total smoky darkness dragging hose with them.

In an attempt to remove the stubborn smoke we called for two extra trucks to bring additional portable fans into use. We set up the fans in relays to draw the smoke from the sub-cellar to the cellar, to an elevator shaft, and then blow it out a hole in the roof created by removing the skylight. This worked fine in theory but in practice the compacted burning paper files below produced smoke faster than we could remove it.

As the battle continued past seven, eight and nine o'clock, it began to take its toll on the men. I spotted one of the men who was due to retire the end of that month and told him to get out of the building and help the pump operators with lines of hose. With his over thirty years on the job I didn't want him getting hurt, or worse, during his last week on the job - not on my watch!

By ten o'clock we had run out of reserve air bottles on the apparatus and the bottle truck was having a difficult time meeting our needs. Four hours after the first alarm, a second alarm was ordered to get some fresh men and more air bottles. We had begun to make headway on the fire and when Engine 10 came in on the second alarm, Captain MacInnes and his crew made it look easy.

Donning their self-contained breathing apparatus, they took over the lead line and pushed it to the core of the cartons of paper files piled to the ceiling in a small room. The overhauling of the paper products took another couple hours and then we returned to the fire house with heads as big as water melons. Dinner was cold but no one was hungry anyhow as everyone had ingested an extremely large belly full of smoke. Another demonstration of why firemen die ten years before their contemporaries.

Every now and then there is a fire that you wish one of the other groups had. It isn't that you do anything wrong, its just that nothing you do seems to come out right. I had one of those fires on a Wednesday December night in the late seventies.

It all began shortly after six o'clock and this time we had finished eating dinner. It was an Automatic Alarm from a building with an address on Washington Street and also West Street. Arriving with Engine 25 and Ladder 17 we checked the Washington Street address. There was a steel roller door blocking the entrance and there was nothing showing so we went up West Street to check there. Either the glass in the door was cloudy or there was a very faint haze inside. We forced entry to find out which. On opening the door there was a slight but distinct odor of burning oil. This is common in a delayed ignition of an oil burner so there was no real concern. As we made our way down the stairs to the cellar and looked around, the oil smell remained steady so we proceeded to the sub-cellar.

As we made our way down those stairs, water was pouring in through a hole in the wall like the open butt of a two and a half inch line and made the stairs look like a miniature waterfall. When we reached the bottom, the water on the floor was a few inches deep and there was still the smell of half burned oil - still not very strong. Visibility was reduced partly by the smoke and partly by steam, but mostly by darkness. In the limited light provided by our Wheat Lights we couldn't determine if the steam was from a leak in a steam line, if there was a break in a water pipe and the spray was striking hot pipes or if a sprinkler was operating and doing the same thing. I didn't think the water pouring down the stairs was a contributing factor to the steam, but who knows?

We had been to this Automatic Alarm many times before but since we had forced entry this time, I told FAO to have the alarm company check again with the customer to be sure he was on his way. On previous Incidents he had arrived in a short time and unlocked the roller door so we didn't have to break it. I wanted to be sure he was on his way.

Since many of the downtown buildings are heated by Edison Steam, I radioed Fire Alarm to have Boston Edison respond to this location because of soaked wires, and also to have Edison Steam report to me, in case it was a broken steam line. The oil burner was not working which could have been caused by the power failure or by rising water. Outside of the steam there was no unusual heat and outside of the oily haze there was no unusual smoke. We checked all the sub-cellar we could see and then returned to the cellar where we found light smoke sneaking out of an electrical room. On investigating we found a little smoke coming up by an electric raceway but that soon subsided. The sprinkler shut off was on that floor and since we found no signs of fire I had the sprinkler system shut down while we waited for Edison to arrive.

As we stood around the area of the shut-off, suddenly fire appeared at the ceiling at a point near where a boxed-in column rose from the floor. I ordered Fire Alarm to strike Box 1461, and the men to open the sprinkler valve. Engine 25 brought in a big line and the fire was put out.

When Deputy O'Mara arrived I briefed him on conditions and what had been done and turned command over to him. Inside, the faint oil smoke remained and the water was still pouring through the hole in the wall and down the cellar stairs adding to the waterfall. I went down to check the sub-cellar and found fire burning on top of the water that was now knee deep. We brought a foam line to the location and quickly extinguished that fire.

We forced entry into the vacant adjacent building and found water there had filled the sub-cellar, the cellar and was starting on the street floor. The only draining was into the fire building next door through the hole that the water had made in the common dividing wall. Apparently a major water line coming into the unheated building had frozen and ruptured releasing thousands of gallons of fresh water which it continued doing.

The Water Department was sent for to shut down the valve in the street. When they arrived and found the valve cover, there was a car parked on it. A call for the police was made and they soon came on sight. They studied the situation and called for a tow truck, which arrived in reasonable time, and removed the vehicle. When the water department men tried to close the valve, the stem broke. Now the only way to stop the flowing water, which was rapidly turning the building into a multilevel swimming pool, was to shut down larger remote mains that were supplying a several block area. This would take a little longer.

Meanwhile conditions at the ranch next door were status quo. We had a big line run to the sub-cellar, one to the cellar and one to the first floor. The trucks and Rescue had begun checking the ten floors above for whatever they might find. Since we had lines of hose in place I asked the deputy for permission to shut down the sprinkler system and see what would happen. He agreed - and for a few minutes nothing happened. Then moderate oil smoke began to develop in the cellar and the first floor and the truckies above radioed that light smoke was developing on the upper floors. I ordered the sprinkler system turned back on and the deputy ordered a Second Alarm, figuring the fire had passed us. I felt certain it hadn't and by the time the second alarm companies began reaching the scene we were back to status quo with nothing showing, inside or out, and the arriving men wondered why they were sent for.

Additional big lines were run as a precaution and the extra men were able to check all the floors above much faster. They found nothing so the sprinkler system was shut down again. In a matter of minutes we had a repeat of the earlier scenario so the sprinklers were turned back on. This on-off combination was tried several more times and always with the same results. When the sprinklers were shut down, smoke built up in the cellar and first floor and on the upper floors. When water was flowing, nothing - except more water in the sub-cellar which was by now getting to be waist deep.

Chief O'Mara was always one to grab paper and pencil and draw pictures to put a problem in proper perspective. We had been unable to find a second stairway into the sub-cellar and in fact the building occupants, who should know, said there wasn't one. Ten o'clock, or 2200 hours, found the chiefs and the store operators standing around a counter with Chief O'Mara using large store bags to draw his pictures of the layout of the rooms in the cellar and sub-cellar. Due to the depth of the water we could not venture beyond the furnace area for safety reasons. Shortly after our arrival I had sent Ladder 17 to check the furnace area and beyond, but sliding a rake in front of them in the water they had come to a point where the floor fell away. I ordered everyone to stay several yards away from the furnace area.

The owner advised us that this building originally had been occupied by quite a few jewelry merchants, and that in the sub-cellar, beyond the furnace, there were a number of unused vault rooms. Our problem had to be coming from that area, but how do we get there? Chief O'Mara decided to have a hole cut in the cellar floor at the front of the building hoping this would provide the needed access to the sub-cellar. He went out to give the necessary orders.

Engine 10 was one of the companies standing by ready in the cellar. There was a small room where the owner said his employees ate lunch and in the room was a door. We had previously asked him where the locked door led to and he said it was just a closet. On a hunch, Captain MacInnes (what a help to have on your team!) forced open the door and was greeted with a blast of smoke. He reached in with his foot and found the floor wasn't level, like a closet. It dropped off. Here was the hidden spiral staircase that had provided the jewelers with a secret way to their vaults.

Donning breathing apparatus, we cautiously made our circular way down into the sub-cellar. At the foot of the stairs we looked across into a room that was in back of the furnace room and there we saw a lazy fire being held in place by the operating sprinklers. In addition to a lot of charred stored lumber and doors, there were four fifty-five gallon drums, all of which had been buckled by the heat. Two had burst open releasing the contents. A few dashes of the big line extinguished the fire. We were wading in water over two feet deep and the sprinklers were soaking us from above. Since the fire was now extinguished, I ordered the sprinkler system once again to be shut down - hopefully for the last time.

Pleased with our discovery and ensuing actions, I left to report our success to Chief O'Mara, while the men began to check the rest of the sub-cellar to make sure there were no other fires. Just then I heard the Third Alarm being struck for Box 1461, and I hurried out to see what the deputy saw that I had missed.

He greeted me with, "The fire got by you Paul and it is up through the building." I protested, "No. We found the fire in the sub-cellar and put it out. In fact I shut down the sprinkler system and Engine 10 is just checking for any possible extension." "Look," he said, and pointed to the upper floors.

Heavy black smoke was rolling out of the ventilated top windows. But as we watched, it subsided and cleared up. Apparently when the sprinkler system was shut down, all the smoke that had been held down by sprinkler water sprays was released and expanded to the upper floors and the opened windows. It was this mass exodus of heavy black smoke that prompted the third alarm. By the time the third alarm companies began reaching the scene there was nothing showing, inside or out, and these arriving men also wondered why they were sent for.

Upon investigating, we determined that the water coming through the wall had made its way into the furnace pit and interfered with the burner firing cycle. Ignition was probably called for several times and oil released to sustain it but no ignition took place because of the rising water. If this happened several times, quite a bit of oil could have been released and then for some reason ignition resulted when it was called for. The burning oil, floating on the water spread to the adjacent room where it ignited the stored lumber and other flammable contents. Sprinklers operated, but the water was deflected by partitions and other stored materials so did not reach the drums that continued to be heated by the burning oil and eventually buckled and the two broke open.

The spilled contents of the drums were flammable and added fuel to the fire. Each time we shut down the sprinklers it allowed the fire to re-intensify, but in the vaporizing stage it released large amounts of smoke which made its way to the upper floors. Each time we opened the sprinkler valve, the fire was knocked down and the evolving smoke was confined to the immediate area - until we played with the sprinkler valve some more.

Anecdote:
A week later Group 2 was back for the Day Tour on Saturday morning and shortly after eight o'clock we had a call for a light

fixture fire in a West Street store opposite where we had spent that Wednesday night. After the fixture was taken care of, we went across the street to take a good look at the sub-cellar where we had been so frustrated. When the fire had been extinguished, many of the men had waded from that back room and crossed in front of the furnace for one reason or another. When we visited the scene that morning, the water had all been pumped out or drained away. We learned that the furnace sat in a deep pit that was bridged with a couple two-by-ten planks. When the several men waded in front of the furnace, they were actually walking on the planks although no one knew it. No one stepped off into the hidden deep water. God is good!

That same afternoon we responded to Box 1461 again. When we turned from Tremont into West Street, black smoke filled the whole area. It was a repeat of the Wednesday night incident but this time we were on familiar ground. It was daylight and we could see, and no wondering firemen had to be called for second and third alarms. One big line in the West Street door and down the rear stairs to the sub-cellar, and a second big line through the Washington Street front door and down the spiral staircase to the sub-cellar. The fire was knocked down in minutes and we were on our way home. Workmen had started to repair the damage caused by the earlier fire and a spark ignited some of the oil-saturated contents. There was an acting deputy with us on that Saturday, and he was impressed with the efficient firefighting of the downtown jakes. He didn't know we had pre-planned that particular building on a previous Wednesday night - for several hours!

Many times, both as a hoseman on Engine 42 and later as a lieutenant on Engine 28, I took part in Pre-Fire Planning at the Plant Shoe factory in the Jamaica Plain section of the city. This was a block long, five to seven story, brick sided factory originally used to manufacture shoes. It fronted on Centre Street with the long sides on Bickford and Walden Streets. As business prospered into the twentieth century, additions were added from time to time and all were of similar construction so from the outside it was one long structure. Inside it was five or six buildings all connected by fire doors on each floor. Automatic sprinklers were included and the buildings were kept in excellent condition.

Hundreds of people were employed there making shoes for many years. In fact, it was there that my dad met my mom.

As shoe manufacturing deteriorated in America, various assorted companies occupied the building. It was still kept in good repair then, but in the sixties and seventies the building started to be occupied by more varied tenants who were not so careful.

All this leads up to a Sunday night in February 1976. Group 2 was working and I was in my office at District 3. In the early evening an automatic sprinkler alarm was struck for a Bickford Street section of the building. On Engine 28's approach they reported heavy fire coming from the Walden Street side of the building. As this came over the department radio, one of the officers stopped by my room and asked, "Did you hear that chief?" My reply was, "Yes, and if I was the chief there now I would skip the intervals and order Fire Alarm to strike a fifth alarm."

He looked surprised and chided me, "How come? You seldom strike a second alarm on a fire building you're looking at." I explained that I knew the building and the type of tenants now occupying it. My reasoning was that probably the fire doors were not being shut every night, so I would immediately strike a fifth alarm to use the manpower. First to go through each floor of the six buildings to remove any blocks and close the fire doors. Then have them run hose lines to each floor and building to stop any fire that may appear. I added that since the alarm was from one side of the involved building and heavy fire was showing from the opposite side it may already be too late, but considering the length of the building, maybe a stop could be made somewhere.

To complete the story for those who don't know, five alarms were sounded, plus many orders for additional companies both from Boston and mutual aid companies. It was raining at the start of the fire but temperatures began dropping and before daybreak everything was covered with ice. Engine 7, which operated its deck guns on the side of the building, was frozen to the ground. At one point there was only one Boston Engine (39) in quarters which regularly ran in the High Pressure District and was familiar with operating the system. This was my territory and I was concerned. I called the Fire Alarm Office to remind them of this situation and told them not to send Engine 39 to the fire

(which they were just about to do as three more engines had been ordered.)

It is just a short jump from winter to summer fires. The "Dog Days of August" is a term that is, or was, applied to late summer when there is a spell of extremely hot and very humid days. These uncomfortable days most often continue into, and through uncomfortable nights. Residents of downtown, and elsewhere in the city, often escape, or delay, the heat of their apartments by staying up late and remaining outdoors. Group 2 was working on one such sultry night when no air was stirring at ground level.

Sometime after midnight we were dispatched to a high rise office building where their Security reported a light haze on the thirty-eighth floor. Going by the SOP we took the elevator to the floor below. On opening the elevator doors we were greeted with a heavier smoke condition and a rubbish fire which had extended. A line was connected to the standpipe system, the fire was knocked down and overhauling was begun. Since the building had operable windows, I ordered some to be opened to help alleviate the smoke condition and provide added ventilation. When the first window was opened, there was practically a gale that came in. Sparks from the overhauling became enflamed and debris blew across the floor. The window was closed until overhauling and wash down were completed.

One small fire, but two big experience lessons. First, in the future I would only use elevators to two floors below the reported Incident floor. Second, although no air was moving at ground level, when one goes a few hundred feet higher, there can be strong winds, and this must be taken into consideration in your fire size up and tactical planning.

I noted these two conditions in my fire report in the hope it would be of help to other firefighters. Because of this experience of mine, plus I am sure similar experiences of many others throughout the country, fire departments now stop elevators two floors below the reported incidents, and in some cities, even three to five floors below,

It is strange how a number of fires will occur in a particular building or street and the same work group will get the repeat business. During my fourteen years in District 3, there were well over two dozen fires on Hancock Street and I only had a couple of them, and one of them I was working for another chief. It turned out to be an arson fire that eventually required my spending several days in court.

On the other hand I had over a half dozen fires in the New City Hall while most of the other District 3 chiefs had none. One of the fires woke up everyone who was listening to their scanners at the time. On the Plaza there was a PT boat that kids played in and one Sunday afternoon we responded to the New Congress Street side of the building, where the PT boat was in flames. In routine fashion, I took the radio and reported to Fire Alarm.

"Car 3 to Fire Alarm."
"Go ahead Car 3."
"At Box 1322 and we have a boat fire. Have the Marine Unit disregard."
Fire Alarm routinely repeated, "OK Car 3. You are at the box and you have a boat fire. The Marine Unit can disregard - - - - you what! Car 3, please repeat your message," which I did.

Another night we responded to the same Box 1322 and on arrival found flame shooting half way across New Congress Street from the City Hall. On one of the upper floors there was a large out door child-care area and the several wooden partitions and padded floor coverings had been ignited. We weren't aware of these exterior furnishings when we first turned the corner from New Sudbury Street and for a moment I thought we were going to be back in the parking lot business.

Over the years I had a few fires in different office machines in the building as well as several one room fires, and a couple of those rooms were quite large and resulted in sizable losses. For an antithesis, we responded one morning to a broken water main between the Hall and 28 State Street that flooded an extensive area. So it would appear that City Hall was Group 2's bailiwick and Hancock Street belonged to others.

Speaking of floods, one of the more unusual happenings that occur when you don't have a camera took place about six o'clock one summer Sunday morning at Washington and School Streets. A major water main had broken under Washington Street, at the top of Water Street, appropriately named in this case. It tore a very large hole in the pavement and thousands of gallons of water gushed forth. Much of it poured down Water Street to Post Office Square, but there was still enough to make Washington Street a river from curb to curb. The fire department responded and while waiting for the Water and Public Works Departments to put in their appearance, I sat with my aide in the car, which was parked blocking School Street.

Not too many people were up and stirring yet in the city, but then a gentleman, who probably had left his bedroom on Boston Common, came sauntering down School Street. He came to Washington Street and for a moment looked like he was going to continue on across. Both my aide and myself started out of the car together to stop him. But at the curb, he stopped. He peered at the water for a moment in disbelief, then knelt down and touched it. Being sure it was not a mirage, he turned around and went over to the door of the Old Corner Book Store. He removed his coat and shirt and hung them on the store doorknob. He then reached into his coat pocket and took out a bar of soap and a comb.

Completely oblivious that he had an audience, he went back to the street curb, unwrapped his soap and proceeded to wash his face, neck, head, hands and arms. Returning to the bookstore, he used the window as a mirror and combed his hair. He put the soap and comb back in his pocket, put on his shirt and coat, checked his appearance in his mirror and sauntered back up School Street, a clean and refreshed man - still unaware that his ablutions had been watched.

Variety is the spice of life so I will add an animal Incident. One winter Sunday afternoon we were called to Boston Common because a Police horse, named Misty, had fallen into an excavation pit. The frightened animal was hanging on to solid ground with his front hoofs and had become exhausted trying to get traction with his hind hoofs to lift himself out of the hole. At the scene there were a lot of spectators who had apparently made attempts to assist, but without success. I think his rider was afraid he would have to shoot his horse to put it out of his misery, but to an old summer farm boy the solution was simple.

I had the men thread a length of two and a half inch hose under the horse's rear end. Using the hose in tug-a-war fashion, I had two teams of firemen and spectators strain in opposite directions. As the space between them widened, the hose lengthened, the horse was raised and he gratefully walked away free and happy. His policeman rider breathed a sigh of relief and was also happy.

In his TV show, Sgt. Friday used to say, "Just give me the facts Ma'am." It would be a big help if the fire department were given the facts when they are called. For some reason, some people are very reluctant to tell firemen everything - or sometimes anything. Maybe they are afraid they will be arrested so they would rather make it a guessing game for the firemen. If we have the facts first, we can spend less time looking and more time doing. We can get out sooner and cause less damage.

One evening we were dispatched to an apartment over a restaurant on Cambridge Street for an odor of smoke. The woman said she could smell smoke in her living room but she had not seen it. There was a fireplace in the room and I asked her if she had used it in the last day or two. She said she had lived there for a few years and the fireplace had never been used. That ruled out a probable cause.

As we talked and watched, a little wisp of smoke came out of an electric outlet in the wall opposite the fireplace. We removed the outlet cover and felt the wires. All was cool to the touch, but every now and then a small puff of smoke was emitted. Since it apparently wasn't electrical, it could be in the wall. In spite of what is thought, firemen do not like to damage property, particularly in a home and on scant evidence. In this case the room was paneled so it was easy to remove a section - after removing the ceiling molding and baseboard. Doing this revealed nothing but a plaster wall and an occasional puff of smoke from the outlet area.

The next step was to put a hole in the plaster to look into the wall, but paneling would cover that when it was replaced. The hole in the wall revealed nothing except to prove that the smoke puffs were not confined solely to the electric box. They were also rising from the floor area, which meant either from the ceiling below or it was in the floor. We went down to the restaurant below and removed some ceiling tiles but found no trace of smoke or fire. This sent us back to the apartment floor.

While the anxious woman looked on, we untacked and rolled up her wall to wall carpeting, and opened up a section of the oak flooring. There the puffs of smoke were larger and more frequent. As we continued ripping up a strip about three boards wide, more smoke became visible and we knew we were on the right track. As we got closer to the fireplace hearth, sparks began to flicker. To make a longer story short, we ended up chopping out the wood rafters that supported the hearth. They had become charred and were like punk from the repeated heating and cooling of the fireplace. It takes many years to reach this point but it is a frequent occurrence with old fireplaces.

We later learned the woman had burned her rubbish in the fireplace almost every night during the few years she had lived there. If we had been told that on arrival, we would have started our investigation there instead of ending it there. "Just the facts Ma'am."

Some people can remain calm in the presence of fire - especially if it isn't their house. Engine 8 and Ladder 1 were sent one summer evening to investigate an unknown fire on a North End street. On arrival, the fire officer rang the bell at the given location and when the door opened, was greeted by the master of the house in his undershirt. He stopped to introduce himself, and then ushered the officer into his home because he had something to show him. He took him into the kitchen where the family was eating their supper. He stopped and introduced the lieutenant to his wife and each of the kids. The guided tour then continued down a long hall to an end bedroom into which the master led the lieutenant. He crossed the room, pulled back the curtains, raised the shade and said, "Look."

What the lieutenant looked at across the yard was the back of another house fully involved in fire. It turned into a two bagger - due to delay in discovery, and delay in alarm.

Anecdote:
The lesson that all that meets the eye is not necessarily true, was demonstrated at this fire. The fire was in a row of three story connected apartments separated by fire walls. Deputy Chief O'Mara, who was in charge, took his proper place in front of the fire building. I was in my proper place directing inside operations. As

we advanced on the fire in the second floor, I could look across an alley and see that the fire had entered the rear of a building on Commercial Street. Rolls of carpeting had been ignited. I promptly informed the Deputy of this by radio. He asked me to look again and make sure because he could see the fire wall from his vantage point in front of the building and that wall should have kept the fire from spreading to an adjacent building. What he couldn't see was that an alley in the rear jutted into the fire building. It was only 6 to 8 feet wide, which is no barrier at all for radiated heat. Firemen, take note of this lesson.

In the early seventies the First National Bank moved into their new building at 100 Federal Street and the old building at Federal and Milk Streets was torn down. All that remained to be removed, before work could begin on the new National Shawmut Bank building, was the vault that had been well constructed with much reinforcing steel. The vault would not yield to the wrecking ball so it was decided to blast it out of existence. Several days were spent in preparations, with many holes being drilled for the placing of explosives. Blasting was scheduled for 7 p.m. on a night Group 2 was working.

I was at the site when the new State Fire Marshal put in his appearance. He had just been appointed and was interested in the first blasting since he took office. I showed him around and shared my limited knowledge of the project with him. He looked around at all the windowed buildings surrounding the canyon where the old First National Bank and the Stone and Webster building once stood and asked how much the bond was. I told him the law required a minimum bond of ten thousand dollars but I didn't know what had been subscribed in this particular case. He said that wasn't enough, and the first thing he was going to do was to have the minimum bond raised.

The blasting time was moved up to eight and then nine o'clock. When it didn't go off then, the Fire Marshal left saying he had more important things to do than waiting around. He should have waited to see his prediction come true. Around eleven, the charges were set off - and glass fell for several minutes. Every window in every building on Federal, Franklin, Devonshire and Milk Streets that faced the canyon were shattered by the explosive waves. It was later determined that the vault was so well reinforced with steel, and there was so much dense concrete, that instead of breaking up the vault, the charges raced back out of the tamp holes. It was determined that the concussion force was equal to thirty-five anti-aircraft shells going off in a confined area and that's why all the broken glass. Incidentally, the law still requires a ten thousand dollar bond.

As a matter of history, mention should be made of the Blizzard of 1978. The snow started in the early afternoon of Monday, February 6th and continued until the night of the 7th. Group 2 worked the Night Tour on the 6th and most of us went in early, first to get there, but also so the Day Tour men could get home. Following the storm, the first relief men, including mine, began to show up starting Wednesday morning. I had then been on duty for over forty-one straight hours. Also, by then the department was holding one officer and seven men on each company, so few men got to go home. Traveling was so difficult that most men were content to stay at the fire house, unless they had problems at home.

The Governor declared a State of Emergency and all non-essential traffic was banned from city streets. The National Guard was mobilized and soldiers controlled traffic points and performed other emergency duties.

The fire department continued to operate as usual but under very trying conditions. Hydrants, and even fire boxes, had to be shoveled out to make them visible and usable. At fires, longer lines of hose had to be laid by hand and ladders carried great distances and over snow banks before they could be put to use. Once again fire houses became places of refuge for stranded people and the kitchens and coffee pots did yeoman duty.

Any work performed under these difficult conditions required an over-taxing of the men's strength. While working at Box 1412 on February 7th, Firefighter John McDonough, of the Lighting Plant, suffered a heart attack and died.

The one pleasant aspect was to see the streets of Boston empty of vehicular traffic. Much of downtown looked like a Currier and Ives scene, as people cross-country skied on the streets of Beacon Hill and the North End, as well as Boston Common and the Public Gardens. Kids coasted down Park Street and onto Tremont

Street on their sleds, or let their parents use them to tow home the groceries. A real spirit of friendliness prevailed throughout the whole city as strangers stopped to talk with strangers and people went out of their way to help one another. It is too bad that it takes thirty inches of snow to make neighbors cordial. On February 14th, Valentine's Day, traffic was again allowed into the city and people returned to their usual selves - an antithesis on this day dedicated to lovers.

On February 4, 1980 the department changed from a five alarm running card to a nine alarm one. Going the distance on either card provided about the same amount of men and apparatus, but under the new system they arrived in smaller increments - like two additional engines on each alarm after the third. As soon as it began, the men started lotteries as to which Group would have the first nine alarm fire.

On March 13th, at 0116 hours, Group 2 responded to an apartment house fire at 121 Salem Street (that same street again), and on arrival I ordered a second alarm because of smoke and fire showing, plus the fact a woman was lying on the sidewalk. I thought she had jumped from an upper floor, but it was just coincidental that she was a pedestrian who had tripped and fallen just as we pulled up.

As we ran lines into the building and made sure all occupants were evacuated, we found the fire racing from floor to floor as fast as we were. On orders of Deputy Chief O'Mara, the alarms were keeping pace with our ascent: 3, 4, 5, 6, 7, and 8 alarms, where he stopped. Some of the men with a stake in the pool were itching for him to go to 9 but we had stopped the fire from extending to any more buildings and we had the upper hand on it. We really didn't need the two more engines a 9th alarm would bring but when I went out to report our progress to Chief O'Mara, I mentioned we were close to 9 and we could use the two engines to relieve some of the earlier companies. He smiled at me and replied, "Eight yes, but I am not going to be the first deputy to strike nine alarms, unless we need it. We can put it out with what we have here. Right Paul?" I agreed.

Anecdote:
*The dubious distinction of having the first Nine Alarm fire in Boston
went to Group One and Deputy Chief Stapleton a few weeks later
when flames raced through a series of storage buildings in Allston.*

A perfect example of having to find the fire before you can fight
it happened on June 17th of the same year. At 0322 hours we
responded to a building on Oliver Street because the night
engineer could smell smoke, and after looking for a while himself
and unable to find it, he called for the fire department. Normally
the men of the two ladder trucks and the Rescue Company would
do the searching while the men on the engine companies stood by
ready with lines of hose. In this case we used everyone in our
search for a trace of the smoke. We could smell it, but we couldn't
find it. The building to which we were called connected with, or
abutted with other buildings on Milk, Franklin and Batterymarch
Streets. After looking for over a half-hour we finally found the fire
at 142 Milk Street. Two separate fires had been set in the
basement and they had extended to the first and second floors
before our discovery. A second alarm was immediately ordered.
Time: 0358 hours.

On November 28, 1981 the firemen in Lynn didn't have to look
for a half hour to find their fire. They responded in the wee hours
of the morning while I was home sleeping, but before their fire
was put out I would add a new first to my firefighting experiences.
Shortly after 0200 hours, the police discovered fire in a building
on Oxford Street. In a few minutes the strong winds had scattered
embers onto roofs and windowsills of nearby buildings and within
a half-hour it was declared a conflagration. The fire was out of
control and spreading indiscriminately from building to building
helped by the radiated heat and firebrands.

By the time the "All Out" was sent on December 14th,
seventeen buildings had been destroyed and others heavily
damaged. Estimated losses were 50 to 70 million dollars. 94 cities
and towns in Massachusetts and New Hampshire responded to
the Mutual Aid call and sent 600 firemen to help their brothers in
need. Boston sent several engine companies along with District 3
in charge of them. When my Aide, Phil "Who," and myself
reported for the Day Tour on Saturday morning, we went directly
to Lynn and relieved the night chief. Fires in most of the buildings

had by then either been knocked down or burnt themselves out, but there was still plenty of work to be done. Phil and I surveyed the destruction and where the Boston companies were working. It was obvious all the men had worked hard to stop the conflagration and they were deserving of a rest.

There was one structure, known as the Vamp Building, which had been a former shoe factory and covered an entire city block. It was an eight story building that had recently been made over into apartments for senior citizens and the first occupants had started to move in. During the early morning hours, fire had gotten into this building by radiated heat and flying embers, but it had been extinguished, or so they thought. Phil and I went through the entire building and as we made our way through the top floor, we detected fire in the cock loft above us. It wasn't visible, but we knew it was there by feeling the ceilings for hot spots and by listening.

It would be a lot of work pulling a block long series of ceilings to get into the cock loft and I thought the men who had worked all night should not be expected to take on the task. There was a standpipe in the stairwell and I had Phil get some men to bring some donut rolls up to the top floor. When the Day Tour men for Engine 50 came on scene, we would start opening ceilings and attack the fire. Meanwhile I would report to the Lynn Chief, who was in charge of the fire, and give him the good news that the fire was in the cock loft, and what I proposed to do about it.

It took a while to locate him and when I did, he was talking to the Governor. He was not happy to hear my news and I think he was reluctant to believe it - and rightfully so, because normally fire walls should prevent the horizontal extension of heat in a building, which I figured had taken place. I persisted, on the theory that the flames had jumped the fire walls, probably through holes that had been made for pipes or wiring chases during renovations. The Governor sensed the problem and our differing opinions. "Would it serve the purpose to go up in my helicopter and look down on the building?" he asked.

Without waiting for the Lynn Chief to respond, I spoke up saying it would be a good way to make certain of conditions, and so a few minutes later we were looking down on the Vamp Building roof from the Governor's helicopter. The fire walls extending through the roof were obvious - and so were the fires burning between them, right across the roof. It turned out to be an excellent way to study the fire's progress in the building. Although this time I was right in my theory, it was no reflection on the Lynn Chief, who I am sure was just hoping against hope that I was wrong when I brought him the news. He already had enough problems with which to contend.

Anecdote:
From the time I became an officer I made it a practice to wear a necktie when working, except in the summer. As a chief, it was partly to set an example for my company officers but in addition the tight neck made it warmer in the winter and so the tie was in place when we went to Lynn that morning. One of those who surveyed the Vamp Building from the helicopter was the State Fire Marshal. Years later our son Bruce was talking with the Marshal on a business matter and in passing mentioned that his father was a Boston Fire Chief. The Marshal asked his name and when Bruce told him "Cook," the Marshal said, "I know Paul Cook in District 3. He is the chief who wears a tie to fires." Strange the impressions made by little things.

During 1981 and into 1982 another tragedy struck the Boston Fire Department - - Proposition 2-1/2.

Engines 25, 43 and Ladder 20 were deactivated on February 4th.
Engines 1, 12, 26, 34, 40, 50, 54 and Ladders 5, 8, 22, 30, 31 and District 2 were deactivated on April 10th.
Engines 11, 36 and Ladder 13, A/Tower 1 and District 13 were deactivated on October 20th.
Engine 49, A/Tower 2 and Rescue 2 were deactivated on January 14, 1982.

Losing these fire protection companies was a tragedy for the citizens of Boston, but it was an even bigger immediate tragedy for many of the faithful firemen and their families. During the summer of 1981, hundreds of men were terminated. Due to the fickleness of the courts there was much uncertainty, so they were reinstated, then terminated again and some were reinstated and others terminated. The effect on officers was not this flexible, but was just as traumatic. On November 10th, 7 district chiefs, 5 captains and 26 lieutenants were demoted.

On March 11, 1982, politics began to stop playing games. The officers' demotions were terminated and some of the firefighters were reinstated. The rest of the men reported to their companies on June 30th. City Hall and the courts patted themselves on the back for putting Humpty Dumpty back together again, but the scars will last for years. Since then, a few of the companies have been placed back in service, but today the department is about one third less the size it was before Proposition 2-1/2 and politics.

Of less serious consequence at this time was the subject of District Chief's Aides. This was an economy measure being studied by fire departments throughout the country. Looking for an excuse to terminate them, or seeking justification to keep them, a request was made for chiefs to submit a paper regarding these valuable assistants. Being long winded with a typewriter, I forwarded my three page epistle on why I needed my aide. Shortly afterwards I was talking with some brass at headquarters and the subject of aides was brought up and my lengthy letter in particular. He said I had been so convincing regarding the value of aides, that headquarters had decided to keep them - and let the chiefs go.

Other district chiefs may not have been so convincing because on December 2, 1981, all aides were reassigned to companies - except District 3.

I started by saying this issue was of less serious consequence, but that is not true. Traffic, parking and the height of multistoried buildings may have given added need for an aide downtown, but in the argument too much emphasis was given to driving the chief's car, which is actually the least of an aide's duties. His real help is at fires and gathering the great amount of information following a fire that is needed for fire reports and public records - so the courts can pick them apart and lawyers can sue.

To expect a chief to concentrate on driving himself through today's city traffic, while also trying to envision the area he is responding to, the buildings that could be involved, location of water sources and life hazards of the neighborhood, is false economy. This was proven in one section of the city when an acting district chief, driving himself, tried to avoid a car that had entered an intersection too fast, and he skidded striking a tree. The department car was demolished, at great expense to the tax payers, and the chief was seriously injured. He spent considerable time in the hospital and recuperating, at great expense to the tax payers, and eventually received a disability pension, also at expense to the tax payers. Like most specific political economies, this one cost more than it saved.

Anecdote:
Shortly after taking office in 1984, Commissioner Stapleton restored the aides to district chiefs. A sensible and appreciated move.

Through the years I have taken part in or been in charge of a few water rescues, but up until a bitterly cold night in January of 1982 they had always taken place out of doors. On that night Engine 4 and Ladder 24 were sent to investigate a reported broken water pipe in a bar not too far from the fire house. On arrival, the senior officer asked for District 3 to respond. Once there I found the four inch sprinkler standpipe in the outside wall had frozen and burst, sending torrents of water down the stairs and into the lower bar. Booths and stools were floating around like unguided cruise ships. The icy water was nearly three feet deep and two young ladies and a gentleman were still at the bar - or rather on it. I ordered the men to rescue them.

One of the shapely ladies had on new expensive designer jeans and rather than get them wet, she removed them for her trip across the perilous waters. The other young lady hopped up on the bar and slipped out of her jumpsuit and shoes, and held them over her head for her marine rescue. The gentleman said he would fend for himself and dove off the bar. When he came to the surface, he began paddling toward the exit. The water was colder than it looked and he began to flounder. We were able to get to him and pull him out. He was rushed to Mass General Hospital where he was admitted in critical condition for hypothermia. Despite the near zero temperatures, when the young lady with the jumpsuit got out of the building, she slipped out of her wet bra and panties there on the sidewalk and back into her jumpsuit, and disappeared into the night.

On another night we responded to a tavern on Lomasney Way to rescue the patrons. It seems one of the imbibers had been shut off and thrown out. There was an extremely heavy stainless steel open padlock hanging on a hasp by the tavern door, and to demonstrate his displeasure with the treatment he received, the inebriated ejectee put the hasp in place and locked all the other patrons in the bar. When I saw the size of the lock there was doubt in my mind as to how quick we could make the rescue, but there was a real giant of a man on Ladder 24. He put the adz end of the Halligan Bar into the shank of the padlock, and with one mighty blow of a maul, he shattered that stainless steel lock into dozens of pieces.

Single rescues are also part of the job. Just about daybreak one morning we were called to a peep show store in the West End. Inside was a man who apparently had been locked in when the proprietor locked up for the night. Since he wasn't going anywhere anyhow, he probably had taken advantage of the unlimited free girlie viewing available to him. We forced the door and let him out. Why he hadn't called earlier is anyone's guess. Before leaving the scene he asked if there was any chance of getting a note from the chief to show to his wife, that it wasn't his fault he was out all night. He didn't get it.

Being a district chief adds another unpleasant, or unproductive, task to an already busy schedule. Going to court! Any number of events that happen in the district while you are working can trigger a court appearance, or I should say appearances in court, because no case is ever settled at the first session - that would be too easy on the tax payers. As a witness for the State you must be there at nine o'clock in the morning, but the judge doesn't come in until ten. He has to sit in his chambers preparing to face the witnesses - the perpetrator of the crime is probably already out on bail thanks to another case. The alleged culprits are always indigent so the court has to appoint public defenders. When they are assigned, they of course have to study the case, so immediately ask for a continuance to another date - which is automatically granted by the yawning magistrate, and this also automatically doubles their fee because it doubles their number of court appearances.

The real reason for asking for a continuance is so they can get back in the public defender's line and pick up another half dozen cases for the morning - which automatically guarantees them tax payers paid fees for twelve appearances. If it stopped there, the tax payers and their pocketbooks could breathe a sigh of relief. Long ago our judicial system forsook the Old English Law it was based on, and adopted the practice of operating on the mathematical principle of multiplication. 1 appearance becomes 2, 2 become 4, 4 become 8, and if there is doubt in the mind of any of the players, it can go to 16. Regardless of this, at some point the money making hocus-pocus goes to a higher court, where it starts all over again.

Meanwhile the alleged criminal is still out on bail and probably practicing his own system of multiplication by repeating his original crime again and again. Each new crime begins a new series of appearances for the public defenders, and a further drain on the tax payers, who knows nothing of what is going on except his taxes keep going up. It is kind of like a semi-legal pyramid club.

Several of the best stories, that I earlier mentioned should not be included in this book, took place in, or were related to court cases, and they have been omitted. But to wrap up this subject, let me conclude with one final scene of justice.

It involved an arson case, and note that it is not an "alleged" arson case as the court jargon would term it. The court always refer to it as "alleged," but as far as the fire department was concerned, the evidence was so overwhelming that there was no doubt in our minds, and we had photos to prove it. In spite of this, we went through the frustrating fanfare of appearances and continuances. The case was dismissed, went to the grand jury and finally on a hot sultry summer afternoon, the winter fire settled into a warm stuffy courtroom for justice to triumph.

I was the first witness "for the State" and the judge grilled me for twenty minutes - like he should have grilled the "alleged" arsonist - but by then he was fast asleep. The second witness was a member of the Arson Squad, and half way through his testimony, His Honor started to nod. Everyone in the courtroom was cognizant of the Arms of Morpheus encompassing His Honor, but the legal procedure continued on schedule. There were questions and answers, examination and cross-examination. Next witness.

When the snickering among the courtroom spectators became too obvious, the court officers sprang into action. One of them, sitting at his desk that was on a raised platform, began opening drawers and banging them shut. Since this repeated overture had no effect, he reached over and kicked his metal waste basket off the platform. It resounded like a clanging cymbal as it crashed to the floor and reverberated as it rolled into a corner. The other officer had a Golden Arch milkshake in an anteroom off the courtroom, and from time to time he would go to the little room, take a gulp of the ice cream drink, slam the door shut and return to the scene of action. Everyone jumped but the judge.

By going for more frequent swigs of his frappe, the officer must have created a draft that chilled the "Fate Decider," because he stirred, pulled his black robe closer around him, rose from the bench and walked around his court. I don't know what he based his decision on, but in the end he pronounced the felony offender "Guilty." Now we could all go home in time for supper - including the guilty party who was released on bail pending an appeal and was the first one out, because he knew his way around the courthouse. My suggestion! If you are looking for Justice, skip the courts, and look elsewhere. Might try the dictionary, it could be found there.

Quite often the fire department is called to a time consuming type of Incident called "odor of gas." This can be a natural gas used for cooking and heating, and which runs in pipes under the ground, or it can be a hydrocarbon product stored in gas stations and elsewhere. Both can be deceiving and misleading. Once in the ground they seek their own level and path of movement. Gasoline especially is elusive as once it leaks from a tank it can end up in remote places for no obvious reasons.

One week in District 3 we were plagued by an "odor of gas" in a waterfront neighborhood. It all ended on a Saturday night when Group 2 was working. A leaking tank had been discovered and steps were in progress for its removal and replacement, but quite a few gallons of the product had seeped into the ground. By that Saturday night, traces of gasoline had shown up in a boat slip on

Commercial Street and it was sealed off with a floating boom. I had an engine and ladder standing by for any eventuality.

The first eventuality was the ship slip. No longer was it traces of gasoline finding its way into the salt water, the entire dammed in slip was turning pale pink, with the influx of the high octane stuff. There were two house boats on styrofoam pontoons that were in the boomed in area and the gasoline was dissolving the floats. The distressed owner wanted the fire department to do something. Just what, he didn't say. Perhaps we could all jump in and hold the boats up.

We had to leave him with his dilemma when the second eventuality happened. Suddenly there was an explosion in a tavern on the other side of the street. We were already heading in that direction with the apparatus when a man came charging at us yelling,
"There is a fire in my place."
"Where is your place?" I asked. It could be two fires.
"Not my place. The fire is in My Place."
"I know its your place, but where is it?"
"It's in My Place, over there," he said, pointing to the site of the explosion.

If I were a drinking man I would have known that "MY PLACE" was a tavern on Commercial Street. If I had followed the Fire Commissioner's order to know every building in my district, I would have known it too.

As soon as the blast took place I notified Fire Alarm to strike the box. When we got to the tavern, the front door had been blown out into the street and the few stunned patrons were making their way to safety. The bartender said it was in the cellar, as he too abandoned "My Place." While Engine 8 began running a big line, I made my way to the cellar to learn the condition. There were several inches of water on the floor but the entire floor area was in flames. Using my portable radio I told Fire Alarm we had an explosion in a tavern and the cellar was fully involved in fire. Engine 8 charged their line and came down the cellar stairs. Where was all the fire I had told them about? It had disappeared as quickly as it had appeared. All we could find was some smoldering cotton floor mops in a wringer pail.

Hearing my radio messages, Chief O'Mara arrived, prepared for the worst - and I had nothing to show him but a busted door. As we put the puzzle pieces together, we concluded that some of the gasoline had floated into the cellar with the rising tide. This was common in the area. On reaching the gas flame of the hot water heater, the vapors ignited and set fire to all the gasoline floating on top of the water. That is why the first time I went into the cellar alone, there was a sea of fire. Since the amount of gasoline was relatively small, the fire burnt itself out almost immediately and when Engine 8 came into the cellar, the cupboard was bare.

Anecdote:
On another occasion we responded to an "odor of gas" in the West End. In the cellar we found a good amount of gasoline on the floor and more coming through the ground. I ordered the three story apartment building to be evacuated. Several days later we found the source to be a leaking underground tank at a gas station two blocks away, not the gas station next to the apartment. Taking pity on his now homeless tenants, the owner made arrangements for them to eat in the nearby Holiday Inn. The first night about six people reported to the dining room Maitre D'. Word of a "free lunch" must have gotten around because the second night about three dozen went to the dining room. This prompted the owner to make other arrangements.

Regarding the waterfront, the Marine Unit, or fire boats, are a most interesting part of District 3. The men assigned to them lived on the boats in close quarters, but this did not hamper their ability or enthusiasm to do their job. Their firefighting concerns are far different from those of land companies but no less important. Constant knowledge of wind speed and direction, and the rise and fall of the tides are paramount to their maneuverability in the harbor. A fire boat responds to every waterfront fire alarm, and once there the powerful pumps can provide thousands of gallons of water a minute from the endless saltwater supply. By using the bateau they can get under piers and attack a fire using an inch and a half line.

Each boat, on each group, has a Master to pilot it and an Engineer to keep it moving. Other members of the crew act as deck hands and operate the guns and lines at fires. On land they maintain the boats and equipment, which needs constant attention because of the salt water. These men save the tax payers money by making their own manila fenders and bow protectors for the cost of the rope alone. These weigh many hundreds of pounds and take months to make in the men's spare time.

Knowing the fire equipment they operate is expensive, and useless when out of service, they spend hours charting and studying the waters and piers around the harbor so as to avoid hitting underwater objects when responding to or working at fires. There is not much left to burn on most of the harbor islands, but the increasing number of marinas being added almost daily in the harbor, house millions of dollars worth of private boats. As these marinas are planned, they make maximum use of the space available, but little thought is given to providing access for the fire boats to reach them in an emergency. It is one more headache for the fire department because the potential dollar loss is staggering.

Anecdote:
When the fireboats respond to a small boat fire, dual action is required by the fire department if the boat is to be saved. First the fire has to be extinguished. This is usually accomplished by one of the monitor guns which quickly pours in hundreds of gallons of sea water, which can also sink the vessel. To counter this, the men must quickly board the boat with a portable pump and eject the water they are pouring in, so the tub stays floating.

Like all fire houses, there is a wide range of talents among the men assigned to the Marine Unit. In my early years in District 3, there were two who were oil paint artists. One of them, who was assigned to my group, began to experiment with portraits and did a very fine one of me in uniform. For a background he included a hazy Boston skyline which was appropriate for District 3. The other artist, on Group 4, made a practice of giving each man who retired from the Marine Unit, a painting of the boat on which he had served. He varied the background according to incidents that happened during the man's career. Some were fire scenes, some were scenes of other locations or activities in the harbor that the man may have participated in. Although I wasn't assigned to the

Marine Unit, the Marine Unit was assigned to me, and I always hoped that if I retired before him, he would honor me with one of his art works. Alas, Gene was a few months older and retired early in 1988. I don't think anyone gave him a painting.

Considering the many talents and marine abilities that the men assigned to the boats brought with them, and then freely used to save money for the public, it is another example of a fringe benefit the tax payers receive from dedicated men. By way of reciprocation, it should be noted that firemen appreciated the public's favorable response on the several occasions we went to the ballot box.

Anecdote:
Following World War II, one of the fire boats was named, "The Joseph J. Luna." It was named after the first Boston Fireman killed in action during the war. He was serving with the Marine Corps in the Pacific and was killed September 15, 1944.

The subway tunnels in District 3 present their own version of challenges and headaches. On the non-fire, but violent side, are the numerous accidents involving a person versus a machine - and the metal giants always win. You are never certain if the victim jumped in front of the train or if he or she accidentally fell. If it was the latter, it is doubly tragic but we'll never know for certain. The men who crawl under the train and raise it up with jacks and air bags to free the victims or to retrieve parts of the body are particularly dedicated. Sometimes there is still life and the paramedics from the city's Emergency Medical Service join the firefighters in trying to preserve something that someone else was trying to throw away. They too are specially dedicated.

Train accidents in the tunnels don't happen very often, thankfully, but when they do it is a trying time for firemen. I had one on the Red Line near Charles Street Station for which a second alarm was struck. There was no fire, but the extra manpower was needed to give medical treatment and carry the many victims out of the tunnel on stretchers. Stumbling over rail tracks and ties while carrying a heavy stretcher, in limited light, is no easy task.

There were no fires in the above Incidents but fires do occur underground. I had a two alarm fire in the Orange Line Washington Street station in the wee hours of a morning. It was a particularly difficult fire to fight because of the limited space for the smoke and heat to go. The men did their part by breathing in as much as they could but there was still plenty left. The fire involved Mother's Bakery and several other shops. The men were taking a beating and we weren't making much progress on the fire. Chief O'Mara told me to take an engine company and see if I could find another way to approach the fire. As it turned out we went down an exit on Hawley Street and walked into the fire on the leeward side. We were able to walk right up to it in clear air and knock the fire down, to everyone's relief. This was before the subway standpipes were in place.

There was a string of other subway fires, mostly involving trains, which resulted in at least one fatality. Dragging long lines of hose down station stairs and then hundreds of feet into the tunnels before the fire could be attacked took considerable time and was a drain on the men. Seeking an alternative, the MBTA and the fire department worked out a system of dry standpipes that now protect all subway stations and extend throughout all train tunnels. When a fire occurs, the fire department fills the standpipe with water, while other men carrying donut rolls move into the tunnel where the fire is located. By connecting to one of the standpipe outlets that are located every one hundred feet, the fire can be attacked with shorter lines of hose, saving time and work.

District 3 provides a varying variety of Incidents. In the progressive process of trying to blow up the bank vault to succeeding in blowing down whole buildings to make way for new construction, impressive scenes are provided for those fortunate enough to view them. The process, called implosion, involves the strategic placing of a number of pounds of explosives, which are then fired as separate blasts, microseconds apart. The intent is to weaken the main supports of the building causing it to all fall down in one pile.

The first building in District 3 to meet this fate was the Hayward Place garage. It was scheduled to fall down at 0700 hours on a Sunday morning but due to lightning storms in the area the night before, the countdown was delayed, but it did come down without a hitch after the delays. Group 2 had worked the Night Tour and I had an engine and ladder company standing by, but they were not needed.

Pictures I have do not indicate an excessive amount of dirt and dust at that one, but several years later the old Hotel Manger was reduced to a story and a half pile of rubble by the same procedure. This one attracted many more spectators, including some chiefs and other officers from headquarters who showed up in their dress uniforms on a summer Sunday morning. Group 2 was working and we had apparatus standing by a couple blocks from the site. Just before the count down, Chief O'Mara went to his car and donned full fire gear. Monkey see; monkey do - so I went to my car and returned in full fire gear. When the blast went off and the hotel came down, a cloud of dirt and dust fifty feet high rolled in every direction. All the spectators, including the dressed up officers from headquarters, looked like they had been hit with bags of flour. All you could see of them were blinking eyes. Thanks to Chief O'Mara, all I had to do was remove my fire gear to look neat.

The fact that I had earned two gold bugles did not abate Herb's relentless desire to see me with a third gold bugle. However, I think he reluctantly realized that three promotions out of a possible four wasn't too bad, and he had done his best to get his kid brother that far up the ladder. He took special interest in the times I acted deputy, hoping it would inspire me to seek the rank permanently.

Alas, in early November 1980, Herb was diagnosed as having cancer on the pulmonary artery. It was inoperable due to its location and it later spread to his lungs. He told me, but kept it from his family until after Thanksgiving. The all too familiar pattern of tests, radiation treatments, chemotherapy and visits to the hospitals for more tests and experiments began and lasted for a year. He had good care and lots of attention at the Brigham and Women's Hospital, because that is where he had volunteered so many thousands of hours in the emergency ward, and which he continued to do even in the first months of his illness. All the staff that knew and respected him empathized with his every concern and stage of his illness.

As his condition deteriorated and he was hospitalized more frequently, he freely discussed his problem with the doctors and volunteered to let them use untried medicines, not expecting it would help him, but hoping they would learn something that might help others. He paid more attention to his vital signs than those attending him, and when he sensed they were failing and the pain became too intense, the nurse found him with all his needles removed and neatly lined up on his bedside table. They were re-inserted, but he died quietly in the afternoon of November 12, 1981. It is quite likely that his years as a working spark contributed to his cancer. Two months later, Rose, his wife of forty-nine years died suddenly of an embolism.

Herb would have really enjoyed watching his little brother later playing deputy at some of the big ones. As the years hastened by, my seniority put me in this role more frequently and I enjoyed it. Too late, I wished I had heeded Herb's constant and final nagging.

One Sunday I was acting deputy and responded to a bakery fire in the North End. The oven section of the bakery was in the first floor of a five story building and the fire started there. Walls had been breached to enlarge the shop and the customer section, with a lunch counter, was in the first floor of an adjacent four story structure. From its origin near the ovens, the fire had spread horizontally into the customer section and vertically in the walls to the second and third floor bathrooms via pipe chases. I had two and a half inch lines working on all three floors. Car 3 had reported fire showing but I had said nothing to Fire Alarm other than reporting my arrival. After several minutes with no additional information, Fire Alarm, per standard procedure, called for a report. I was quite certain all was under control and I wanted to report I had a fire in a five story building extended to a four story building and all companies working. This news would have brought every scanner listener to attention (like the boat fire at City Hall) and many to the North End. But in case there was a surprise waiting for me, it was better to err on the side of caution, so I reported fire knocked down and holding all companies. We were there for another hour overhauling and wetting down - and there were no surprises. In hindsight, I wish I had let go my first report - just to see the reaction!

The fact that strange events often happened, when Cook was acting deputy, stirred the curiosity of the men on Group 2 and they would wonder, "What will it be this tour of duty?" Many times they didn't have to wait long to find out, and it was quite often something out of the ordinary. It was kind of a repeat of what Chief Ainsworth had said nearly forty years before.

On January 2, 1984 I had the first Boston Westin Hotel fire, which had all the makings of a chief's nightmare: fire in a high rise hotel with heavy smoke throughout the building; electrical failure so elevators were not usable; people peering and waving from upper floors to get attention; windows beyond the reach of our longest ladders being broken by frightened occupants ready to jump, regardless of the height and certain consequences. At the time, Mayor Raymond Flynn was being sworn in for his first term, and he left his Inauguration to come see what young Cookie was up to.

Anecdote:
A few days later I was talking to a deputy and in passing he remarked, "I was listening to my scanner the other day when you had the Westin Hotel fire and I was sure glad you were having it and not me."

On January 20th of the same year I had the infamous pier fire in back of North Station that fouled up commuter rail transportation to the North Shore for a year, but more about that in a later chapter.

If he was listening, Herb must have been grinning from ear to ear as his kid brother answered to "C-6," even if he was only acting deputy.

Anecdote:
An interesting footnote is that of the 199 men who were appointed on January 22, 1947, 12 became District Chiefs, 11 became Captains and 32 became Lieutenants. On January 29th, 198 more men were appointed and of these, four became District Chiefs, four became Captains and 22 became Lieutenants. This is the good news. The sad news is that three appointed on January 22nd and five the next week died in the Line of Duty.

Promotion to District Fire Chief, July 28, 1971.
L-R, Commissioner George Paul, wife Dorothy, Chief Cook, mom,
brother Herbert who pushed me to this day, Rev. Arnold Olsen.

Anecdote:
*The Line of Duty Deaths of Hoseman Barnard and PMS Cady at 70
Chauncy Street on the night of October 22, 1946 assured a Yes
vote on Question 4, and thus also assured my appointment to the
fire department. Likewise, the Crawford-Hollidge store fire provided
my appointment to captain and Chief McLaughlin's injuries
provided a vacancy for district chief. It is sad and ironic that these
three fires which had a bearing on my career all involved stores
selling furs.*

Hotel Vendome, June 17, 1972.
Nine firemen killed, including Lt. Tommy Carroll of our youthful days on old Engine 42.

Engine 7, morning after Plant Shoe Factory fire, February 1976.

Lynn Conflagration, November 28, 1981.
Chief Cook, back to photo on right side, reports extension of fire
in Vamp Building to Lynn Chief Joseph Scanlon, as Governor Ed
King, in suit, listens. He offered his helicopter to fly over the sight
to gain a better perspective. We did – a first! 94 cities and towns
from Massachusetts and New Hampshire sent Mutual Aid.

(Photo by Walter Hoey, *Daily Evening Item*, whose picture
appeared in, "A City in Flames, Lynn's Second Great Fire.")

Lynn Conflagration, November 28, 1981.
Chief Cook, Lieut. Messina (Engine 50) and Aide Phil LaCascia.
Note tie the State Fire Marshall remarked about.

(Photo by Walter Hoey, *Daily Evening Item*, whose picture
appeared in, "A City in Flames, Lynn's Second Great Fire.")

One of my several fires at Boston City Hall. Mayor Raymond
Flynn in white shirt.

Acting Deputy Chief Cook receives radio report from a Company Officer before ordering an additional alarm at South Boston fire.

Deputy Chief Harrison sits on apparatus observing operations.

Last fire I responded to as Commander of District 3.
L-R, Deputy Chief Edward Kenney, Captain George McCafferty,
District Chief Paul Cook.

14

HERE, THERE AND EVERYWHERE

(or, We'll Go Anywhere)

The Marines advertise that they are looking for a few good men. The fire service has a lot of good men and they are not limited to one city or to one state or even to one country. The thing that the two units have in common is "esprit de corps" but in the case of fire departments it crosses all boundaries and even leaps behind the "Iron Curtain." It is a bond that recognizes no language, political or cultural difference. It is melded and welded by mutual concerns and dangers and is fraught with the realization that we share a perilous occupation, always with the possible fate of a date with destiny.

The friendship fraternity that exists within the Boston Fire Department was described earlier but it is also manifested among "visiting firemen." Most firemen on vacation will stop in at the local fire house to introduce themselves - and often end up spending several hours. This is why firemen need patient and understanding wives. On the other hand, if a fireman runs into any type of difficulty when away from home and in a strange place, he can always get a sympathetic ear and a helping hand from his fellow wearers of the Maltese Cross.

Anecdote:
The Maltese Cross is a symbol of protection - a badge of honor. Its story is hundreds of years old and goes back to when a courageous band of Crusaders known, as the Knights of St. John, fought the Saracens for possession of the Holy Land and they encountered a new weapon unknown to European warriors. It was a simple, but horrible device of war; it wrought excruciating pain

and agonizing death upon the brave fighters of the Cross. The Saracens' weapon was fire!

As the Crusaders advanced on the walls of the city, they were attacked by glass bombs containing naphtha. When they became saturated with the highly flammable liquid, the Saracens hurled a flaming tree into their midst.

Hundreds of Knights were burned alive. Others risked their lives to save their brothers in arms from dying painful deaths. Thus, these men became the first Fire Fighters - and the first of a long list of courageous Fire Fighters. Their heroic efforts were recognized by fellow Crusaders who awarded each hero with a badge of honor - a cross similar to the one Fire Fighters wear today. Since the Knights of St. John lived for nearly four centuries on a little island in the Mediterranean Sea, named Malta, the Cross became known as the Maltese Cross.

The Maltese Cross is a symbol of protection. It means that the Fire Fighter who wears this Cross is willing to lay down his life, just as the Crusaders sacrificed their lives for their fellow men so many years ago.

The Maltese Cross is a Fire Fighter's Badge of Courage - a ladder-rung away from death.

(Credit: The Pittsburgh Fire Fighter)

Being a renowned medical center, Boston attracts many people in their hours of physical need. Some have to stay for extended periods or keep coming back for repeated treatments. Many of them are members of firemen's families from all over the country and in their frightened loneliness they turn to their brothers in blue to help see them through their difficult times. District 3 near the Mass. General Hospital and Shriner's Burn Center, District 4 near University and New England Medical Centers, District 5 near Brigham & Women's and the Beth Israel Hospitals, as well as District 11 near St. Elizabeth's Hospital. These are the main gathering points for medical visitors, but it could be any fire house, or any medical facility in the city. At a minimum they can be informed about reasonable places to stay and eat, and at maximum they may spend a few days in a fire house. Hospital costs for the sick are high enough but adding food and lodging for a loved one to accompany them is often prohibitive. Sometimes the men's private homes are offered as a solution. Life long friendships are started, and followed up with nationwide visits among families that share a common hazardous job.

Wives and children of firemen are instructed that if they run into any kind of trouble in a strange city, head to the nearest fire house and identify themselves. There are no strangers among firemen; only friends that may not have yet met.

Firefighters in every country are interested in learning about the way things are done in other departments. They are interested in the hours worked and the pay received by others for the same work they do. They want to know about the latest equipment innovations others have and whether they are a real improvement or just a change. They want to learn about the big ones, that got away - fires not fish - and tell of their triumphs - both the prompt ones and those delayed. They want to talk shop, but mostly they want to extend the hand of fraternal friendship.

1972 was the year of our Twenty-fifth Wedding Anniversary and I had promised Dot we would visit her beloved England - provided we could also visit my beloved Paris. We spent a week in England seeing all the things that tourists look at, plus a fire house full of engines. In that country it is a National Fire Service - so you have to behave yourself or you could have a very long commute to work.

Then on to "Gay Paree" for a week where we celebrated our Silver Anniversary with French Champagne at a Montmartre Cafe. I was able to show Dot the city that many of her daily letters went to twenty-eight years before. Also the street corner near La Place de L'Opera where, on a night right after the "Liberation," a German sniper fired a few rounds seconds after I left, killing the G.I. I had been talking with. We stopped into the Hotel D'Iena, where I had been billeted for a while, and talked with the manager. It was then a hotel occupied mostly by retired people, but the sliding roof over the grand dining room still worked.

The heavily reinforced concrete bunker that the Germans had built in the early forties, and we took over and made into an Intelligence Center, was just then being demolished. They were having as much trouble dismantling that concrete bunker as we had with the First National Bank vault.

We went on this vacation with a couple who were neighbors. One day we walked along the Seine River looking for a place to have lunch. As we strolled, I spotted a familiar looking vessel and a sign reading, "Brigade De Sapeurs-Pompiers De Paris." The old fire horse in me was aroused - I was home. It was a fireboat of the Paris Fire Department. As we stopped to look and take pictures, one of the crew came over and struck up a conversation - the brotherhood is international. In a few minutes we were touring the boat and then sitting in the galley with a cold drink. They were preparing a delicious looking lunch and I knew enough French to decipher that they were wondering if it could be stretched for four more. It couldn't, and we politely begged off their sacrificing offer.

In Paris the fire department is part of the military and the one who had struck up the conversation was Corporal Henri Leroux, who was the pilot on the fireboat. Naturally he was interested in Boston's fireboats and I was glad that they were part of my district so I could talk intelligently about the boats, even if he couldn't fathom all of my French. Before our debarking, he gave me badges of the French and Paris fire service, as well as a red trimmed uniform hat, worn by all French fireman. In return he wanted an American fire badge. I explained that badges weren't so easily come by in Boston, but that I would send him something.

The something turned out to be an officer's uniform hat. It included a shiney silver chin strap and the polished insignia of a lieutenant - one silver bugle. When Henri received it, he sent me a flowery letter of thanks, and he must have proudly displayed it around the whole Paris Fire Brigade, because I was suddenly inundated with mail from Paris requesting hats.

The following June we went back to England again. The travel bug had bitten us and we wanted to see how our youngest, Jonathan who was then aged nine, would travel. He did just fine and so for the next few years we traveled overseas every Spring and Fall. Sometimes it was with a couple of our children, sometimes with all four of them and sometimes with our neighbors or other friends, but always our sightseeing included at least one fire house.

On October 14, 1973, Chelsea, Massachusetts experienced another conflagration and Boston sent ten Engine and three Ladder Companies along with three chiefs. One of them was an acting chief covering my vacation. At the time, Dot and I were in Italy, but Herb represented the Cook family as he worked with the Red Cross Disaster Unit. It was appropriate for Herb to be there because he had missed the 1908 Chelsea conflagration because of his age, as mentioned earlier.

We were again with our neighbors and this time on a bus between Florence and Sorrento, Italy. One of the passengers finished his American newspaper and handed it to me. I asked him if there was any interesting news and he replied, "Yes. There is an article that tells about a Boston Fire Chief fiddling his time away in Rome while Chelsea burns." It turned out that he was a district fire chief from Lynn, Mass. I don't know just how he knew I was a Boston chief, except there are no strangers among firemen, and for the rest of trip we compared notes and talked shop.

The first airplane ride for our daughter Janna was when the whole family went to Japan in the spring of 1974. The trip was memorable for several reasons. First, we spent several days in Kyoto, which is also a Sister City to Boston. Kotaro Ito is a member of the Kyoto Fire Department and he had been sent to Boston University a few years before to learn English. While alone in Boston, he spent a few evenings and weekends with Engine 10, which was a reasonable thing for a visiting firemen to do. I didn't get to meet him while he was here, but I was fortunate to be the recipient of his appreciation of courtesies shown him by Boston firefighters.

Before going to Japan I did correspond with Kotaro and it was agreed that I should call him when we arrived in Kyoto. The phone call was made on a Sunday afternoon and shortly after breakfast on Monday morning he was at our hotel with a department red car. Cars there are mostly of the compact size so only Bruce and Jonathan went with us. Dot, Janna and Frank went shopping. I enjoyed what I did more, and it cost less, - but Japanese pearls are beautiful.

Our first stop was their Fire Alarm Office. At that time, Kotaro was assigned there but he has since been transferred back to fire duty and promoted to lieutenant. Compared to Boston, Kyoto's fire alarm office was modern and included all the latest in electronic communication equipment, but it was no more efficient than Boston's, which was the first central fire alarm system in our country. It was opened for business at noon on April 28, 1852 and the first alarm was received on April 29th at 8:25 P.M. for a house fire at Charlestown (now North Washington) and Causeway Streets.

From their Fire Alarm Office we went to Fire Headquarters where we had morning tea with the Chief of the Kyoto Fire Department. We spent several minutes discussing the two departments, through Kotaro who translated for us. Before leaving headquarters I was given several mementos, including a Chief's badge, and from the Mayor, a picture book of Kyoto, reserved for visiting dignitaries. The inscription reads, "This is a pictorial book of Kyoto, the spiritual home of all Japanese. It is my pleasure to present this to you as a token memento of your visit to Kyoto," signed, Motoki Funahashi, Mayor of Kyoto.

Anecdote:
The Japanese people take great delight in giving gifts, and the custom, known as "NO," requires that a return gift be given (this can go on for centuries). We knew this before we went and took several possible presents with us, but I had neglected to think in terms of the fire department. When the Chief gave me the badge, the only symbol of the fire department I had was the tie tack I was wearing. It was in the shape of two gold bugles, indicative of my rank. Several times during our conversation I had noticed him eyeing it so before leaving, I took it off and gave it to him.

In typical fashion of "esprit de corps," I was assigned a car and a deputy chief as guide, for as long as I wanted them. They had planned to include a ride over the area in the department's new helicopter but it was being serviced. We did visit several of the shrines that help to make Kyoto the "spiritual home of all Japanese" and stopped at City Hall Plaza to see the Beacon Hill gas lamp, a gift from the people of Boston to the people of our Sister City, Kyoto.

From there we went to the Shimogyo Fire Station, which also serves as their Fire Prevention Headquarters. For the "visiting dignitary," the men put on a demonstration of how firemen do things in Japan. It included demonstrating their new 150 foot ladder truck. One unique innovation was the elevator on it that rode up on the spars of the ladder and was capable of carrying two people. It was a practical application and not just a gimmick, for by the time a man climbs up a hundred and fifty feet in full gear, he has already expended much energy and is limited as to what he can further accomplish. If a rescue is involved, carrying a victim back down the 150 foot ladder could be exhausting. The elevator made sense.

Anecdote:

While there we noticed one or more large colorful paper fish flying from a flagpole or otherwise attached to many of the houses. Jonathan, who was then eleven, asked our assigned driver about the meaning of it. He explained that in Japan it was "Boy's Day" and on each house a fish was flown for each boy in the family. He asked Jonathan how many brothers he had and he replied two. While we were watching the demonstration, the driver disappeared and later returned and gave Jonathan three colorful paper fish that could be attached to his house when he got home.

In anticipation of our visit, Kotaro had taken a series of slide pictures of Kyoto Fire Department activities and interlaced them with some beautiful slides of the city. He thought they might be used in our academy to demonstrate foreign evolutions and backgrounds. He made up a book describing each slide and the reason for including it. By then the gifts and printed fire information we had collected had become quite cumbersome so Kotaro tied them all together in a "furoshiki," which made the items easier to manage.

Anecdote:

In the afternoon, Kotaro returned us to Kyoto's "Handicraft Shopping Center," where we had prearranged to meet Dot - and rescue my handicapped wallet. In parting, Kotaro removed his tie tack and gave it to me. It was in the shape of a helicopter, symbol of that branch of the Kyoto Fire Department.

The other memorable event in Japan was experiencing an earthquake. We were in Hakone, in the Japanese Alps, at the time and had just finished eating breakfast in our hotel. We were in the lobby studying an unusual fountain which by a series of chutes sent water cascading in several directions. At first it sounded and felt like a subway train passing under us, but then we realized there are no subways in the mountains. Suddenly, the fountain, and everything else - including us - began to shake, and water went cascading in directions other than that intended by the fountain designer. We watched to see what the natives did in an earthquake, and when the rumbling continued, we saw them pick up the cash box and head for outdoors. We were right behind them. It stopped as quickly as it began and everything was back to normal. We later learned that it measured six on the Richter Scale and the center was on the Izu Peninsula, not too far away, where there were fatalities and much property damage.

While visiting in Denmark, I did catch a fire in the capital city of Copenhagen. It wasn't that spectacular a blaze but it gave opportunity to compare notes with another group of brothers. I went back to the fire house with them and learned a couple things. First, their district chief's cars were Mercedes. Second, they had a much faster way of letting their fire alarm office know the status of apparatus. There was a cable on each piece of apparatus, and a second cable that was suspended from the ceiling over each piece of apparatus in the fire house. When in quarters, the two cables were connected. On responding, the movement of apparatus separated the cables and fire alarm knew they had left quarters. On returning, the plugs were reconnected and fire alarm knew they were in service for another run.

After visiting Japan, Turkey and a few other remote spots, Janna said, "Enough of the family going to outlandish places." If we wanted her company, it would have to be to a less alien location. So we let her choose our next destination, and it was off to Ireland for a very relaxing and enjoyable vacation. In Cork, I visited a brand new fire house on a Saturday night. The men were in the final stages of getting it ready for dedication the next day. I learned that they use oxygen in their self-contained breathing apparatus and the bottles are made of aluminum - both no-nos in our country, at the time. Now we do use aluminum alloy air bottles, but it is highly unlikely we will ever use oxygen in close proximity to our fires. They don't mix, - or rather, they mix too well.

In Hong Kong, my visit to a fire house was in the mid-afternoon of a hot humid day. They were still drilling outdoors in the yard, and although there was much perspiration visible, they seemed to be going about it in routine and expected fashion. Incidentally, if you go to Hong Kong and travel by cab, be careful not to pick a radio cab. We made the mistake one morning when we were in a hurry and paid seventeen dollars for a seventy-five cent ride. Better still, take the Kowloon Ferry, it only cost seven cents - First Class.

In Rome, I learned that their new recruit training is much stricter and more strenuous than what is practiced in Boston. Dot was intrigued by the cooking odors of the fire house. Mama mia!

In the fall of 1974 we went to Romania, behind the Iron Curtain. The travel club we belonged to had offered Russia, but there were so many takers that the USSR canceled all of them. As an alternative, the club offered Romania. We accepted and were among the first Westerners to go behind the Iron Curtain and visit that interesting land. In a lot of ways the country was backward and primitive, but in other ways, it set examples that could be well copied by ourselves. But this is a book about fires, firemen, fire departments and families so we will not dwell on ideologies.

In Brasov I learned that Fire Prevention Regulations vary from country to country. We went to dinner one evening in one of their popular nightclubs, known as "The Carpathian Stag." From the start it was obvious that news about Boston's Cocoanut Grove disaster had never made it past the front door of the Iron Curtain.

The banquet room we ate in was the former vault in the basement of this bank building. There was only one stairway down, and once in the dining area, there was only one exit from the gallery. There were long tables, family style, and illumination for the room was by candles stuck in wine bottles. That was enough of a nightmare for a boy who had seen the Cocoanut Grove - but there was more! Over the tables, and running the length of the room, were wires about five feet above the tables, and at each place setting there was a stack of rolled paper streamers. As wine bottles were uncorked and toasts offered, the diners threw the paper streamers over the wires to form a paper tent over the tables and candles. The resulting heat under the ceiling of streamers would turn a rare steak into well done. Despite the hazardous surroundings, which were probably noticed only by Chief Cook and his family, it was an enjoyable meal and the show that was put on afterwards was spectacular. Nevertheless, we were glad to get back on the street and into fresh air, with two exits.

We spent several days in Bucharest, the capital city. Parts of it were modern, or tried to be, by Americanizing with gaudy orange and purple plastic fixtures and furnishings, as in Hotel Modern where they assigned us. Their old world stone buildings, with stained glass windows and ornate woodwork, were much more charming and attractive, and they should stick with them.

Anecdote:
A few years after we were there, the Hotel Modern totally collapsed during an earthquake.

When we signed up for the trip we were given pages of information and instruction. Romania was a Socialist country with strong emphasis on the military. This was made clearer when our Tarom plane landed on a runway lined with anti-aircraft guns. Once in the country, we would be under control of Carpati, the national tourist agency of Romania, and we would be departing on a certain Thursday. Picture taking was allowed but not of anything national or military.

Around noon on the Wednesday before our slated departure, they put up a notice in the hotel lobby advising that "Wake Up" time would be two-thirty A.M. and departure for the airport would be four-thirty A.M., on Thursday.

Most evenings the electricity in the city failed for varying lengths of time so we decided it best to pack by daylight and not risk a power failure our last night. We did this right after lunch and then we had most of the afternoon free. Checking some literature they had given us, I noticed that there was a Fire

Museum not far from our hotel. What better place is there for a visiting fireman and his family to spend an afternoon?

Walking there was no problem as it turned out to be only a few blocks away from our hotel. It was a round brick building six stories high and long ago it had been used as a tower for spotting fires in Bucharest. Across the street from it was a field filled with ancient fire apparatus, most of it rusting away.

My methodical mind said to take a picture of the field of dilapidated fire engines, then turn a hundred and eighty degrees and take a picture of the fire tower museum. I took the first picture, turned a hundred and eighty degrees, and - whoops! All I could see in the camera's viewfinder was a soldier in khaki, rushing toward me with his Soviet AK-47 pointed in my direction, and yelling at me! He took my camera and yelled some more. Dot was ready to leave - if they would let her. Coward!

Apparently the fire museum was National, or Military, and pictures weren't allowed. I asked him if we could see his museum anyhow, and he grunted. Once in the museum they put us in an elevator and took us to the top floor, from where we walked out onto the roof. What a magnificent view of the city lay before us - I wished I had my camera! It was obvious why they had chosen that high spot for the fire observation tower.

From there we walked down, floor by floor. Each one was filled with artifacts and history of the Bucharest Fire Department and even though we couldn't read the many inscriptions and explanations it was clear to me what we were looking at - and all the time an armed guard followed us. At this point Dot was not too interested in the history or the ancient equipment of this fire department. She just wanted "out" and was about a floor ahead of me. I could see the guard was getting itchy over this arrangement and called her back and said he might shoot one of us to make his task easier.

Now that we were all walking together again, we asked the guard if he spoke, "English ?"   "Nyet !"
                              "German ?"   "Nyet !"
                              "French ?"   "Nyet !"
                              "Italian ?"   "Nyet !"
                              "American ?"   "Nyet !"

Since he didn't speak any languages, I thought to try a picture and showed him my fire department I.D. that had my photo in uniform. He looked, grunted and said nothing - not even, "Nyet." But as we continued the downward trail he would step behind some of the displays and illuminate them or call attention to other displays with a pointer.

Back at ground level, a guard motioned us over to the largest Visitor's Book I have ever seen. It was leather bound, a good two inches thick, and must have measured two by three feet. He handed me a pen, but just as I began to write, the guard that had followed us, and could only grunt and say "Nyet," came over and slammed the book shut. He walked away with it, but shortly returned with a book about half the size. He placed it on the table, opened it and handed me a pen. He must have been a very smart man, for in that short time he had learned English and he said, "For you."

The smaller Visitor's Book was for firemen only. Firefighters from all over the world, who had visited the Bucharest Fire Museum, had left their mark in it, and I was privileged to add mine. If not the first American Fire Chief to sign that fraternal book, I was at least the first one in many years. That bond among firemen that recognizes no boundaries, politics or languages, had penetrated the Iron Curtain.

To answer the question in many of your minds, as I was signing the book, the soldier that had seized my camera spoke to his superior, and as I put down the pen, he handed me back my camera with the film intact. I couldn't wait to get outside and get that picture of the tower, but by then Dot had covered half of the blocks back to the hotel and I had to run to catch up with her. Coward!

In Egypt all of our flights were on MisR Air. It was interesting to fly over many miles of desert and then see a small black strip of macadam appear. Each time we landed, the airport fire department would pull out and standby near the runway. As we were landing at Abu Simbel late one afternoon, the lone fire truck was at the runway, but it was afternoon prayer time and all the firemen were on their prayer rugs facing Mecca, with their backs to the runway as we glided onto the tarmac.

Lest it appear that I only visited foreign fire houses, let me just add that I sailed under the Golden Gate Bridge and visited Alcatraz, courtesy of the San Francisco FD Marine Unit. I also visited a fire house in Colorado, that was dug into a mountain, and a primarily glass, open-ended fire house on the island of Kauai.

I could go on with this travelogue, but in this book, it is getting late and by now you should be getting the picture of why I feel the way I do about firefighting, firemen and fire departments. The camaraderie is part of it. A big part, and yet, a small part!

Old apparatus at Fire Museum in Bucharest, Romania, October 1974. For this photo my camera was confiscated.

"Brigade De Sapeurs-Pompiers De Paris"
Fireboat on Seine River, Paris, France, May 1972.
Corporal Henri Leroux is to my left.

A PIER FIRE

(or, The Trains Won't Be Running This Morning)

In an earlier chapter, reference was made to a pier fire. It is included here for multiple reasons. First, I hope it will be an interesting story of what went on one cold night while most people were home sleeping. Some of them awoke to find their usual means of getting to work was out of order, and would be for a long time. Second, it will give lay people an idea of the variety of problems that a fire department can be faced with in quick order, and the loneliness of the man who is ultimately responsible for making the decisions. Third, Civil Service no longer includes this type of fire problem in exams, but that doesn't stop them from happening. Fourth, it is included as a guide for fire students on how to fight a pier fire - or how not to. I will let them decide.

Much of this is taken from a report I wrote while the night was still fresh in my mind. It appeared in *Fire Engineering* magazine, in disguised form that was barely recognizable after their editing.

Boston had not had a serious pier fire for many years until the Night Tour of January 19, 1984. The first notification was a telephone report of a "small" outside fire at the rear of the Spaulding Rehabilitation Hospital at 125 Nashua Street in the old West End section of the city. This was at 0337 hours and Fire Alarm sent a Still Alarm assignment consisting of Engine 4, Ladder 24 and District 3, under command of Acting District Chief George McCafferty (George generally covered me when I was Acting Deputy). Just prior to this reported fire, these three units had responded to a series of false alarms in an area not far from the hospital.

Approaching the hospital, the acting chief observed a column of black smoke rising from behind the hospital and he first thought it could be an automobile fire, as Boston has several hundred of these each year. Many of them are deliberately burned for insurance claims. On reaching the location he saw a large outside fire which included a forty foot trailer, used as an office and positioned in the hospital parking lot which was located on a portion of the pier. He ordered Fire Alarm to strike Box 1341 to get a full first alarm response, consisting of Engine 8 and Ladder 1 from the North End and Engine 50 from Charlestown, plus Division One, which in this case was me. Rescue 1 is normally included in this first alarm assignment but they had been sent to a two alarm fire in the Roslindale section of the city. Phil LaCascia (now my regular aide in District 3) reported that the fire was also involving pilings under the pier and Acting District Chief McCafferty ordered a second alarm just as I arrived to assume command at 0346 hours.

In sizing up the situation it became apparent that the visible fire on the pier, including the trailer and other sheds, was only "the tip of the iceberg." The main body of fire was under the pier and eventually involved hundreds of creosoted pilings with the accompanying cap-logs and built up wood piers topped with asphalt paving on the northern end of the pier. I ordered the Marine Units to be sent to the fire.

Engine 4 (a two piece Engine Company) connected the pump to a hydrant at the rear of the hospital and ran a 2-1/2" line to begin attacking the fire in the structures located on the pier. Engine 8 (a two piece Engine Company) connected their pump to a hydrant in front of the hospital and ran a 2-1/2" line to the pier and began attacking the fire there. Engine 50 connected to a hydrant at the right of the hospital and ran a 3" line to a portable deluge gun. Since there was no venting, axe duty or overhauling to be done at this point, Ladders 1 and 24 stretched 2-1/2" and 3" lines and set up a portable deluge gun. The initial attempt was to break up the large amount of radiated heat being emitted from the intensely burning structures on the pier.

Aide LaCascia continued investigating and reported to me that the fire was extending rapidly under the pier in a southerly direction, as evidenced by the spreading fire lapping up over the edge of the pier. It was extending toward a reported 10,000 volt transformer.

Based on this information and my own observations, I issued a quick series of orders to Fire Alarm:
1. Strike a third alarm (0355 hours).
2. Send an additional district chief (Tom Shea of District 4) and have him respond via Accolon Way to the rear of the North Station (which connects with the southern end of the pier). I wanted him to direct operations for the companies that would soon be arriving in that area.
3. Second alarm companies - Engines 7, 10, 33 and Ladder 17 to respond to Accolon Way and report to Chief Shea.
4. Ordered Fire Alarm to request the Port Authority fireboat to respond and also to contact the U. S. Coast Guard Base to send whatever boats they had with firefighting capability. Both agencies cooperated and responded promptly, with Mass. Port sending their 75' boat (sister ship to Boston's Marine Unit 2) and the Coast Guard providing six smaller boats, plus a liaison team to coordinate communications and operations with the Chief in Charge - me! These marine firefighting units remained at the scene for several days.

As the second alarm companies arrived at Accolon Way they began attacking the fire extending south along the pier. Engines 7 and 33 stretched 3" lines to portable deluge guns set up in this area. Fire was burning from underneath and reaching through the pier in two places. I had Engine 10 relay water through 3" lines from a High Pressure hydrant to supplement Engine 7's pump. Meanwhile, Engine 3 and Ladder 15 responded to the rear of the hospital where the Engine ran two 2-1/2" lines to their deluge gun. Ladder 15 assisted in running lines and then began cutting holes in the pier for eventual use of Bresnan rotating nozzles which would be lowered below the pier to reach the fire there.

The Boston Marine Unit arrived and began to operate bow and deck guns on the fire under the pier which was continuing to spread, assisted by moderate winds in the thirteen degree temperature which gave a wind-chill factor below zero degrees Fahrenheit. When the Port Authority and Coast Guard boats arrived on scene, full use of their bow and deck guns, as well as hand lines, were made in hitting the fire below the pier and the areas above. Initial approach by the marine units was at the southern end of the pier. Later when the trestle was opened, they were able to maneuver the full length of the pier, about 700 feet, but it was with great difficulty because of zero visibility caused by the heavy black smoke from the burning creosoted pilings.

Here a brief description of the topography of the area could be helpful to better understand the problems facing the fire department. The Spaulding Rehab Hospital is a ten story building which is set back several hundred feet from Nashua Street. The three hydrants used by the first alarm companies are located within fifty feet of the hospital and additional hydrants are available a few hundred feet away on Nashua Street and Accolon Way, south of the pier. A three story addition had recently been added to the rear of the main hospital building. This addition rests on concrete support columns visible on the pier. At the rear of the hospital, to the left, was a covered over area of the pier used for parking cars. Also on the pier at the time of the fire was the construction trailer already mentioned, which was used as an office. In addition there were smaller sheds used for various storage purposes.

To the right rear of the hospital, the pier extended several hundred feet. This pier area connects with the rear of the North Station, a railway connection for trains running north out of Boston. This was formerly the Boston and Maine Railroad, but the commuter trains are now a subsidiary of the MBTA, who owns the property and runs the trains. Commuter trains reach the North Station via a drawbridge trestle that crosses the Charles River. The trestle connects the North bound tracks in Cambridge to the ten sets of tracks extending to the North Station. These tracks are on the pier to the right rear of the hospital. There are about 1300 wood pilings supporting the approach to the trestle on the Boston side.

In this area, in addition to normal pier construction, there is the added gravel track road bed, wood ties and railroad tracks which amounts to considerable weight, compounded by the water and ice build up. These factors had to be taken into consideration with regards the safety of the firefighters working on the pier.

Getting back to the fire, the third alarm companies, Engines 17 and 14, set up portable deck guns at the rear in an adjacent parking lot and started to attack the fire under the parking lot pier. Engine 17's gun was supplied with 2-1/2" lines and Engine 14's with 4-1/2" hose. Engine 14 later supplied three 2-1/2" lines to the Aerial Tower when it was released from the fire in Roslindale at 0600 hours and came directly to my fire. Ladder 18 assisted in running lines and then in cutting holes in the pier.

With the third alarm companies committed and the marine units in operation, I ordered the fourth alarm to be struck at 0401 hours. This brought Engines 5 and 32 to the location. Members of Engine 5 were placed aboard the Port Authority boat to assist in operations of monitor guns and hand lines. Members of Engine 32 were placed aboard Marine Unit 2, with the same assignment. I called for the SCUBA TEAM to be alerted and report to me. I wanted them available at the scene should something unforeseen occur. There was no intention of putting them into the water during the night, except in the event of a life saving emergency.

At this point District 4 was supervising operations on the southern front and District 3 was supervising operation on the north. I remained in overall command and at 0412 hours ordered a fifth alarm, bringing Engines 18 and 21 and Ladder 7 to my outdoor fire. On the striking of the fifth alarm, Mutual Aid companies from surrounding cities and towns in Metro-Fire began covering Boston fire houses on a pre-arranged schedule. At the fire, Engine 18 ran 1200' of 2-1/2" hose and 300' of 3" hose to their deluge gun directed toward the still growing fire on and under the pier, at the rear of the hospital. Engine 21 connected a 2-1/2" line to the hospital standpipe and with a Bresnan nozzle, operated their line below the pier by means of the holes previously cut by the ladder companies. Ladder 7 assisted in cutting additional holes.

A unit of the Boston Fire Arson Squad responds to all multiple alarm fires in Boston, and any other fire when called. On their arrival, there was little investigative work they could do at this point. These two officers were instructed to take up a position on the tenth floor of the hospital where they could look down on the entire operational scene and keep me informed, by radio, of the progress being made by the fire. Their view of this fire was similar to the one I had from the helicopter at the Lynn conflagration. Looking down from their lofty advantage point, they reported the fire involved an area of six to seven hundred feet along the pier, with the depth probably up to three hundred feet. I ordered the sixth alarm at 0422 hours. Engines 22, 9 and 39 responded. Members of Engine 9 and 22 were put aboard marine and Coast Guard boats to assist their crews.

It was about this time that the oil saturated lumber of the pier was beginning to really heat up. It produced extremely large amounts of heavy black smoke that further hampered operations, and reduced visibility for the boats to mere inches. As if I didn't have enough concerns to occupy my mind at the time, one of my marine liaisons reported that Marine Unit 2 and one of the other fireboats had collided in the smoke. It appeared the bigger Boston fireboat was taking on water. All I needed! I called them on the radio and asked for a report. It seemed longer, but in a few minutes the report came in that all was well. They had bumped but no real damage and they would continue to float. "Praise the Lord" and pass the water!

The fire had now extended to the trestle, due to the delay in raising it. When we first arrived on the scene, Phil had told me the bridge was down and I requested it to be opened, but because of a power failure it could not be raised electrically. I sent Engine 39 to the Cambridge side to investigate conditions there and instructed them to advise me if additional companies were needed there. Aide Phil, who was familiar with the area, went with them. Lieutenant Ralph Reis, Jr., who was in command of Engine 39, found a yard hydrant, which was frozen, close to the trestle. Using their Ross Thawing Device, his crew quickly melted the ice in the barrel of the hydrant, connected the pump to it, stretched 2-1/2" lines of hose and placed their portable gun in operation to knock down the fire extending toward them across the trestle.

Once they were able to extinguish the main body of fire, they ran a 1-1/2" line to complete the mopping up of the burned railroad ties. At this point the railroad workmen were able to raise the trestle manually, preventing further fire damage to it, and allowing the fireboats to pass beyond it so they could attack the burning northern portion of the pier.

Anecdote:
Lieutenant Ralph Reis, Jr., mentioned above, is the son of the Ralph Reis mentioned earlier, as one of the Famous "96," and who fascinated me when he came to church in his new blue fire uniform.

By now there were thirteen deluge guns and hand lines being used by the land companies, plus, the numerous water throwing devices being employed by the eight boats. Heavy black smoke, from the creosoted pilings, was blowing mostly away from the land operating companies. This was good for them, but it made visibility and maneuverability for the marine units most difficult and uncomfortable. With the large number of heavy stream appliances being operated from the boats in the limited visibility, they were concerned about their heavy streams striking brother firefighters working on the pier. It was from the elevated observation post on the tenth floor of the hospital that safe direction and assurance could be given to the men on the boats.

This is the fire fighting tactic that would be used until daylight, when hopefully a clearer view of the situation would be revealed.

With the temperature well below freezing, ice quickly built up on men and equipment causing frequent falls by the men, but no serious injuries occurred. As the ice layers increased most everywhere, I was cognizant of the fact that it remained slushy on much of the northern end of the pier. This indicated to me that a high degree fire temperature existed below the pier, and with this amount of burning there would be a weakening of the sub-structure. Watching the area, I noticed the growing pool of water on the pier and ordered all men off that section. Shortly afterwards, a large section of the burning pier collapsed, including the area used for parking. Only a portion of the pier fell into the water and was extinguished. The rest cantilevered into various configurations depending on the degree of burn and collapse of the supporting pilings. This added to the total extinguishing problem because it restricted hose line penetration.

The above synopsis outlines the firefighting tactics to this point, but it does not depict the entire problem facing the first arriving firefighters. This section of Boston's waterfront is actually on the Charles River, which empties into Boston Harbor. The

Army Corps of Engineers built a series of locks to keep salt water from the ocean separated from the fresh water of the river. The locks are maintained and operated by the Metropolitan District Commission, a state agency. Pleasure boats, which moor in the river, use these locks to traverse into Boston Harbor, and by the same means the fire department's marine units can only enter the Charles River via these locks. As previously noted, the railroad trestle carrying the commuter trains crosses the river above these locks.

This trestle was down when the fire was discovered, and on arrival I ordered the bridge to be opened for two reasons. First, the bridge opened from the Cambridge end and I wanted to prevent the fire extending across it from Boston. Second, it was necessary to raise it in order for the marine units to pass through and enable them to attack the fire on a wider front and reach the far northern end of the pier. There the wind would be at the men's back, the visibility would be improved and the smoke less annoying, and thus provide safer and faster operations from the decks. One reason for the delay in opening the bridge was the heavy smoke that pervaded the trestle area, and there was reluctance to move it knowing men and boats were operating in the vicinity. After assurance that all firefighters were clear of the bridge, an attempt was made to open it electrically but it failed. Pins had to be removed manually and this took time in the extreme cold. These delays allowed the fire to extend to the trestle and also prevented the marine units from passing by and hitting the fire that was now involving the northern pier.

Life safety is always the first consideration of the fire ground commander, and here a constant, life threatening, situation nagged at me. The hospital contained over 200 bed patients, most in serious condition, and many in terminal stages. The hospital personnel and administration were fearful of having to evacuate this many patients in the freezing weather but were aware that fire or smoke conditions might necessitate it. Their one question to me was, "How much notice can you give us before evacuation will be necessary?"

It was not that easy to answer. As far as smoke was concerned, evacuation would not be needed if the wind continued blowing toward the water as it presently did, but if it shifted to the reverse, the only time I would be able to give is "Evacuate now!" Meanwhile, I suggested they shut down air intakes to help prevent any smoke being drawn into the hospital. Provisions were made for thirty ambulances to be ready on standby should evacuation become necessary. The Heli-pad adjacent to the hospital was cleared to be available. The Coast Guard liaison team advised the wind direction in Boston should remain constant, away from the hospital, for the next two or three days - but naturally could not guarantee it. Evacuation never was ordered, but it remained a nagging threat for me, the hospital staff and the fire personnel for a couple days.

Another major concern of the fire ground commander was the foundation under the hospital. It was noted that wood pilings supported the covered pier on which the train tracks ran to the North Station. Fire under this southern section had already burned through to the railroad ties in two or more places and the wooden pilings supporting the northern sector had burned through, dropping part of their parking lot into the drink. Was it possible these wooden pilings extended under the hospital and could possibly allow the fire to burn through emitting smoke and fire directly into the hospital? More important, if these wooden pilings were helping to support the hospital, how much were they being affected by the fire?

Since no one in the hospital was certain of the foundation, I requested they send for their resident engineer who was present when construction of the addition was in progress. He arrived sometime after 0600 hours and assured me the addition was built on a solid foundation. In the meantime, I had ordered ladder companies to cut a series of holes along the pier bordering the hospital so that cellar pipes could be brought into use to cool the area and prevent fire from extending under the hospital if construction was such. It is this myriad of uncertain and adverse conditions at a fire that makes the loneliness of command evident to the chief, if no one else.

Shortly after 0800 hours on Friday morning, Deputy Chief Hart and his Group 3 Day Tour arrived to take over operations. The SCUBA TEAM entered the frigid waters and with a 1-1/2" line was able to get under the pier and begin working on the fire burning the pilings. They also investigated a considerable distance under the pier, reporting heavy charring and structural damage to an extent that it was unsafe for the SCUBA TEAM to continue their subterranean search. They did report the presence of a granite sea wall that ran adjacent to the hospital. This was reassuring. On a rotating basis, two men from the TEAM were kept at the scene for several days. As the surface fire was extinguished, and the extent of fire under the pier was determined and isolated, the number of land companies and Coast Guard units were gradually reduced.

At 1800 hours on Friday, Deputy Chief Stapleton and his Group 1 Night Tour took over command of operations, and at 0800 hours on Saturday morning I relieved him, and Group 2 was back at the scene of our crime. We walked around surveying the still smoldering pier and looked at the gaping holes and collapsed pilings. About then he said to me, "There are a lot of chiefs who have made parking lots in Boston, but you are the first chief to go down in the annals of the fire department, to lose one!" This reputation will probably outlive me.

Anecdote:
A few days later, on February 1, 1984, Deputy Chief Stapleton was appointed Commissioner and Chief of the Boston Fire Department.

Chief Stapleton called for a meeting with all parties involved. After discussion with demolition experts, it was decided against using explosives to demolish the remaining pier under which there was still a considerable amount of fire. It was agreed with the MBTA, who owned the pier, to have the Perini Company cut the tracks on the southern section and then with cranes and other heavy equipment, knock down the burning pier for a distance about twenty feet wide beyond the sea wall. This would reduce the smoking pier to an island and assure no further extension of the fire to the pilings beyond the sea wall. Work continued through the day and into the night with portable lights providing illumination. The Marine Unit 2 continued to monitor and pour water onto this island fire for several days. The All Out was sounded at 2237 hours on January 22, the box having been in for 66 hours and 56 minutes - by no means a record. An engine company detail remained at the location until 1800 hours on January 25th. The final frozen hose was removed from the pier on February 20th.

I estimated the loss at $7,000,000 and listed the immediate cause as Undetermined. It had been reported that work had been done in the area of the pier and trestle in days preceding the fire. Work requiring the use of acetylene torches had been done under the pier with men working from a scaffolding, and there were reports of vagrants using this platform as a shelter at night. It is common practice for workmen to burn wood in old drums to keep warm and there was evidence of this in the area, but supposedly snow or water was used to extinguish the barrel fires before workmen left. Also it is common practice in cold weather to use a gas line to thaw track switches. Someone reported there was a blue flame under the pier before the fire. There is a 4000 volt electric cable that ran along the sea wall. There were attempts by various workmen to put out a fire prior to notification to the fire department, but there was a time discrepancy. Finally, the trestle was insured for $14,000,000 in early 1984.

O.K. students, you have seen the fire. Now using information provided above, determine the cause and give your reasons.

Anecdote:
On April 20, 1985, a new MBTA North Station Trestle was dedicated and commuter travel to the north was restored. The Boston Fire Department was not invited to the ceremony, maybe for justifiable reasons. A few days later a stranger dropped by my office at Fire Headquarters and gave me one of the souvenirs that were given out at the dedication. It was a marble paperweight with a brass plate noting the event. His comment was that since I was in charge of the fire that provided the new trestle, he thought it appropriate that I at least get a remembrance of it. To the donor, if you read this, my thanks. It is now part of my collection of memorabilia.

Pier Fire, January 19, 1984.
Fireboat and land companies attacking fire.

Pier Fire, January 19, 1984.
Vast area involved. Connecting trestle has been raised.

Pier Fire, January 19, 1984.
L-R, Acting District Chief George McCafferty, District 3, District Chief Thomas Shea, District 4, Acting Deputy Chief Paul Cook, Division 1.

PENTAGON

(or, The Puzzle Factory)

As you have been reading these pages you should be aware of the changes that have slowly taken place in the fire service in Boston. The workweek has been shortened and the paycheck has been lengthened. The older ornate fire houses have been replaced with more efficient one or two story sterile buildings. The apparatus has become streamlined and equipment modernized. Centrifugal pumps have replaced the rotary gear ones. The pumps have more capacity and the ladders reach higher, but they still come far short of reaching the top of a lot of the buildings that are changing Boston's skyline.

Pictures of fires taken a hundred years ago look quite similar to those being taken today. Men still have to advance long lines of hose into fiery furnaces that should be reserved for only the devil.

Protective clothing that once consisted of a black fire coat with large metal buckles, leather helmet and rubber boots has been replaced with a variety of safer and more colorful turnout gear. The old filter type masks have been outlawed and in their place men wear self-contained breathing apparatus which are much heavier and more cumbersome but, provide better breathing protection. In some cities, plastic headgear in space-age shapes, with extensions to protect the ears and neck, and clear shields to protect the eyes, make the men look more like they are prepared to go to Mars than to a hot stinking cellar fire.

All this is within the context of saying that changes were about to take place in my career too. In early 1985, due to a retirement, there was an opening for a chief officer to head the Planning and

Logistics Division at headquarters (or the Pentagon). It had the dual role of also being the Civil Defense Director for the city.

When one considered all the involvement that the job entailed, it presented a real challenge. After interviews with the Chief of Operations and the Fire Commissioner, during which the extensive duties were outlined, I was offered the position and given a week to contemplate. It was not an easy decision to make, and although Dot had her own ideas about it, again she remained silent. She knew that if she tried to influence my decision and it turned out I wasn't happy at the Pentagon, she would never hear the end of it. She probably figured right.

It would be a total change. Instead of working the forty-two hour week with day and night shifts, it would be a five day week like most civilized people work. That part was not particularly appealing to me. True, weekends, holidays and nights off were part of it, but I never considered these to be persuading perks. Actually it would not be a normal five day week. As Head of a Division and also Boston's Civil Defense Director I would be on call twenty-four hours a day, three hundred and sixty-five days a year. A hurricane, snowstorm or other emergency could keep me at the city Emergency Center until things were back to normal.

Anecdote:
To jump ahead a bit, during Hurricane Gloria in September 1985, I was in my place at the Emergency Center in City Hall. The news media (bless them) kept flashing across their boob tube screens for the public to contact the Civil Defense Director if they had any problems with wires down, flooding, fallen trees blocking roads or other emergency. They gave a number to call. Inadvertently, they posted the Civil Director's home phone rather than City Hall. Dot was besieged with calls she knew nothing about and the Emergency Center had a quiet afternoon. Eventually it was straightened out and Dot had a quiet evening and the Emergency Center was besieged with calls.

Resuming, the mental wrestle was more with what I would give up than what I would gain. From boyhood I have loved firefighting, and for the last fourteen years I had thrived on, and daily looked forward to the challenge of downtown District 3.

However, things were changing on the firefighting front too. Places to live, whether buying or renting, were harder to come by and property values had escalated, making people more careful with regards to fire and their property. Older buildings were being demolished and replaced with structures that are supposedly more fire safe. The increased use of smoke detectors and automatic sprinklers in both residential and commercial buildings were reducing the number of structure fires, but not the number of "bell alarms." Most of the men I had worked with comfortably for many years were retiring, and the younger replacements appeared to me to be slower in accepting the traditional ways of the fire service. I found myself growing impatient and a little bit frustrated at times.

On the other hand, the job at headquarters would provide me with an opportunity to pioneer in some new areas, and its complex duties would allow me to continue going to fires and other Incidents, both as an observer and a participant. It also included a reasonable pay increase and since pension factors include the last three years salary average, it would include a fringe benefit after retirement.

I am not certain just what the deciding factor was for me, but I told the Commissioner "yes" and on April 1, 1985 I took up my new duties. No one was more surprised and pleased with my decision than Dot. I would not have chosen to spend my entire career at the Pentagon, but the last three and a half years were rewarding in ways that were far different than the rewards of firefighting.

At the start, let me point out that the Planning and Logistics Division was there before me and will remain after I leave. Some of the projects I finished were inherited with the job and were well on their way, started by dedicated predecessors. Some were started and completed during my tenure. Others were started by the writer and will be completed by those who follow in the position.

One of the tasks of P & L is implementing measures to prevent future problems. If the fire department learned one thing from the Cocoanut Grove disaster, it was to do everything within its powers to protect the public - and the fire department. One problem is that all people, and all agencies, do not see eye to eye with the fire department. Of course they are often encumbered with the financial obligations, whereas the fire department thinks solely in terms of public safety, and these two viewpoints often don't go hand in hand.

My first task was to work in the area of Civil Defense. In fact the entire work of P & L deals with the realistic objectives of Civil Defense which is to reduce potential human losses and material damages. Throughout most of the state, the work of Civil Defense had been given low priority since Proposition 2-1/2 and other cuts in funding that came with it. However, Federal law says that every city and town in the nation will have both a Civil Defense Director and a Comprehensive Emergency Management Plan. This Plan became one of my priorities, but it was not accomplished overnight. It took much time and a lot of concerned people from various city departments, working with state planners, to assemble all the required data, but before I retire it will be in place.

One of the reasons I accepted the position at the Pentagon was because I saw it as an opportunity to repay the tax payers in another way for their goodness to me, and my family. They may never know of my efforts, and that doesn't matter, but many times I have felt like a voice crying in the wilderness on their behalf, and for public safety. Perhaps I have tried to think and act as an idealist, but if so, it was not for selfish reasons. My day to day duties were made easier by the fact that once given the parameters in which to work, there was no added interference or restrictions from the Boss. In many cases, my on the spot decisions determined department policy to a degree, and Commissioner Stapleton backed me to the hilt. Naturally I never tried to overstep my bounds or assume more authority than was mine, but public safety and the welfare of the people were always paramount during discussions, and in decisions made by me.

Hydrants are an important part of firefighting and in Boston there are about thirteen thousand of them. They are owned and serviced by the Boston Water and Sewer Commission. The fire department just uses them for public safety purposes (when the kids aren't using them).

In the fall of each year the fire department does make a visual inspection of every hydrant in the city. During these examinations, missing gaskets are replaced, caps are oiled, they are checked for defects and it is determined if there is water in the barrel, which could make for a freezing problem in the winter. Daily communication is maintained between the water agency and P & L so that defects are reported and repairs promptly made. In the last three years, in a joint effort, all hydrant locations have been identified, numbered and computerized so that we talk a common language between the two departments.

One issue that is of major concern to the fire department, and should be to the general public, is the illegal use of hydrants. Much of this takes place in the summer when selfish people open hydrants to cool off their kids and sometimes themselves. Much money has been spent in an attempt to discourage this type of misuse by installing expensive tamper proof devices on some hydrants. It is sad to report, but in some cases when this deterrent worked, revenge has been taken by destroying the hydrants.

In some instances, when a major fire was in progress, it has been necessary to strike extra alarms and use these companies to go around closing hydrants that were being illegally used. Again, the rate payers take it on the chin by having to pay for this wasted water. But of greater importance is the waste of a commodity that may be in short supply in the not too distant future. It is too bad that this message can't be impressed upon those that are responsible for these selfish acts, for they too will suffer in the shortage that they are helping to create.

Anecdote:
In Chapter 12 I wrote that pumps are not connected to high pressure hydrants. This was so when few buildings exceeded 12 stories. With the addition of many buildings in Boston reaching heights greater than 40 stories, water pressure sometime becomes a problem. P & L spent a few Sundays at the Prudential Center with several engine companies testing the theory that increasing the pressure of the water going into the standpipe system would improve water flow on the upper floors. This was accomplished by connecting a pumper to a high pressure hydrant and then laying a line of hose to the standpipe connection. This increased the water pressure to the building's fire pumps. We also experimented with relaying water to a second pumper, before supplying the building.

Both of these experiments proved most effective at extreme heights, and now pumpers are connected to high pressure hydrants under certain conditions.

Another part of P & L is liaison with city and state agencies and with public utilities in matters involving the fire department and safety. It involves a lot of time at a lot of meetings and is frequently frustrating. Many of the issues seem simple to the fire department, but they do get complicated when others become involved. But slow as it may seem at times, progress continues to be made and projects do get completed. Many of them require continual follow up once they are turned over to the involved fire district.

One aspect of P & L that has expanded in the last three years has to do with the many building projects that are going on in the city. Being fresh from District 3, I was well aware of most of the problems that had to be contended with by the fire suppression forces and the importance of improvement in the water distribution system for fighting fires.

Working closely with the Inspectional Services Department, all building plans pass through P & L where they are carefully examined for fire safety features. Drawings are checked for installation of automatic sprinklers, standpipes and heat and smoke detectors when required. Compliance with the Elevator Regulations and the Boston Fire Prevention Code are verified and corrections made when needed.

Working closely with the Boston Water and Sewer Commission, it is made certain that adequate water supplies will be available for domestic and fire needs.

Working with the Transportation Department, access to all buildings for firefighting purposes is guaranteed. This process is not always welcome by builders and developers, but in the long run it can save them time and expensive changes later, if they were not corrected in the planning stage by this system. I wish state agencies understood our thinking as well, but they have plenty of money for expensive changes later on - your money! The sad part is that sometimes the public has to get hurt or killed before they will make the expensive changes that could, and should, have been avoided.

On the brighter side, today the public is better protected because of improvements made in the water systems of the Callahan and Sumner tunnels, the MBTA tunnels, and soon the Mystic Tobin Bridge. These were not accomplished overnight either, but that is history. The improvements have been made and the public can commute more safely. Drills are held in the various MBTA subway stations in the wee hours of the morning after the trains stop running. These serve a dual purpose. First it is an opportunity for firemen to get familiar with the underground caverns and the third rail electric system. Second, it serves as a test of the below ground standpipe as the men practice charging the system and operating lines of hose from it. Several mechanical shortcomings were discovered during early drills, but that was the purpose, and corrections were made.

Major fire protection measures have been completed at the Commercial Point LNG tank facility and all Boston firefighters have undergone a familiarization and training program in cooperation with the Boston Gas Company.

Included in P & L is responsibility for the Underwater Dive Team. These regular firefighters respond to water emergencies including accidents and fires. Cars that have gone off piers or bridges are checked for occupants in both the passenger compartment and the trunk. At pier fires they swim between the pilings with small monitor guns to attack fires, and further save the tax payers money. They regularly survey the hulls of the fireboats and remove tangled debris on propeller shafts and rudders.

The Emergency Medical Services of the fire department are also part of P & L. There are over a hundred EMTs and Paramedics in the department. They are assigned to the companies and work regular shifts. Training and state re-certification are provided for as well as updating the latest accepted emergency procedures. Trauma kits carried on apparatus are checked twice a day and shortages reported to P & L so used items can be replaced. In 1987 there were 6,484 emergency medical Incidents that the fire department answered and in 1988 they are running almost 45% ahead of that figure.

Records of responses by the department are maintained and computerized. Members that may be exposed to communicable diseases are followed up.

When the question of emergency treatment of possible AIDS victims became a subject matter, the Boston Fire Department was one of the first in the nation to put Infectious Disease Kits on all apparatus. Included in the waterproof metal boxes are rubber gloves, eye goggles, face shields and one way micro-shields for mouth to mouth resuscitation.

One of the fun assignments to me has been involvement in the designing, and looking after the department's interests in, two new fire houses. They are both unique in that they will be located in private buildings and leased to the city. The one closest to fruition is the Division One Headquarters on Purchase Street. It will house the same companies that are presently in the Oliver Street fire house, namely Engine 10, Rescue 1, Aerial Tower 1, the Squirt and Haz-Mat Unit. Move in date for the fire department is planned for the summer of 1989 with the fire house occupying the first two floors of a nine story building, part of the 125 High Street Development.

In Chapter 9, I mentioned that if ever it were my prerogative, a new fire house would include all new furnishings. Little did I then expect that such an occasion would ever arise, but now it was happening twice. Both of these new fire houses will have all new fixtures and furnishings on opening day.

My fifty years experience of living and working in fire houses, paid and unpaid, was put to good use in a design attempt to meet the needs of the fire department, and the men who will occupy them. Since the Boston Fire Department has pioneered in several areas, and been copied by many large and small departments throughout the country, it is quite likely that this fire house will also be copied, and could become a new standard of efficiency for new big city fire houses. Knowing firefighters, I will likely be considered a failure as a designer soon after it opens, but if all goes as planned, it will have several interesting innovations and be closer to the Taj Mahal than the one described in Chapter 4.

Before construction of this new fire house and the office complex could begin, it was necessary to remove the Traveler's

Insurance Building which then occupied most of the land. It was brought down by implosion on March 20, 1988. I was invited to view the spectacular event from an inside vantage point, and remembering the amount of dust created by the Hotel Manger's demise, I accepted. When the countdown ended and the nineteen story building came down without a hitch, the cloud of dirt that went up was almost as high, and covered several blocks. I had made the right decision in accepting the invitation to view it from the sheltered location.

The other fire house to be built is also in my old District 3 and is for the Marine Unit. When completed, the boats will tie up at their old location, but with a new name - Burroughs Wharf. While the boats will still float on the water, the men, for the first time in over forty years, will have living quarters on dry land in a first floor condo. The verdict on that one will also be interesting.

About the same time, the apparatus floor at Engine 8 and Ladder 1 on Hanover Street developed serious cracks. Further investigation revealed the floor was structurally unsafe for apparatus and must be replaced.

Some folk in the North End thought it was a ruse by the City to remove the fire apparatus, close their fire house and sell the land to a developer. It took several heated neighborhood meetings to convince them otherwise. As chief in District 3 I had dealt with neighborhood meetings for fourteen years and most residents had come to respect my honesty with them. Some were skeptical of my new role, as I was no longer part of their neighborhood. They wanted the men and apparatus to remain locally visible. I had done my homework and promised them the apparatus would be returned to Hanover Street as soon as the new floor would support it. In the meantime I had made arrangements for the apparatus to respond from the old Brink's garage (mentioned in Chapter 8) at 600 Commercial Street. Finally, they agreed.

The following Saturday (five day week - Ha) I was at the garage. I had two mobile house trailers delivered and placed in the building. One would be the "Bunk Room." The other would be the Patrol Desk and kitchen - so there would be no break in round table discussions and solving world problems. The Fire Alarm Shop made the needed connections to receive alarms and the department electricians did the necessary wiring to make life somewhat comfortable. This worked reasonably well for the several weeks it took to install and cure the new floor, but the men and residents were glad to see the fire engines rolling from Hanover Street again.

While at the Pentagon I spent a week of my 1987 vacation in New York City helping NYFD develop new standards for their future fire houses. On leaving I was told that my "perspective brought about considerable changes in the thinking of all concerned." A considerable achievement - but I am not sure they bought it all. I think it was their way of saying, "Thanks, but your ideas are too progressive, and too expensive." It is my contention that fire houses usually have a life expectancy of over a hundred years, so a few extra dollars spent on efficiency and comfort at the start is money well spent.

Of serious concern to the fire department is the matter of public safety in regard to elevators in buildings. This "headache" also is part of P & L. I am sure most people are all familiar with the sign beside elevators stating that they are not to be used in the event of a fire in the building. There is good reason for this. Several fires throughout the country have resulted in injuries and/or deaths involving elevators. Excessive heat often causes the electronics of elevators to function erratically and may even bring the car to the fire floor. If you have paid attention to news reports of Hi-Rise fires, you are aware that in many of them there have been elevator failures.

The fire department is aware of this, and stresses that anytime there is an alarm of fire from a building containing elevators, the cars are to automatically be brought down to the first floor - or an alternate floor in the event the alarm originated at the first floor. This automatic recall should take place regardless of the alarm origin. This includes alarms from a water flow (automatic sprinkler), heat or smoke detector, or by a manual pull box. We believe this is in the best interests of the public and will continue to insist on it.

There are those who argue that this is not necessary, because the public might be inconvenienced by accidental alarms. Their solution is to have the cars descend only when two smoke detectors in the elevator lobby are activated. The fallacy of this is that if the lobby is air tight, as many are, a raging fire could involve an entire floor and due to the efficiency of the insulation, smoke would not reach the lobby detectors to activate them and return the elevators.

Anecdote:

There is a Hi-Rise building in downtown Boston that has a sign by the elevator reading, "In the event of fire, do not use this elevator. Do not use stairs." I called this to the attention of management several times, but it still remained.

Another matter of great concern to firefighters is the so called blind elevator shafts in which cars ride nonstop to speed passengers to upper floors in high rise buildings. This is another reason for the automatic removal of elevators for passenger use in emergencies. At a recent Hi-rise fire in a Boston office building, this became a problem as people were trapped in an elevator somewhere in the shaft. First it was necessary to determine the location of the car and then members of the department rappelled down the dark shaft to rescue the trapped occupants. You can understand why at least these men would like to see attention given to improving access to blind shafts, but the same people who don't want automatic recall of elevators, don't want this bucket-of-worms opened either.

One other ongoing project that merited increased priority three years ago was the need for additional water at Deer Island. The two present major occupants of the island are the House of Correction and the sewer treatment plant. Both desperately need water and although it is a very, very long story, and will get longer, suffice it to say that the much needed solution is a few steps closer. But if rate payers are watching, the combined package deal is going to cost!

The pros and cons of the Depressed Central Artery and the Third Harbor Tunnel is not a matter of official discussion for the fire department, or this book. P & L's role has been to work within the context of the planning, and provide guidance in terms of public safety and fire protection.

Paramount to public safety is the matter of vehicles carrying hazardous materials. It is the contention of fire departments that hazardous cargoes should be banned from tunnels, but in this case we are dealing in terms of Boston, and it is a hard policy to sell. There have been enough fires in vehicular tunnels, both in this country and throughout the world, to make the wisdom of such a ban elementary, but there are those in the state who think otherwise.

I can appreciate the complacency of the designers regarding hazardous cargoes because their immediate concerns involve the multitude of construction details that have to be worked out and incorporated into the final designs. The fire department knows that what ever is built, we will have to live with it for a long time. Firefighters will have to contend with Incidents in the eight miles of tunnels that will eventually catacomb beneath Boston streets.

Anecdote:
This is one of those battles that began to intensify during my time as head of P & L. The fire department finally did persuade the State to prohibit vehicles carrying "Dangerous Articles" from using tunnels. After a long hard battle, the public is the winner. For me, this decision for the people, at least partly made up for the three and a half years I gave up in District 3 to serve in headquarters.

It should be made clear that the P & L section is not a one man operation. There were conscientious dedicated members working in P & L when I took command, and although most of those have retired in the last three years, I have been most fortunate in the caliber of men and officers who have replaced them. They have been quick to adapt to the strange schedule of working five days a week, but more important, to grasp the sense of the job that has to be done. They have shown ingenuity and a tenacity that benefits the citizens of Boston and the fire department. I hesitate to mention names, but I want to acknowledge that they too made me look good in my position, and I appreciate every one of them.

In Chapter 8, I told how the idea of being in the spotlight at the Ball never again entered my head, but when the Board of Merit met for their yearly meeting in early 1988, they chose me to be honored at the Ball with an Award of Recognition. And so on May 27th at the 109th Annual Ball, my last as an active member, and with Dot and our kids and their spouses watching, I proudly stood in the spotlight that I had erased from my mind nearly forty years before. The award reads:

FIRE DEPARTMENT

Award of Recognition

In addition to his multiple duties as Director of Civil Defense, he has successfully developed and completed numerous programs that have had a most positive effect on the operation and efficiency of the department, including: improved fire protection services at the Boston Gas LNG Facility, Commercial Point, enhanced water supplies for fire fighting city-wide, improved fire protection on all M.B.T.A. sites and the Sumner and Callahan Tunnels, design of a new fire station for Fort Hill Square, renovation of the Hanover Street fire station, development of an evacuation plan for the city, increased protection at Deer Island House of Correction, exclusion of hazardous cargoes from the proposed depressed artery and several other progressive achievements.

His forty-one years of service, both in fire fighting and headquarters activities are a credit to himself and the Boston Fire Department, therefore, the Award of Recognition is hereby awarded to

District Fire Chief Paul F. Cook
A Member of the Communications Division
Planning and Logistics Section

In Witness Whereof, this certificate is given under hand and seal of His Honor the Mayor, duly attested by the Fire Commissioner, Boston, Massachusetts, this twenty-seventh day of May, nineteen hundred and eighty-eight.

Fire Commissioner   Mayor

Whether by inheritance or environment, our son Jonathan would loved to have followed in his father's footsteps as a Boston firefighter. Being a WASP in Boston, he would qualify as a minority in Webster's dictionary, but not in the eyes of the courts that had its own select interpretation of who was a minority. Fortunately he was high enough on his list to be one of four appointed to the Westwood Fire Department in 1988.

Because the class starting at the Mass. Fire Academy for Men on Probation was filled, they would have to wait for the next class. Boston was just starting a class of new recruits and there was room for four from Westwood. The graduation exercises were held at Florian Hall. John Sheehy, Chief of the Westwood Fire Department gave me the honor and privilege of pinning Jonathan's new badge on his uniform.

Anecdote:
FFOP Morley Carter who was appointed with me, and later became my brother-in-law, made lieutenant and followed me to Brighton. Later he made captain and returned to Engine 42. His son Richard became a Westwood firefighter on June 1, 1977 and was joined by Jonathan a year later. Comparing his starting salary with mine, and if he were to receive raises and promotions to match my career, at the end of forty years Jonathan's salary will be in excess of six hundred thousand dollars a year. If it happens, every one will be in financial trouble.

These two events were certainly high points in my career, but what I consider another honor, was yet to come my way. As mentioned earlier in this chapter, one of the fun assignments dealt with the two new fire houses in District 3. In September the Commissioner called me to his office and asked if I was available to go to France to represent the department. After stopping to consider the offer - for a full split-second, I told him I was prepared to obey any order of my superiors and accept any assignment given to me, no matter how distasteful it might be.

It seems that Strasbourg, France, which is also a Sister City to Boston, would be inaugurating a new State-of-the-Art fire house and Training Center in their city on September 21st and they had invited three members of the Boston Fire Department to join them for the occasion. They requested that at least one Boston jake being sent should be knowledgeable about fire house design and planning. Lucky me! Also lucky, the tax payers of Boston because our Sister City and Air France took care of all details of our trip - including expenses.

And so on Sunday evening, September 18th, Chief of Operations John White, Lieutenant Curtis Holzendorf of Engine Company 33 and yours truly, reluctantly settled into First Class seats on Air France Flight 012 for our flight from Boston to Paris.

We spent Monday in Paris Fire Headquarters comparing notes with our brother "Sapeurs and Pompiers." It was interesting to learn that the City of Paris has seven thousand firefighters. They respond to 300,000 incidents a year and average fifty building fires a day in the "City of Light." We learned that though three thousand plus miles separated us, the problems and experiences of both departments are similar. As we broke bread with them, that fraternal bond that binds firefighters was evident, and except for a little language difficulty and a slight variance in uniforms, one would never know we had left home.

On Tuesday we flew to Strasbourg where we were received royally by our brothers in blue and immediately welcomed with a luncheon in a private dining room at the airport. On reaching the city we were met by an interpreter who was assigned to us for our three day stay. Tina was a very attractive blonde from California who had gone to school in Strasbourg. While there she met and married a Strasbourg firefighter, Ted Wolff. Their enthusiasm, cordiality, hospitality, and help with the language added much to smoothing our visit.

In the afternoon we were taken to the Air France office where we each were presented with one of the latest type fire helmets worn in France, provided by the manufacturer. They were for our use while there, and for our evaluation when we returned to Boston. The design and features are a big change from the leather helmets we wear and have merit, but American firefighters are slow to change some things and even slower to break with tradition so I do not anticipate a rapid change over to the space age type helmet. That evening we were guests at a reception given by the City of Strasbourg and Air France.

On Wednesday noon we were guests of the mayor for lunch at a fine restaurant. Wednesday evening was the Inauguration of the new fire house. It was a gala and spectacular event as the city and fire department together went all out to proudly open and show off their new State-of-the-Art fire house. Looking at the marble floors and stairs, the lobby elevator, the eighteen foot deep swimming (I mean training) pool, the gymnasium with full size basketball court, the carpeted TV room with dozens of lounge chairs, the large auditorium with the latest electronic teaching equipment, the huge stainless steel kitchen with all the newest culinary aids that a First Class hotel would be envious of, and the two bars - one for the officers and one for the men, made me feel that I somehow had fallen short in the fire houses I worked on for my brother Boston firefighters. Of course, theirs did cost $17,000,000 - so maybe I wasn't a complete failure at my work on our new Taj Mahal.

In typical French architectural style, the fire house buildings are built around a court yard and it was in this area that they put on a two hour water, colored fountains and laser light show. The Strasbourg City Orchestra provided a concert and the firemen provided an historic demonstration of apparatus, uniforms and equipment of their fire department through the years. The long finale included a spectacular fire in their training building and rappelling by three men, with dogs, down their hundred and fifty foot drill tower while Blue, White and Red floodlights engulfed them in the dramatic French Tri-color. As the orchestra struck a patriotic note, fireworks were set off from the tower and the training building. The visiting firemen from Boston were given a place of honor in the front row seats to view this amazing presentation.

Following the public tour of the new facilities there was a collation served in the gym that included everything imaginable in food and drink. Those in attendance included firefighters from all over Europe, as well as Canada and the U.S. It was a night that was all about the fraternal friendship. There was the common camaraderie, the bond which recognizes no boundaries or languages, the desire to share like experiences, the hunger and thirst to listen and talk shop among brothers who share a common danger, the exchanging of addresses, the invitations to visit work places and homes of otherwise strangers, and the reluctance to terminate relations that began that night, which were new, but eternally old. It all lasted well into the night - - or was it Thursday daybreak!

Later on Thursday morning we had an informal and friendly visit with Colonel Dollinger, Chief of the Strasbourg Fire Department, and a slower private tour of the new facilities. In the Officer's bar we toasted the new fire house and union of the Sister Cities. We gave their Chief gifts from our Commissioner and the Boston Fire Department including a clock, with a Maltese Cross, from Curt's fire house. There was a plaque with the helmet shields and ranks of the Boston brothers. Colonel Dollinger then led us to a room that had already been designated the "Boston Room." Our gifts would become part of the room's decor and he assured us the room would always be open and available to visiting firemen from Boston.

In return, we were made Honorary Firefighters of the Strasbourg Fire Department. We were given badges and tri-color work shirts of our new department and presented with the Military Aiguillettes. In all of France, only members of the Strasbourg Fire Department are entitled to wear it. This was an honor bestowed only on the Strasbourg Fire Department by the military, in recognition of their particular service in battle during World War II. It is a blue, white and red woven cord with a metal tipped cord extension and is worn on the left shoulder and drapes under the arm. I am proud to have it – but never dared wear it with my department uniform in Boston.

On Friday we drove to Reims where we were entertained and fed by the fire department there. After returning from dinner in a hotel, we again sat up until about three in the morning comparing departments and swapping stories.

On Saturday we returned to Paris by car with our police escort. To me it was a most fitting finale for my last days in the Boston Fire Department. As mentioned before, my first sight of Paris was with Patton's Third Army in August 1944. Perhaps it was my tender age and the romance of being in Paris, but I came to love that city then and have always had a warm place in my heart for it. Something has drawn me back there several times in the passing years and I have always experienced a nostalgia for that place - somehow to belong and be a part of it.

As part of our visit and exchange of information among fire departments, we took our helmets and fire gear with us. At Paris Fire Headquarters there was a display of fire helmets from several cities and countries around the world, but no leather helmets from America. As a parting gesture, I donated my helmet to their collection.

Hopefully, for the next few hundred years, a white leather fire helmet with a shield reading "DISTRICT CHIEF, BOSTON" and bearing two crossed gold bugles will be on display in a glass case in Paris Fire Headquarters. Later an inscription was placed beside my helmet noting that it was, donated by District Chief Paul Cook of BFD, who also took part in the Liberation of Paris in 1944. It will be a bit of Bostonian Americana that will be seen by visiting firemen - and hopefully by generations of future visiting Cooks. It is a symbolic uniting in one fond place of two important parts of my life - that which took place as a young soldier in the battle for democracy, and that which took place over forty-one years later in the battle for public safety.

On Sunday, we returned to Boston via Air France, First Class. Recognition at the Ball and a nostalgic trip to France. What a delightful way to close my brief Pentagon years.

Anecdote:

When the new Division I fire house was dedicated in September 1989, it was my privilege to be instrumental in having the Boston-Strasbourg Sister City Association arrange for Chief Dollinger to attend. He was accompanied by Monsieur Jean Meyer, Deputy Mayor of Strasbourg.

On the Wednesday before my retirement there was a noontime gathering at headquarters to recognize my years in the department. Prior to lunch, the "Commish" said the following,

"Next Monday, October 31st, marks the retirement of Paul Cook. This brings to a close what I consider to be one of the most outstanding careers in the history of the Fire Department.

For those of you who have only come to know Chief Cook since he arrived at Headquarters three years ago, you should also know that what he accomplished here really only scratches the surface of what he did throughout the thirty-eight years of firefighting he performed before he accepted this assignment.

He exemplified what we think a truly dedicated firefighter should be in each rank that he served and his fourteen years in command of District 3, the largest and most difficult to administer, serves as a model for every member who reaches the rank of District Fire Chief.

If I started listing all of his major accomplishments in Planning and Logistics, and if I read them all we would have a very late lunch. But I must mention his work as Civil Defense Director, his accomplishments at the LNG facility at Commercial Point, the design of two new fire houses, his work on the Central Artery Project, the MBTA fire protection system, the water supply system at Deer Island and the Title III Disaster Drill we had last month.

I have been a member of the Board of Merit for twenty years. The Board consists of all Deputy Fire Chiefs and we meet annually in February to vote on awards to be given at the Relief Fund Ball in May of each year. This year, when Paul Cook's name was submitted as a candidate for the City of Boston Award of Recognition, it was the fastest unanimous Yes decision that I have seen in those twenty years.

I think that all retirements that are mandatory involve sadness and joy in equal amounts, and I know I certainly feel both of those emotions in this case. Sadness that Paul must leave the department after all of these outstanding years of service, but joy because he is receiving the retirement he so richly deserves and both he and Dot are healthy enough and happy enough to really enjoy the future.

Best Wishes"

Leo D. Stapleton
Fire Commissioner
Chief of Department

Visiting North American firefighters with Colonel Dollinger, Chief of the Strasbourg Fire Department, at their new Training Center.

We receive our French fire helmets.

THE FORUM

(or, Dying Embers From An Old Chief)

When starting this book I expected the Forum would be the longest chapter. First, because of the uncertainty as to how many events could be recalled, and second, because of my pent-up opinions that were withheld from discussions around the fire house tables for the last thirty years. As it turned out, when I began to write, the thoughts flowed freely and the pen moved more smoothly than expected. Actually, for each story included, two or three others have been omitted because of space. So as the rest of the book grew, so now this chapter will be abbreviated, but regardless of the length of this chapter, the thoughts are strictly my own, and after forty years, I believe I am entitled to them.

It doesn't matter what the subject, nor at which table it occurs, firemen's discussions often revolve around diametric positions and thus become wide open debates. At the start of this book I suggested that my input might be added to the forum and I promised some history. All of the following should fall into one of these two categories.

Included in the Gloss---ary is WASP - White Anglo-Saxon Protestant. Through no fault or favor of my own, I am included in this caste. This is mentioned to bear out a point about today's society, which is really an enigma, for while it has become very legalistic in some ways, it breaks and ignores more laws and rules than has any previous generation.

Even though a WASP, I was able to rise to my elevated position in a department that has been wrongly accused of being a restricted Irish Catholic domain. That I didn't get to be a district chief faster, or go higher, was my own doing, or undoing. It was the opportunity, available to all, and not a court ordered minority WASP quota that motivated and propelled me into the department and through its ranks.

In the same vein, it is encouraging today to see some of the minority firefighters placing high on promotional lists and being promoted as vacancies occur. It is to their credit, and the way it should be for the public's best interests! I hope our courts will allow this legitimate, democratic and enterprising American process to continue, without their restrictive rules and quotas.

On the next subject, you may feel that I am not consistent, but that is a matter of opinion. It may, in some eyes, lack consistency in regards to equal rights, but it doesn't in regards to my major concern - the tax payers. As a father of four I have always been grateful for having been appointed to the fire department and been able to devote a lifetime to a career that I wanted and respected. My appreciation to the public has already been expressed and I have tried for over forty-one years to give them their money's worth in return.

The fact that my career and those of many other men have spanned many years, has spared tax payers the cost of training frequent replacements and providing them with personal equipment and eventually with pensions. The public has also profited by the years of continuing available experience of these men. In the Gloss---ary, under FIREMAN, I stated it was a man's job and it always will be. This is my personal conviction and through the years I have seen no reason to change it. Though the ladies may, or may not, make pretty additions to fire houses, and though they may physically be able (although this has my doubts) to do the job for a few years, I cannot picture any of them putting in thirty or forty years of fire duty for the tax payers. It is also my conviction that tax payers are entitled to a dollars worth of service for every dollar they pay and now they are being cheated.

Can you, who are paying the bills, picture a sixty year old woman, or even forty, climbing a hundred foot icy ladder on a winter night, then entering a window and groping around a hot dark smoky tenement, and then carrying a two hundred pound unconscious person back down to the street? It is part of the job regardless of age and, it is done daily by dedicated men right up to their sixty-fifth birthday!

And what of the ladies who marry and bear children. How long should they be expected to stay working, or how long can they safely continue to work under such unhealthy conditions and not harm their unborn? And if they should stay beyond motherhood, how about the childhood diseases and other problems that are part of everyone's growing up? Can you also picture a good mother not wanting to be home with an ailing child? Do you think if there is a sick child at home, she can be at work and give full attention to the public's safety (for which she is being paid), and her own safety, as well as that of other firefighters with whom she should be sharing responsibility? It is hard enough for many men to do it, but they do not have that inborn maternal concern.

A pregnant woman will not expect (nor should she) to continue fire duty once she learns of her condition and for some time after delivery. The extra time-off she needs will steal protection from the tax payers, but may not save them the expense. It will also put an added work burden on the men in her group. In most jobs, mothers-to-be are allowed a few weeks of maternity leave, which may or may not be with pay. In the fire department it adds up to a year or more of maternity leave. Some departments state this leave will be "with loss" (not paid).

I have spoken with some of these women and they talk in terms of going back to school after they earn some money, seeking a desk job to get away from fire duty, or leaving altogether and trying some other lark. It is my calculated opinion that all they do is satisfy the court's dictum that they are as capable as men of taking the job - but not of doing it for very long. There are many men who would love to fulfill their boyhood dream and become firemen to serve the tax payers for a life time, but they are passed over because "political correctness" dictates that females be given the job. I repeat, all the ladies and courts are doing, is depriving some men of the job. In so doing, they are robbing tax payers and piling unfair financial burden on them.

Mention was made of Proposition 2-1/2. This was an attempt by the public in the early eighties to slow down the pace of the politicians robbing them by way of special interest projects. They were aware that a lot of their money was being spent by their elected leaders on inflated programs that may or may not be productive. Since the elected officials would not listen to their cries, the public went to the ballot and passed the referendum, but what they could not pass, was how it would be administered. To show their displeasure and contempt for the public's concerns and their voting, the politicians, instead of eliminating their pet projects, made drastic cuts in services effecting the voting tax payers. Schools, library hours, rubbish collections and public safety departments were all cut so the public would know their insistence on less spending had not fallen on deaf ears.

In the fire department, fire houses were closed, companies were deactivated, officers were demoted and firemen fired. Using the long established and accepted labor practice of "last hired, first fired," men with up to a couple years service were let go. Many of them were men who had recently been hired under a court ordered minority quota program. When these men were let go, the courts stepped in and ordered that the quota system be maintained, regardless of seniority. The result was that men with little seniority and experience were taken back and other men with more experience were let go. It should be pointed out that some minorities at first refused to come back if it meant others would be let go to make room for them, but their good intentions were defeated by the bureaucracy. When they tried to collect unemployment insurance because they were laid off, they were denied it, because they had been offered back their jobs and they had refused them. The reason they refused was not taken into consideration, and so to feed their children they had to abandon their good honest intentions and return to work. No one should blame them for this.

Some men who were fired ended up losing their cars and homes because they were unable to make payments. Domestic and other problems increased and resentments grew.

In an attempt to reduce the number of men to be let go, the city offered a financial incentive to men with longevity who would take an early retirement. Sentiments were running high and talk of a strike was mounting. It never materialized, but many men who loved the job did not want to be put in the position of having to make a strike decision, so they took the incentive and retired early. Once again the tax payers were hit in their pocketbooks.

When the elected officials thought their message had sufficiently gotten through to the voters, all the let-go firemen were offered back their jobs. Most of the men returned, but it was to a job that had lost much of the old spirit. Wounds had been opened that probably will not close until all the men who were involved have completed their careers.

This matter has been included strictly as an event of history. If the esprit de corps in the fire department remains scarred, historians may pinpoint these years as a probable cause. The real tragedy is that it was unnecessary - and the men were the victims, along with the public. In desperation the men may have accused one another, but it was the selfish, heartless politicians who were to blame - and they still resent any restrictions placed on them by the voters. When they feel the time is right, they will likely find an excuse and means of doing away with Proposition 2-1/2, either by nibbles or in one fell swoop. Then they will have had their revenge on the voters, and they can return to their spendthrift ways big time! In the meantime, they can use voter approved overrides to spend more of our money. Will tax payers ever wake up?

To change the subject, which is done quite frequently around the fire house kitchen tables, the exams that we took for entrance and promotion over a twenty-five year period all had the same similarity. The material that we had to study had a practical application in preparing us for the work we would do, the equipment to be used and the critical decisions to be made. I have already mentioned that my first Red Book was purchased as a teenager. It described fire apparatus and included pictures of equipment and appliances used by firemen. It explained the duties and pointed out the dangers of the job. It probably weeded out some men who on learning what the job was all about, decided it wasn't for them. That is the way it should be.

Material for promotional exams went into more detail and expanded on the knowledge that is vital for an officer to know. The entire exam process was handled by the state Civil Service Commission, which operated on a stringent policy and a strict timetable that was understood by all concerned.

Some years ago the Commonwealth relegated Civil Service to a less dominant role and instituted, or substituted, the state

Department of Personnel Administration. To me it appeared, and remains, a disaster as there appears to be no rhyme, reason or consistency in its operation. It is like Madison Avenue's "new and improved, with the smell of lemon added," that turns out to be a more expensive but inferior product that the tax payers get stuck with. About this time, and in conjunction with a court's ruling, the Red Book was eliminated as being immaterial and irrelevant. Using the same logic, medical books should be removed from the curriculum for those studying to become doctors.

To make the marking process simpler and to limit the appeal practice, exams have been reduced to all multiple choice which are easier to mark but give no real indication of a man's knowledge or ability to understand and address problems he will face in the field. Without studying, a lucky individual can guess his way to a job or promotion. The end result is a lot of men with the same high mark and a lottery to see who gets the job. Since experience has been reduced to an insignificant quotient, men are able to rise to chief's rank in a relatively short time. It is my belief that a man should be in each grade for five years before being allowed to take an exam for the next rank. On this basis, most officers would have twenty years experience before becoming a chief, which again, in my opinion, is about right for a man who is to be entrusted with other men's lives and the tax payer's property.

In all fairness to the men who are making the meteoric rise in the fire service, it should be pointed out that they are intelligent and ambitious. They would be applying themselves with the same dedicated determination if they were in another field, where the financial rewards would probably be much greater. Further, they are not breaking any rules, just taking advantage of the present available system. In my opinion, it is the system that is at fault, not the men working under it.

Most firemen are thought to be conservative in their thinking and their talking - but I am not sure about their voting. If they are conservative, it is because of their closeness to reality, as they go about their daily duties. All too often, at least in Boston, they are witnesses to sorrowful situations that are the results of liberal thinking, liberal courts and liberal policies.

As an example, my wife was called for jury duty and went through the process of being considered as a jurist on a serious felony case. As the defense studied the panel, Dot was rejected - because her husband was a firefighter. I wonder where the court's application of equal rights for women was in this case? She was not dealt with in her own right as a women and as an individual, but only as the wife of one who is lumped into a group that are considered conservatives - and conservatives are thought by liberals to be too strong on justice. Therefore, conservatives should not be allowed to be part of the jury making decisions in criminal cases.

It is a sad comment on today's America that this is the norm in local courts, but the same liberal philosophy causes elected politicians to vote against confirming potential judges who still believe in the principles of our founding fathers and Justice. It's called "Politically Correct."

And now, the news media. "I disapprove of what you say, but I will defend to the death your right to say it," is attributed to Francois Voltaire. Noble words and a real democratic approach. Perhaps this remark, along with Freedom of Speech as provided in the First Amendment, has been seized - no, stolen, by the Fourth Estate, as license to report what they want and in the way they want it slanted. As I view it, the media long ago ceased to be satisfied with reporting the news, and became the self-appointed regents to make the news. It is similar to our courts that have determined their duty is to make laws rather than enforce the legislature enacted ones, as our founding fathers prescribed. My dealings with the media have not been on earth-shaking issues, but one thing I have observed, the media is consistent - they are more interested in ratings than accuracy.

As chief in charge of many Incidents, it was often necessary for me to meet with the media and issue statements. When possible, I would delay the confrontation with them until all fire concerns had been completed, which was my proper duty. I also hoped they would get tired of waiting for me and go bother someone else. Besides, I had noticed that there was little difference in their stories whether or not they talked with me. In the beginning I preferred TV reporters because the voice and message were mine. I soon learned that sometimes much of the tape ended up on the cutting room floor, and my picture and remarks were out of context, if it better suited the story the media wanted to present.

The first request is always for your name – and "how do you spell it?" (Cook is such a difficult name to spell, but they often managed to somehow disguise it). Once they have a name, they write what they please and attribute the remarks to the name. Quite often one would try to goad me into saying something that would be more newsworthy from their perspective - never mind if it wasn't true. I recall having two minor subway fires only minutes apart. They were on two different subway lines and two different type fires. One was an electrical fire, and the other a small rubbish fire. They did have a common cause - simple overheating on a hot, humid summer afternoon. The reporters prompted and almost pleaded with me to connect the two fires. They just knew it had to be arson, or perhaps even sabotage or terrorism. They left disappointed and no mention at all was made of the Incidents by the news media.

A reporter came to my office one evening to interview me for a human interest article on the neighborhood fire chief. In the article that appeared in print, the reporter had every right to describe my quarters, and surroundings, as seen through the writer's eyes - even if I didn't recognize them. When I also had difficulty recognizing the answers I had given, it made me wonder if there shouldn't be some limitation on journalistic liberties. In the courtroom, a witness is only allowed to testify as to what he said or did. Anything else is hearsay and is not admissible as evidence. Shouldn't the media also be required to include a "truth in reporting" statement, and declare that most of what is reported is only hearsay?

Anecdote:
To illustrate "Freedom of the Press," I am including some remarks regarding "Voltaire's quotation" that appears in Bergen Evans, "Dictionary of Quotations." Speaking of the quotation, he says,

"The phrase has enough exaggeration to be striking and enough paradox to seem vaguely witty. And as Voltaire was a champion of freedom of speech, it seems 'in keeping.'

In reality, however, Voltaire clung to his life with zest and was not prepared to give it up to defend any piece of senseless babble - or anything at all, whether he disapproved or approved. He was a reasonable man, not a martyr. What he actually said in his 'Essay on Tolerence,' the words that Miss Tallentyre 'paraphrased' into the pompous utterance so often attributed to him, was 'Think for yourselves and let others enjoy the privilege of doing so too.' That is something different."

One further comment around this forum coffee table. I am glad that my school days in Boston were during a time when patriotism and respect for God and Country were inalienable rights, and practiced. Each day, our teachers read from the Holy Bible and together we stood and saluted our country's flag. No one questioned it or thought their rights or freedoms were being trampled upon. The flag wasn't allowed to touch the ground, let alone be worn on the seat of one's pants. We were learning respect and responsibility, and developing a pride in God, country and flag. It was this pride in our country and faith in God that saw millions of boys rush to the recruiting offices to defend that flag on December 8, 1941. It was that pride and responsibility that inspired the Marines to raise the flag at Mount Surabachi against tremendous odds, and millions of other inspired Americans to perform heroic deeds on land, air and sea in battles all over the world, to preserve democracy and freedom for all people.

It annoys me greatly that all we hear about today is "people's rights" with no mention of "people's responsibilities." One's rights and responsibilities should go hand in hand. Those who are yelling the loudest about "rights" are doing the most to destroy them in our country. I have seen and I have read, and it is my considered opinion, that as tax payers we should insist that government funding be stopped for those individuals and organizations who feign to defend civil liberties. It would be interesting to see just how many of them would continue their "cause" if they were taken off the public dole. As tax payers, it makes no sense to finance our own destruction, which we are doing, and it should be stopped.

The Rule Book of the department states that religion or politics will not be discussed in the fire house. Naturally this rule is strictly adhered to, like all the others, so I will withhold my comments on religion until later. As for politics - it stinks - - and "politically correct" is putrid! When historians write "The Rise and Fall of America," and they will if major changes aren't made soon, "politically correct" will be a dominant cause! Politicians take note.

A subject that is much in the headlines these days is the disease, or condition, known as AIDS. There is no question that this is a frightening matter to many people, and as far as I am concerned, to firefighters who are daily called to rescue and treat people who are victims of accidents and other mishaps. As "First Responders" we are expected to, and do, give immediate attention to all unfortunate victims without thought of any personal dangers at the time. The fear sometimes comes later, with a call from a hospital advising that a treated victim showed signs of a contagious disease.

Following instructions and the example set by trained and informed medical personnel, the fire department has adopted the now standard practice of attempting to avoid exposure to body fluids of other people by the use of gloves, masks and eye shields, when handling accident victims. But even with all precautions taken, there is often the nagging uncertainty of whether the measures were adequate. Generally the firefighters' concerns are not for themselves, but rather for their families and loved ones, whom they fear may somehow be exposed to some contagious disease through them. It is well known that some people have become innocent victims of dread diseases by blood transfusions before the need for additional testing was realized. These, and the innocent babies born with the AIDS factor, are the real tragedies.

This book has pointed out that statistics consistently show that firefighters have an above average propensity of developing cancer, and at an earlier age than their contemporaries. Statistics also indicate that a growing number of people in all walks of life come down with what is referred to as the "Big C." Even though medical progress has been made in research and treatment in recent years, for many - if not most, cancer is still a long, agonizing terminal disease for the individual and the family. As more and more families experience the shattering effects, and long costly treatments, when a member of the family is diagnosed as having cancer, there has developed a growing cry for the government to invest larger sums of money in an all-out attempt to learn the cause, and then eradicate cancer. In spite of the universal concern, it has fallen on deaf ears. Only relatively small amounts have been voted and expended.

On the other hand, because of the publicity and lobbying of AIDS victims and friends, and the politicians' inclination to cater to the "squeaking wheel" groups, larger and larger amounts are voted for AIDS research and treatment because this is "politically correct." After watching many of my fellow firefighters fall victim to cancer, it is my personal "Forum" feeling that most of these funds should be transferred to cancer research, that would benefit all mankind.

As I am leaving the fire department, new turnout gear is being introduced. Although too new to be a kitchen table discussion subject yet, I believe their merits, and/or non-merits, will have its day both in fire houses and official circles. They do have OSHA and the manufacturer's approval, but I don't think all firemen will find it the same panacea.

I have waded through too many cellars in water well over my knees to see any merit in abandoning hip boots. Remember the bar with water deep enough to dive into?

Beyond a doubt there is a time and place for the new gear, but there are also times and places when they are not practical, in my opinion. For much of my career, summer firefighting gear was optional, and thus minimal because of the added weight and discomfort when working in confined heated atmospheres. We could work longer and more efficiently. I am aware that many man made products in use today do produce more hazardous smoke, and that has to be taken into consideration, but in some instances a healthful compromise is possible.

Since the jury is still out on this modern turnout gear I will say no more now, but when the men who wear it as they fight fires begin to have their say, remember you first read about it in this book.

Of course fire house round table discussions include the daily newspaper and TV renderings of world and local happenings, sports, deaths, movies, books and everything else that is likewise discussed around various office water coolers elsewhere. When necessary each subject is bisected and dissected and sometimes if it ends in agreement, the subject is quickly changed so the Forum can go on, but this one is ended.

Now my pent-up thoughts have finally been released. As at the fire house kitchen table, I do not expect everyone to agree with my opinions, but I have a right to express them. In some matters I feel it is a responsibility, because of my concern for tax payers - of which I am one.

2002 Note: With the passing of time, and with 20/20 hindsight, my thoughts on some of these subjects may have strengthened, tempered or changed, but they remain as originally written.

AND OMEGA

(or, God Doesn't Make Parking Lots)

If you have been reading this book as it was written, by now you should have laughed (or at least smiled) a couple times and maybe shed a tear or two. You may have learned something you did not know before and knowledge is always helpful. But better still, maybe these stories have triggered your own memory to recapture long forgotten events in your own life that are mentally worth recalling and sharing with your family.

Although all these pages may in one sense be a worthy accomplishment, I do feel this much written text should go a bit further since it is part biography. So now, a word from the sponsor.

If you do not believe in God, or if you have strong feelings that even a touch of religion has no place in a book such as this, then I ask you to please bear with me for the next couple pages. If you prefer, skip them and go on. God has been an important part of my life since before birth and I would not feel right leaving Him out of my book.

Earlier I pointed out that "environment" may have played a major role in my becoming a working spark and eventually fulfilling my dream to be a fireman. God gave us life that we might enjoy all things, and then He gave us all things that we might enjoy life. Despite the sad moments, that are part of every life, I must say that by God's Grace my life cup has been filled, packed down and overflowed. The serious part of my life has been influenced by both "environment" and "inheritance."

Briefly, my Roots. My grandfather, John E. Cook, came to America in 1858 with his parents and siblings as a German immigrant family and settled in Pennsylvania. He was 13 years old. I will not burden you with all the details of his life but just say the family was God-fearing and put into practice what they read in their Bible. So here is where "inheritance" plays its role.

When the War Between the States erupted, he joined Company M of the Seventeenth Pennsylvania Cavalry and fought in fifty-two major campaigns (his name is engraved on the Pennsylvania Monument at Gettysburg).

Afterwards he married, became an interior decorator and raised a family that included my Dad. He was most active in the Baptist Church in Honesdale, Pennsylvania where he served as a deacon and in many other tasks. In that church there is now a stained glass window in honor of his, and his wife's, faithful service to God. They did their utmost to raise their children "in the way they should go."

During World War II it was acknowledged that, "There are no atheists in foxholes." It has been my observation that this also applies to the foxholes of firefighting. In general, I found most of my fellow firefighters to be devout men who believe in God and rely on Him to see them through their dangerous careers. I suspect their loved ones also depend on the power of prayer and God's faithfulness to keep their husbands, fathers and sons safe.

It has been a long time since I have slept in a fire house bunk room so I cannot vouch for today, but I clearly remember my first nights in the bunk room at Egleston Square. Some men demonstrated their faith in God by kneeling at their bunks and praying before crawling in to bed (maybe they were just praying for an all-night in). I was impressed by this bedtime ritual when my teen age sparking reached the "bunking in" stage, because here were grown men whom I respected, still doing the same thing my mother had taught her sons.

Probably those firemen had also been taught to pray by their parents, and now they continued to offer up prayer, even when not seen by their families. It was convincing evidence to me that those early teachings at my home were not an isolated family affair, but rather were part of a widely accepted practice in

America in those days. Regardless of what religious creed an individual held to, it was "training up a child in the way he should go."

Through the years other men were less open about showing their faith, but that did not necessarily mean that it was lacking. I have seen many men, loaded with equipment, stop and bless themselves before entering a burning building to fight a fire, and I do not believe it was an idle gesture on their part. In fact, it made me feel better knowing that men I shared danger with also recognized their dependence on someone higher than the Chief in charge of the fire.

When heavy smoke banked down, indicating a possible back draft build-up, or strange creaking sounds were heard in a burning structure, I sensed that other prayers for protection, besides mine, were hurriedly being offered up to a Supreme Being even as the men, without hesitation, continued their dangerous duty. Most often our prayers were heard and answered, but sometimes God had other plans, like at Lyceum Hall, Trumbull Street and the Hotel Vendome, plus a lot of other single and multiple firefighter fatalities.

All Line of Duty deaths are traumatic tragedies for the families involved, but I still believe there are no accidents in God's planning - only timing that we do not understand now. As individuals we just have to be patient and wait to learn His plan for our life.

God had His plan when He called my Dad home at age fifty-four, when I was eight years old. I couldn't understand it then - and I still am not sure of His timing, but I accept it. Dad's death made a tremendous void in our family, and left Mom with the enormous task of not only having to provide for the physical needs of her sons, but also to look after our more important spiritual needs.

In the then typical American tradition, my Dad continued to trust in God as he raised his own family. He had no reservations about leaving this life before his three score and ten years allotted in the Bible, because he had lived long enough to see all four of his sons accept Christ as their personal Savior. He did not live long enough to see his sons Charles and Richard become Baptist ministers but I am sure he knows and is proud of them.

I remember my Dad, as best as any eight year old could, but he had many friends who admired and respected him for what he believed, stood for and practiced. As I was growing up, they made a point of regularly reminding me of the great man my Dad was, and all agreed that the epitaph on his gravestone was most fitting. Chiseled into the bottom of that gray Quincy Granite stone in a Brookline Cemetery are the words, "FAITHFUL IN ALL THINGS."

Growing up, I was impressed by the effect my Dad had on so many people as to make them collectively think of him in such exemplary terms even years after his death. I became determined, that while I didn't know all the reasons others had for this profound respect, I would do my best to honor him by also trying to be faithful in as many things as possible during my life.

When I joined the fire department, my superiors stressed the importance of adherence to the department Rule Book. As a young boy my parents stressed the importance of adherence to life's rule book, the Bible. It tells us that man's life is three score years and ten, or seventy years. Perhaps by strength it might stretch ten or more years, but on the other hand, as with firefighters, it might end ten years sooner, as statistics indicate. Regardless of the number of years we are given, the important thing is that we don't make empty parking lots of our lives.

Perhaps one reason the fire department Rule Book states that religion will not be discussed in the fire house is because of the theory that one's religious convictions are personal, and to a degree it is true. My religious belief is personal - a personal knowledge and relationship with Jesus Christ as presented in the Bible, and as lived out in the lives of my parents as an example.

With a touch of humor, this book has pointed out how some parking lots are made and has referenced from Joyce Kilmer's poem "that only God can make a tree." The comparative analysis could be that God doesn't make parking lots - only we do --and you don't have to be a Chief to do it.

In the Foreword I suggested that while this life and this book may be fun, there is the realization that someday I too will have to stand before God and give an account of the serious things of my life. With this realization, I have tried to walk the straight and narrow, and love my neighbor.

In the Book of Proverbs we read, "Trust in the Lord with all thine heart; and lean not unto thine own understanding. In all thy ways acknowledge Him, and He shall direct thy paths."

I am not sure about all of my brother firemen, but for me the courage to face the day to day dangers of firefighting was grounded in my boyhood decision to trust in the Lord and be content knowing my future, of whatever length, was secure in God's hand.

With the knowledge that He would direct my paths, I have been **READY TO ROLL ... READY TO DIE.** Not only ready to die as a firefighter, but ready to die as an individual because of His assurance that for believers "to be absent from the body is to be present with the Lord."

I appreciate the "environment" in which I grew up, but I am even more grateful for the "inheritance" that is mine. I hope our children can always be as thankful of their dad as I am of my father and grandfather. Dot and I fervently pray that by the lives they live, their children will be equally proud of them.

We will end this short chapter with the following, because it typifies the Roots from which I came, and sets the example I still strive to attain.

After the death of my grandfather in 1914, Mr. W. J. Barnes of Honesdale wrote the following words:

Lines Upon The Death of J. E. Cook

Yes, I always loved to meet him in my walks upon the street,
Also in his house of worship with his kindly smile to greet,
And his honest look of frankness as my hand he warmly shook
Showed the purity of spirit of our brother, J. E. Cook

He was brave, and true, and honest, both in matters great and small,
And he never flinched or faltered when he heard his country's call
To the front, to face the cannon, and the musket, and the sword
He left home and friends and loved ones dear to battle for the Lord

Yes, he's gone, but not forgotten - we can't stop the falling tear,
As we look upon the casket, something says, "He is not here!"
So we take the "house" he lived in, gently lay it 'neath the sod,
But the "tenant" now rejoices in the Paradise of God.

BACKWORD

(or, Now I Have Said It)

In science the theory is advanced that the Universe revolves on a system of checks and balances. For every movement, there must be a compensating movement. Every action results in a counter-action. For each addition somewhere, there needs to be a subtraction somewhere else ... for every day on one side of the world, a night on the other side ... for every evening, a dawning ... for every tide, an ebb and flow ... for every ocean, some land ... for every flood, a drought ... for every cloud, the sun ... for every desert, an oasis ... for every mountain, a valley ... for every wind, a calm ... for every storm, a clearing ... for every advance, a withdrawal ... for every attack, a defense ... for every victory, a defeat ... for every war, a peace ... for every birth, a death ... for every in, an out ... for every up, a down ... and for every fire, an All Out!

Therefore it is scientifically logical that since this book began with a Foreword, it should end with a Backword.

Since you are reading these last pages, I trust you have also read the first pages - and looked at the pictures.

If you have found this book long and hard to read, take consolation in the fact that it was longer and harder for me to write.

On the other hand, if you have enjoyed it, or found it amusing, interesting or informative, then my time has been well compensated.

It has been a most rewarding experience for me to recall and write about lo these many years, but it cannot begin to compare with the joy and pleasure of having actually lived them.

If through this book you have found my life a bit fascinating, and you are young enough (or old enough), I urge you to consider the vocation of a firefighter. There are still many fires to be fought ... hose lines to be run ... ladders to be raised and climbed ... windows to be broken ... buildings to be ventilated ... locks to be forced ... inspections to be made ... firemen to be appointed ... rescues to be made ... books to be opened ... lessons to be learned ... medals to be earned ... promotions to be made ... arsonists to be caught ... terrorists to be coped with ... jokes to be played ... lives to be spared ... souls to be saved ... parking lots to be made ... and a life time of friendships to be accumulated.

If you seek, and are accepted for the position of firefighter anywhere, you will have to assume the responsibility of being a part of, and perhaps even adding to, the heritage and traditions of the fire service. So "I beseech you that you walk worthy of the vocation to which you are called."

If you do choose this path, I commend - and envy you. I would love to walk it again.

But for now the fires have all been extinguished ... The over hauling is completed ... The buildings are secured ... The apparatus has returned to the barn ... The hose has been dried and repacked, ready for the next alarm ... All the equipment has been cleaned and checked ... Air cylinders have been refilled ... The fires have been critiqued ... The House Journal has been written ... The fire reports have been made and forwarded to headquarters ... The tax payers have been repayed ... The last cup of fire house coffee has been poured and is being savored ... The men are –

READY TO ROLL ... READY TO DIE!

Now my desk and locker have been cleaned out.

My white fire coat and white fire helmet have been put away.

The last cup of coffee is empty.

That which began fifty plus years ago has ended.

There is no more work for this Chief to do, so as of 2400 hours Monday, October 31, 1988, I am ordering the "All Out" on this book

<< << << <<

and on this career!

REKINDLE
(or, Back To The Fire Barn)

The accompanying picture is that of the Firemen's Memorial statue in Boston's Forest Hill Cemetery. On the second Sunday of June each year, a Memorial Service is held there to remember in particular those men who have answered their Last Alarm in an act of unselfish devotion to the citizens of Boston, whom they chose to serve.

The monument was dedicated on Sunday, June 13, 1909. The bronze figure is of a fireman in helmet and fire coat of his generation. He stands fourteen feet tall and rests on a twelve-foot granite base. It was designed by John Wilson, as were the four bronze tablets which are attached to the four sides of the base. The tablets depict a Steamer, a Hook and Ladder, a Protective Wagon and an Old-time Hand Tub. Cut into the base are the words,

IN MEMORY OF DEPARTED COMRADES

THIS MONUMENT IS ERECTED BY THE MEMBERS AND FRIENDS OF

THE BOSTON FIRE DEPARTMENT

JUNE 1909

There are presently 116 deceased firefighters interred in these hallowed grounds. The first Line of Duty deaths to be buried there were Francis I. Cutting and John W. Tuttle, both of Tremont 12. They were killed by falling walls while fighting a fire at 113-139 Federal Street on May 2, 1858.

The last Line of Duty death to be buried there is Firefighter Edward R. Connolly, Aide to District Chief, who was killed on March 21, 1986 at Box 7413 (9 alarms).

Firemen's Memorial Statue
Forest Hills Cemetery, Boston.

Regarding the 1909 Dedication, newspapers reported that 700 veteran and regular firemen gathered for the services while 5,000 spectators were in attendance. The Orator of the Day was the Honorable John R. Murphy, who spoke as follows:

"We have gathered here today to dedicate this Memorial in honor of the men of the Boston Fire Department. It is fitting that it should be erected amidst the graves where sleep so many of the dead that have served our city. It is a memorial of beautiful and simple design, yet noble in its simplicity, symbols of the brave deeds of the men in whose honor it was erected. It will tell to future generations that Boston Firemen died that their fellow man might live."

In 1990 I was chosen by Commissioner Stapleton to be the second retired fireman to be "The Orator of the Day." It was an honor I never expected.

FIREMEN'S MEMORIAL SUNDAY
June 10, 1990

"Mayor Flynn, Fire Commissioner Stapleton, Police Commissioner Roache, Senior Chaplain Keating, President Fitzgerald, Officers and members of Local 718 of the International Association of Fire Fighters, President Hughes and Trustees of the Boston Firemen's Relief Fund, fellow firefighters both active and retired, and finally each of you who have taken time to be at this ninety-seventh anniversary of Firemen's Memorial Sunday, in this historic Forest Hills Cemetery.

Another year has flown by and once again we have assembled here to be still that we might reflect and remember. This day is one of distinct honor for me personally, and for my family. For as I stand before this rostrum in the privileged position of Orator of the Day, my thoughts go back to many past Memorial Ceremonies which I have attended at this serene spot.

Each visit has been similar, and yet each a little different, because of the ever changing names and faces of those individuals who, as they pass through the department, and perhaps rise in rank, unselfishly give of their time to serve on various committees and in varied capacities. The scene and sentiments have often been altered by events that transpired in the department's history from year to year, but our emblematic hero has remained steadfast in his stance and symbol.

For me this day is a nostalgic journey as my mind goes back well over fifty years to when I was a pre-teen age spark and attended my first solemn service on these hallowed grounds. As I first looked at that bronze "hoseman" who represents the dedicated spirit of all firefighters, past, present and future, I was impressed with its undaunted appearance and its somber representation, and the sight of it, lo these many years later, still stirs my heart.

On that first visit, I stood on the side lines as an unrelated spectator, but one who had already developed a love and respect for the fire department and for the men who serve in it. Through the many years, that have passed too quickly, my attendance at these ceremonies has been fairly regular and has taken on a mixture of appearances. As already mentioned, first as a spark coming by bicycle, later as a World War II veteran recently returned from the European Theatre of Operations, still sparky and still wanting so much to belong, and then with great pride for nearly forty-two years as an active member.

At times I came because I was detailed, and for a few years as a Trustee of the Charitable Association. Some years my group was working and I was unable to attend in person - but my thoughts were still here. For the remaining years, as I rose in rank to District Chief, I came partly out of duty, but mostly because of my respect for the department and my fellow firefighters, and also to view again the solemn significance of that silent sentry.

I have observed attendance at these exercises wax and wane, and regretfully, in recent years they have waned more than they have waxed. In the time immediately following World War II, when the department was comprised of men who had been on before the war, and those of us who were hired for the forty-eight hour work week, large numbers met at Engine 3 on Harrison Avenue for coffee and doughnuts and then we came on several buses to the familiar Morton Street entrance.

Perhaps it was because we were new and young and so proud to be part of the comradeship and spirit that special efforts were made to turn out for department functions. The excuse is now given that life was less hectic in those days - and maybe it was. In any event, at the entrance we formed into several units and marched to this special lot of land. On those occasions there were more men than graves to be decorated, and so there was a rush to have the honor of being one of those chosen to place flowers on the grave of a hero.

Following the tragic events of the Lyceum Hall fire in 1942, Trumbull Street in 1964 and the Hotel Vendome in 1972, each of which took the lives of several firefighters, there were larger than usual turn-outs on the following second Sundays in June, as men were drawn closer to the realities of our 'high calling' and felt a desire to pay respect, and to remember with a dignity befitting the gallant efforts of those fallen comrades. Sadly, in more recent years, there have been too many times when the uniformed ranks have been mostly detailed members and each has had to decorate several graves.

As I recall, most of the second Sundays in June have been clear and warm, unlike today. Through the years we have marched from the beautiful entrance of this cemetery, with the colorful rhododendrons in full bloom, past the quiet pond, up the hill - and then to this Firemen's lot. We have performed this ritual to the rhythmic blare of the once large Boston Fire Department Band and Color Guard. We have moved to the ruffle of school drum-and-bugle corps. We have stepped off with bagpipes, and at times we have almost silently shuffled to the beat of a single drummer. For some reason our feet have not always been in step with the one in front of us, but more important, our hearts have always been in step.

And now my being at this ninety-seventh anniversary brings me full circle, for again I stand not in my cherished blue uniform, but neither as an unrelated spectator now, for my presence before you today culminates in what I shall forever consider a high honor and profound privilege.

But you have not come to hear of my memoirs. We have come to this peaceful place that we might pause and remember those of our fraternal family who served well their paymasters, and the citizens of Boston, and who in some instances paid with their lives. Those members did not choose the date or details of their departure, but to their credit, they went about fulfilling their daily duties, mindful of lurking dangers, yet, with a determination to leave their destinies in the hands of a higher authority, and ask no questions.

Over the years there have been a variety of speakers on these Memorial Sundays, but in 1988, John Jennings stood in this place and told us the history of the monument and the day it was first unveiled and dedicated in 1909. It is unanimously agreed that his was an outstanding report, and still stands as a most worthy reminder of the devotion and enthusiasm which first inspired those firemen, as well as other citizens of Boston, to recognize the unselfish role of firefighters in the life of the city.

It is a role that has become a tradition in which every member of the department is expected, not only to live up to, but who, if called upon, has an obligation to add another chapter. The faithful fulfilling of this tradition continues to bring honor to the department, but more important, it adds years to the lives of those people who firefighters seek to serve and protect.

Just a little over two weeks ago we gathered at the Park Plaza Hotel to honor those members of the department who had performed meritorious acts during 1989, and lest we be tempted to rest on our laurels, we were reminded within the same weekend of the frailty of life, and the sometimes limitation of our abilities and heroics, as six members of a family perished in a dwelling house fire in the Roslindale section of the city.

As we quietly pause before this monument, let us study the details of it for a moment. First, we are pleased to see it complete again, for since we last gathered a year ago, a part of it was vandalized, no, desecrated is the more appropriate term, by person or persons who were ignorant of, or cared not, for the lives and sacrifices it represents. They removed a smaller base plaque probably hoping for financial gain. We are indeed grateful to the individuals who had a part in getting back that plaque so our monument could be restored to its original splendor.

As we consider what this monument represents, we are reminded of the changing role of the firemen as depicted by it. To begin with, we have become firefighters rather than firemen - and this may have been a prophetic change as it took place prior to the ladies being added to the ranks. Although our bronze example is properly dressed for the role he played in his day, he would be out of uniform responding today, for fire department tasks have become more complex in today's changing technical society. His leather helmet, without eye and ear protectors, his shirt and pants that are not fire retardant, his rubber coat that is not nomex treated, and the absence of protective gloves and self contained breathing apparatus would prevent him from properly performing his job in the hazards of fighting fires today.

We cannot criticize his absence of steel-toed boots, for in his day, the only protection provided firemen by the city were leather helmets and rubber coats. Perhaps on his meager salary he was raising a passel of kids, as firefighters are still prone to do, and he could not, or would not, afford the luxury of protection for himself.

Our example is depicted in a state of readiness for fire suppression which was his main responsibility in those earlier days. We are all aware this is not the only duty of today's firefighters. The multiple assigned tasks, plus what the public has come to expect from their fire departments, have expanded to the point where today's firefighters are 'first responders' to almost every whim of the public. Whether a vehicle accident requiring extrication and immediate medical attention, a cardiac arrest where prompt CPR is needed, a choking child, handling persons with communicable diseases, entrapments of every kind, downed electrical wires, boating accidents and drownings, Haz-Mat incidents and now even shooting, stabbing and physical assaults, and of course, still fires - whether in manholes or high rise buildings, whether by accident or by arson, on land or on water, the public has learned well the lesson that help in their time of need is only as far away as the nearest red fire box.

The function of fire prevention has expanded too, and the results obtained thus far have gone a long way in reducing fire losses, but again more important, in saving lives. Legislation has been relentlessly pursued by fire departments with the positive results of smoke detector and automatic sprinkler laws for both new and existing buildings over seventy feet high. Sprinklers are now required in buildings of four or more residential units in Boston, regardless of height, and hopefully before long, the mandatory installation of sprinklers will be further extended to include even single family dwellings.

In other areas as well, fire departments are diligently working to have public safety issues addressed in the design stages for structures rather than waiting for them to be added later at extra cost. In a way, firefighters are engaged in a battle in which they are trying hard to put themselves out of business. We know this will never be fully accomplished, but not many professions can claim that as a goal toward which they are striving. If we even come close to being successful, once again it will be the public, whom we have always sought to serve, who will be the real beneficiary of the firefighter's efforts.

These are worthwhile endeavors, but we have not met here to heap praise upon ourselves. Rather we have come to remember those of our numbers who have responded to their "Last Alarm." Again we look to that lofty monument and we do not forget that some of our brothers died in the performance of their duty. There are one hundred sixty-eight of these heroes in the Boston Fire Department. Some are buried here and some have been laid to rest in family lots elsewhere, but regardless of their final resting places, surely they can all claim those verses from the Gospel of John, which reads, 'This is my commandment that ye love one another, as I have loved you. Greater love hath no man than this, that a man lay down his life for his friends.' Our comrades demonstrated that love, and their devotion to duty, by laying down their lives, not just for friends, but usually for total strangers. Most assuredly, they share a special place in our Father's mansions.

Today we meet and remember all of our members who have passed on to their reward. Many had premature deaths because of injuries received while serving the public. We can say of them, 'They have fought a good fight, they have finished their course, they have kept the faith; henceforth there is laid up for them a crown of righteousness which the Lord, the righteous judge, shall give at that day.'

And while on this day we remember our dead, we do not forget today's active firefighters. Those of you who have been handed the torch, so to speak, and are continuing to hold to the heritage passed on by your predecessors. You who still respond with that same love for your fellowman and that same devotion to duty, without concern for personal safety. We are thankful to you, and ask for God's mercy upon you and your loved ones, and pray that He will continue to hold you in the hollow of His hand.

On the second Sunday in June each year, there is a flurry of activity here and many people are at this special place for just a brief few minutes. This is proper, and we must continue to come and remember. But in essence, that is all we can do, for if I may paraphrase what President Lincoln said at the dedication of the cemetery at Gettysburg, 'Brave men have consecrated this place far above our power to add or detract.'

Soon the graves of fallen comrades will be decorated. We will stand with bowed heads while Taps is sounded. Bouquets will be placed at the base of the monument and pictures will be taken. We will pause to greet old friends and associates for a short while, and then re-group to march again from this Fireman's lot. We will go down the hill, by the quiet pond, past the colorful rhododendrons in full bloom, through the arch and out of the cemetery. By tradition, and now after years of practice, most of our feet will again be out of step - but our hearts will not be.

If you glance back as we leave, you will see that the bronze hoseman, revered emblem of our profession and guardian of this lot, has again resumed his lonely vigil over his fallen comrades - and he will faithfully stand his silent watch, until we return next year.

Thank you."

LINE OF DUTY DEATHS

(or, In The Hollow Of His Hand)

1	Mr. John Smith	Hydrant Co 2	Feb 12, 1852
2	Mr. Ezra J Wiley	Engine 11	Sept 17, 1853
3	Ladderman Charles T Warren	Ladder 3	July 29, 1856
4	Hoseman Francis Cutting	Tremont 12	May 2, 1858
5	Hoseman John Tuttle	Tremont 12	May 2, 1858
6	Captain Charles E Dunton	Hose Co 1	Feb 18, 1860
7	Ladderman Charles Carter	Ladder 1	Feb 18, 1860
8	Hoseman Reuben Hanaford	Hose Co 5	Feb 24, 1862
9	Hoseman George N Abercrombie	Engine 7	July 11, 1862
10	Ladderman George H Golliff	Ladder 1	May 11, 1868
11	Hoseman George F C Hamilton	Engine 8	June 5, 1869
12	Hoseman Jacob Smith	Hose Co 2	Nov 5, 1869
13	Hoseman Thomas Young	Engine 6	Nov 5, 1872
14	Foreman William Farry	Ladder 4	Nov 10, 1872
15	Asst Foreman Daniel Cochrane	Ladder 4	Nov 10, 1872
16	Hoseman Brown P Stowell	Engine 15	Feb 27, 1873
17	Hoseman James Sturks	Engine 15	Feb 27, 1873
18	Hoseman John Prince Jr	Engine 15	Feb 27, 1873
19	Hoseman William S Hill	Engine 25	Mar 11, 1874
20	Hoseman Mark W Hayes	Engine 26	July 31, 1874
21	Ladderman John H Kelley	Ladder 4	June 16, 1875
22	Ladderman Frederick A W Gay	Ladder 3	Jan 5, 1878
23	Deck Hand Thomas J Tobey	(FB) Flanders	April 15, 1881
24	Hoseman Joseph Pierce	Engine 4	Aug 13, 1884
25	Hoseman James Quigley	Engine 4	Aug 13, 1884
26	Ladderman William H Flavell	Ladder 8	Nov 25,1886
27	Driver/Charge Michael Murnan	Hose Co 7	Nov 28, 1889
28	Hoseman John J Brooks Jr	Hose Co 7	Nov 28, 1889
29	Ladderman Frank P Loker	Ladder 3	Nov 28, 1889
30	Ladderman Daniel J Buckley	Ladder 3	Nov 28, 1889
31	Edward E Whiting		Nov 28, 1889
32	Engineer Patrick M Crotty	Engine 26	July 3, 1890
33	Ladderman James M Powers	Ladder 4	Aug 3, 1893
34	Hoseman Michael Lamb	Engine 42	Sept 21, 1894
35	Superintendent Henry Demary	Repair Shop	May 9, 1896
36	Hoseman William H Chapman	Engine 1	July 31, 1896
37	Captain William G Blanchard	Engine 20	Sept 19, 1896
38	Hoseman Joseph F Collins	Engine 26/35	Apr 10, 1897
39	District Chief Joseph F Egan	District 3	Feb 5, 1898
40	Captain James H Victory	Engine 38/39	Feb 5, 1898
41	Lieutenant George J Gottwald	Engine 38/39	Feb 5, 1898
42	Hoseman Patrick H Disken	Engine 38/39	Feb 5, 1898
43	Hoseman John J Mulhern	Engine 38/39	Feb 5, 1898
44	Hoseman William J Welch	Engine 38/39	Feb 5, 1898
45	Hoseman Martin F McDonald	Engine 13	Jan 23, 1899
46	Hoseman Patrick J McCarthy	Engine 8	Mar 11, 1900
47	Hoseman Herbert Pierce	Engine 42	Nov 8, 1900
48	Lieutenant Solomon P Russell	Chemical 1	Apr 3, 1902
49	Aide-to-Chief Daniel Shea	District 5	Sept 22, 1902

50	Captain John Ready	Engine 54	Mar 27, 1903
51	Hoseman John J O'Brien	Engine 36	Apr 23, 1903
52	Captain John F O'Connell	Engine 16	Aug 16, 1903
53	Ladderman James Killian	Ladder 14	Apr 21, 1904
54	Chief of Dept William T Cheswell		Feb 15, 1906
55	Captain Edward D Pope	Engine 27	May 22, 1907
56	Hoseman Cornelius H Tagen	Engine 14	Jun 17, 1907
57	Ladderman Daniel T Dineen	Ladder 17	Jan 29, 1909
58	Hoseman James B Akerly	Engine 11	Nov 11, 1909
59	Captain Patrick W Lanegan	Ladder 13	Mar 12, 1910
60	Ladderman Leroy James	Ladder 13	May 24, 1912
61	Ladderman Phillip T Smith	Ladder 14	Aug 21, 1912
62	Engineer William H Clay	Engine 30	Dec 3, 1912
63	District Chief Robert Ritchie	District 13	Dec 22, 1912
64	Lieutenant Michael D Greene	Engine 33	Jan 13, 1913
65	Hoseman John J Goff	Engine 45	July 19, 1913
66	Aide-to-Chief Joseph Hackett	Division 2	Jan 14, 1914
67	Lieutenant William H Hughes	Engine 27	Feb 24, 1914
68	Lieutenant William H Magner	Ladder 9	Dec 18, 1914
69	Hoseman Thomas W Devaney	Engine 38/39	Dec 25, 1914
70	District Chief Michael Walsh	District 9	Feb 20, 1915
71	Deputy Chief Charles H W Pope	Division 2	July 15, 1915
72	Hoseman Charles Willett	Engine 10	Dec 21, 1915
73	Hoseman Dennis A Walsh	Engine 10	Dec 21, 1915
74	Hoseman Alexander F Mitchell	Engine 1	Feb 13, 1917
75	Hoseman Frank Lailer	Engine 31 (FB)	Dec 27, 1917
76	Hoseman Thomas H McAndrews	Engine 26	Oct 26, 1918
77	Hoseman George Layhe	Engine 31 (FB)	Jan 15, 1919
78	Ladderman Thomas J Stevens	Ladder 11	Feb 15, 1919
79	Ladderman William J Cox	Ladder 29	Dec 6, 1920
80	Captain William J Swan	Ladder 15	Sept 22, 1922
81	Aide-to-Chief Owen T Martin	District 10	May 22, 1925
82	Hoseman Michael J Travers	Engine 7	July 1, 1926
83	Lieutenant Joseph F Donovan	Engine 9	Mar 23, 1927
84	Lieutenant James Gavagan	Ladder 19	Dec 8, 1927
85	Ladderman Martin J Callahan	Ladder 1	Nov 28, 1928
86	Captain Florence J Sullivan	Engine 32	Nov 29, 1929
87	Ladderman William E Emmel	Ladder 8	Dec 26, 1929
88	Hoseman George J Corcoran	Engine 13	Sept 16, 1930
89	Ladderman Michael A Riley	Ladder 24	Jan 20, 1931
90	Asst Chief of Dept Henry Power		Aug 18, 1932
91	Captain Michael J Gilligan	Engine 34	Mar 17, 1935
92	Ladder Albert F Mitchell	Ladder 8	Aug 9, 1935
93	Hoseman Francis F Parkes	Engine 21	Aug 21, 1935
94	Hoseman John T Murphy	Engine 36	Mar 31, 1937
95	Captain Edward S Humphreys	Engine 39	May 17, 1937
96	Hoseman Edward R Lynn	Engine 18	July 28, 1937
97	Hoseman Cornelius Noonan	Engine 33	Feb 10, 1938
98	Hoseman John J Moriarty	Engine 6	Apr 19, 1942
99	Ladderman Lawrence J Harvey	Ladder 9	Aug 12, 1942
100	Hoseman Francis J Degan	Engine 3	Nov 15, 1942
101	Hoseman John F Foley	Engine 3	Nov 15, 1942
102	Hoseman Edward F Macomber	Engine 12	Nov 15, 1942
103	Ladderman Daniel E McGuire	Ladder 2	Nov 15, 1942

104	Hoseman Peter F McMorrow	Engine 50	Nov 15, 1942
105	Hoseman Malachi Reddington	Engine 33	Nov 15, 1942
106	Lieutenant Daniel F N Mahoney	Ladder 9	Mar 26, 1943
107	District Chief Timothy Donovan	District 12	Dec 29, 1944
108	Lieutenant John J Murphy	Ladder 22	Apr 17, 1945
109	Ladderman Harold Bishop	Ladder 2	Jan 19, 1946
110	Captain Stephen Gunn	Engine 2	Feb 3, 1946
111	Hoseman Edward J Barrett	Engine 2	Feb 3, 1946
112	Captain John J Morgan	Engine 20	Apr 20, 1946
113	Hoseman Warren E Barnard	Rescue 1	Oct 22, 1946
114	P.M.S. Patrick J Cady	Engine 39	Oct 22, 1946
115	Lieutenant John J McDonough	Engine 6	Nov 21, 1946
116	Hoseman Charles A Buchanan	Rescue 2	Mar 24, 1947
117	Prov. Fireman Joseph Sullivan	Ladder 19	Dec 3, 1947
118	District Chief Daniel Crowley	District 5	Oct 25, 1949
119	Hoseman Joseph C Morgan	Engine 49	May 4, 1950
120	Lieutenant Roy E Burrill	Ladder 14	Sept 23, 1950
121	Ladderman William R Benson	Ladder 14	Sept 23, 1950
122	Ladderman Daniel McLaughlin	Ladder 20	May 12, 1953
123	Hoseman Arthur E Gately	Engine 30	Oct 19, 1953
124	FF Robert J Quinn	Engine 18	July 5, 1955
125	FF Thomas J Slattery	Engine 40	Jan 29, 1956
126	F Lieutenant Michael Langone	Engine 40	Feb 2, 1956
127	F Lieutenant Frederick J Ford	Rescue Co	Apr 14, 1957
128	FF Arthur P Spacone	Engine 2	Dec 25, 1959
129	FF James Walsh	Engine 42	Jan 13, 1960
130	FF Arnold Reis	Engine 3	Jan 20, 1961
131	FF Richard ConCannon	Ladder 15	Jan 23, 1961
132	FF James Sexton	Ladder 4	Dec 7, 1962
133	F Lieutenant John J McCorkle	Engine 24	Oct 1, 1964
134	F Lieutenant John J Geswell	Ladder 26	Oct 1, 1964
135	FF Francis L Murphy	Engine 24	Oct 1, 1964
136	FF James B Sheedy	Ladder 4	Oct 1, 1964
137	FF Robert Clougherty	Engine 3	Oct 1, 1964
138	F Lieutenant Warren T Lynch	Engine Sq 18	Nov 23, 1967
139	F Lieutenant George J Gottwald	Rescue-Pump	Mar 3, 1970
140	F Lieutenant Joseph J Downing	Engine 2	Oct 16, 1970
141	FF Edwin Foley	Engine 30	Dec 30, 1970
142	FF Jeremiah Collins	Engine 45	July 4, 1971
143	F Lieutenant Daniel T McInness	Engine 8	Aug 17, 1971
144	FF James F Doneghey	Ladder 30	Nov 5, 1971
145	FF Patrick Kelly	Engine 26	Nov 22, 1971
146	FF John Hopkins	Engine 34	May 11, 1972
147	F Lieutenant Thomas J Carroll	Engine 32	June 17, 1972
148	FF Paul J Murphy	Engine 32	June 17, 1972
149	FF Thomas Beckwith	Engine 32	June 17, 1972
150	F Lieutenant John E Hanbury	Ladder 13	June 17, 1972
151	FF John E Jameson	Ladder 13	June 17, 1972
152	FF Joseph P Saniuk	Ladder 13	June 17, 1972
153	FF Charles E Dolan	Ladder 13	June 17, 1972
154	FF Richard Magee	Ladder 13	June 17, 1972
155	FF Joseph Boucher, Jr	Engine 22	June 17, 1972
156	FF Vincent Dimino	Ladder 30	June 19, 1972
157	FF Arthur Ceurvels	Ladder 20	Feb 2, 1973

158	FF John Carlson	Engine 28	Oct 14, 1973
159	FF Bernard G Tully	Engine 30	Jan 22, 1974
160	F Lieutenant James Flahive *	Rescue 1	Mar 6, 1974
161	F Lieutenant Hubert F Moran	Ladder 6	June 4, 1975
162	FF Richard Sheridan	Ladder 16	Oct 23, 1976
163	FF Hugh F O'Brien	Ladder 5	Apr 11, 1977
164	Wrkg Foreman Walter McGuire	F A Constr	Apr 20, 1977
165	FF John McDonough	Light Plant 1	Feb 7, 1978
166	FF Robert M Greene	Ladder 23	Nov 27, 1978
167	F Lieutenant Paul M Lentini	Engine 37	Jan 6, 1981
168	FF James Gibbons	Engine 37	Jan 6, 1981
169	FF Edward J Donovan	Rescue 1	Nov 6, 1983
170	FF James Ealey	Engine 3	Sept 5, 1985
171	FF Thomas L Conley	Engine 41	Jan 7, 1986
172	Aide-to-Chief Edward Connolly	Ladder 17	Mar 21, 1986
173	FF Francis J Baker	Engine 16	Nov 26, 1993
174	F Lieutenant Stephen F Minehan	Ladder 15	June 24, 1994
175	FF James A Ellis	Engine 14	Dec 23, 1996
176	Aide-to-Chief Joseph Murphy	District 9	Jan 29, 1999
177	FF David L Packard	Engine 48	Mar 16, 1999

(FB) - Fireboat

* Lieutenant Flahive was injured at the Chauncy Street fire on October 22, 1946 which took the lives of Firemen Barnard and Cady. His brain was deprived of necessary oxygen for too long a period. He existed until March 6, 1974.

"Greater love hath no man this, that a man lay down his life for his friends," is a familiar quotation from the Bible (John 15:13). These firemen demonstrated that love. They were ready, and rolled to one more alarm, not knowing it would be their last. For some, death came swift and without pain. They were the fortunate ones. For others, death was just as certain, but took a much longer time, as in the case of Lieutenant Flahive.

While each of these deaths had a tremendous impact among fellow firefighters, it was the families of these brave men who faced the devastating tragedy that can never be amply compensated for, and the reality, which created voids that can never be filled. Firefighters and their families live with this possibility, but this makes it no less shocking or tragic when it happens.   Nevertheless, the men are still

READY TO ROLL ...
READY TO DIE.